FORAGING TEXAS

Finding, Identifying, and Preparing
Edible Wild Foods in Texas

ERIC M. KNIGHT WITH STACY M. COPLIN

T0346539

FALCONGUIDES

GUILFORD, CONNECTICUT

FALCONGUIDES®

An imprint of Globe Pequot, the trade division of The Rowman & Littlefield Publishing Group, Inc.
4501 Forbes Blvd., Ste. 200
Lanham, MD 20706
Falcon.com

Falcon and FalconGuides are registered trademarks and Make Adventure Your Story is a trademark of The Rowman & Littlefield Publishing Group, Inc.

Distributed by NATIONAL BOOK NETWORK

Photos by Eric Knight except the following: pp. 76 (bottom right), 265 by Sam Kieschnick; p. 172 (bottom) by Frances and Clark Hancock; p. 160 (top) by Suzanne Dingwell; p. 123 by Whitney Arostegui.

Gould Ecoregions of Texas map reprinted with permission from Texas A&M AgriLife and Texas Parks & Wildlife.

British Library Cataloguing-in-Publication Information available

Library of Congress Cataloging in Publication Data available

ISBN 978-1-4930-5609-5 (paperback)
ISBN 978-1-4930-5610-1 (e-book)

∞™ The paper used in this publication meets the minimum requirements of American National Standard for Information Sciences—Permanence of Paper for Printed Library Materials, ANSI/NISO Z39.48-1992.

CONTENTS

Note: Asterisk (*) denotes invasive or otherwise nonnative species.

ACKNOWLEDGMENTS

First, we would like to thank our family and friends for their ongoing love, support, and encouragement. We'd especially like to thank Eric's parents (Steve and Mary) and Stacy's parents (Lennard and Boots) for encouraging an interest and respect for nature early on. Being outside and participating in the natural world has always been part of our lives and it's thanks to them.

Developing the skills, knowledge, experience, and confidence to forage wild edible plants is a lifelong pursuit. We are continually learning new methods of preparation, honing our botany skills, and learning about new-to-us species (whether edible or not). We would like to take a moment to acknowledge some of the important mentors, teachers, peers, and elders who have helped us along the way.

Thank you to Ingwe for the wisdom, poetry, and stories that have inspired and enriched us over the years. Ingwe's words have been a source of grounded reason and strength in our lives, and we take his words to heart: "The wilderness holds all truth and knowledge." Thank you.

Thank you to the Austin Nature & Science Center, where the authors met and fell in love while working together as environmental educators. Special thanks to Dave and Michel Scott, who founded Earth Native Wilderness School in Bastrop, Texas. Eric was one of their first students when they opened the school and learned and honed many of his "primitive" skills both while apprenticing under them and then while leading classes as part of their staff. Dave has been an important mentor, and we truly appreciate his drive to connect his students to the natural world. Also, a huge thank-you to Dave for putting us in contact with FalconGuides to begin this whole process.

Special thanks to the late Texas botany giant Dr. Billie Lee Turner, Director Emeritus of the University of Texas (UT) herbarium and the Botanical Research Institute of Texas (BRIT). Dr. Turner described numerous new plant species and significantly influenced Texas botany throughout his career. We corresponded with Dr. Turner a number of times over the years, and he never failed to inspire us and encourage Eric in particular to pursue botany and field botany. Thank you, Dr. Turner—you will be missed!

Thank you to herbalist Nicole Telkes of the Wildflower School of Botanical Medicine. Nicole was Eric's first herbalism teacher, and we thank her for her knowledge, wisdom, and encouragement. Thanks also to herbalists Sam Coffman (The Human Path) and Ginger Webb (Sacred Journey School of Medicine) for sharing their expertise with us.

Thank you also to all the preceding edible plant authors and experts including Euell Gibbons, Michael Moore, Bradford Angier, Scooter Cheatham, Samuel

Thayer, Delena Tull, Jon Young, John Slatterly, Charles Kane, Mark "Merriwether" Vorderbruggen, Tom Elpel, John Kallas, Steve Brill, and Green Deane. We have learned from all of you through various field guides, talks, and websites over the years; thank you for sharing your knowledge and experience.

A huge thank-you to the Lady Bird Johnson Wildflower Center for providing opportunities for Eric to lead edible plant walks on-site and for helping him develop his botany skills while volunteering on vegetation surveys with Dick Davis and crew. And fun fact: We got married in a large live oak grove at the center.

Thank you to our past and future students at the Austin Nature & Science Center, Earth Native Wilderness School, Lady Bird Johnson Wildflower Center, and Local Leaf for humbling us and allowing us to share our experiences. A certain Latin proverb comes to mind: *docendo discimus*—"by teaching, we learn." We also want to thank all the plant identification experts who have helped us identify plants over the years. Thank you especially to botanist Nathan Taylor (for his assistance with identifying several species in this book) and Texas Parks & Wildlife's Sam Kieschnick (for his broad base of plant knowledge and photos used in this book). Thanks also to iNaturalist contributors Frances and Clark Hancock and Suzanne Dingwell for letting us use some of their photos in this book, and to Texas A&M AgriLife and the Texas Parks & Wildlife Department for permission to reprint the Gould Ecoregions of Texas map. And a special thank-you to the renowned forager Samuel Thayer for reviewing the draft manuscript of this book and providing valuable insight and feedback.

Thank you to our editor Katie O'Dell at Falcon for guiding us on this bookwriting adventure and keeping our wild ideas in check.

We would also like to send out a special thank-you to our collective ancestors. No matter your ethnicity, race, or heritage, someone in your lineage passed down vital knowledge of the plant world to future generations. Thanks for passing it on; we're here to keep it going. Specifically, though, we would like to acknowledge that none of this book would have been possible without the deep knowledge of the native plants shared by the past and current indigenous people of what is now called Texas. Further, this land that we live on and the beautiful lands we have traveled to for plant photos and harvests over the years were originally stolen from or (at best) coercively ceded by one or another indigenous tribe. Our hearts ache for what was done to our indigenous brothers and sisters, and a profound respect and gratitude goes out to them for sharing their intimate knowledge of the plant world.

And lastly, a profound thank-you to the non-human beings we interact with on a daily basis. The live oak trees, mockingbirds, grackles, salamanders, bats, yaupon, and limestone of this special spot along the Colorado River, where the Edwards Plateau meets the Blackland Prairie, keep us sane and grounded. Thank you.

PREFACE

In nature's infinite book of secrecy
A little I can read.

—Soothsayer in William Shakespeare's *Antony and Cleopatra*

This book seeks to unlock for the reader many of the secrets of the plant world. Sadly, many Texans cannot reliably identify more than one or two wild edible plants much less know the potentially dangerous plants to avoid. In place of this void of knowledge, many Texans have a fear of wild plants and the thought of eating a wild plant is often, quite literally, off the table. This book was written to help fill the void with sound, useful information to take away the fear and apprehension and allow for greater understanding and awareness.

Knowing well even one wild edible plant can break down the mysterious "green wall" around us, allowing us to look at nature, and plants in particular, in a different light. Given what has been going on in the world recently, nature is screaming for us to listen and take note of Western civilization's destructive tendencies. The better we understand and appreciate nature, the better we can hear the natural world's anguish and take action. As the naturalist Jon Young says, we need a naturalist on every street corner. The more people we have that know the natural world intimately and understand its rhythms and nuances, the better chance we have as a species and the better chance we have for life on Earth to recover and thrive.

We hope this compilation of information accumulated through our experiences, domestic and international travels, cultural exchanges, and inherited knowledge resonates and instills an awareness of our natural world and its gifts. And because this book only scratches the surface of the ways in which we can positively interact with our plant allies, we hope it also inspires a curiosity and hunger to unlock more of the natural mysteries that still abound.

Nature knows all the secrets but won't tell all.

—Andrew Yelenosky (Eric's grandfather)

INTRODUCTION

This book is an introduction to the wild edible plants of Texas but also serves as a useful reference for the seasoned forager. It outlines the basics that any forager will need to master in order to confidently obtain food from the wild plants of Texas. This book is not intended to contain every conceivably edible plant in Texas nor every harvesting, processing, and preparation method possible. A book of that scope would surely amount to at least fifteen volumes and would be a mighty pain to lug around. Luckily for us all, Scooter Cheatham et al. are pursuing this very endeavor with their exhaustive account of the plants of Texas in *The Useful Wild Plants of Texas, the Southeastern and Southwestern United States, the Southern Plains, and Northern Mexico* [1]. As of the date of this publication, they have published four out of the fifteen planned volumes. So, as we wait for the completion of that gargantuan and important work, this guide details ninety-two of the more common, interesting, and useful edible wild plants that Texas has to offer in a more portable format.

About This Book
The state of Texas contains an array of different habitats, climates, and geology that equate to a similarly wide variety of plant species. Because there is an enormous number of edible plants in Texas, we unavoidably came to the difficult decision of which plants to showcase and which to exclude. To narrow down the selection process, we picked plants that meet the following general criteria:

1. They are safe to consume if proper precautions are taken.
2. They are generally common in at least one region of Texas.
3. They are plants that the authors have had direct consumptive experience with.
4. They are not threatened, endangered, or otherwise at risk.

For plant genera with multiple edible species occurring in Texas, we tried to showcase either the most commonly encountered species in Texas *or* an invasive species to promote its consumption. There were also times when this decision was difficult, so we picked the species that we had the most experience with, thought was most interesting, or otherwise preferred.

Even though we could only showcase a relatively small number of the edible species in Texas, we wanted to include as many of them as possible while still including enough detail regarding the best ways of identifying, harvesting, processing, and preparing each plant. To address this, we endeavored to list many of the other related edible species in each genus in the "Related edible species" section of each account. Generally, in Texas, most of the species in a given genus have similar edible uses. In cases where this is not true, we either do not list the non-edible species or make a point to call out the non-edible species. So, even though there are ninety-two species accounts in this book, many more are actually covered at least to some extent through the "Related edible species" section and through Appendix A, which lists other edible species in Texas for which you will have to do further research due to the space constraints of this book.

Also notice that several species accounts do not list a specific epithet and instead simply name the genus (for example as with *Tradescantia* spp.). The "spp." after the genus indicates that we are referring to more than one species in that genus; spp. is a shorthand abbreviation that means "multiple species." In this book, this was done in cases where it is difficult for most people (including the authors) to distinguish between different species in the same genus. When used in the edible species accounts, it is essentially saying that all species in that genus found in Texas can be considered edible in some way *and* that it is often difficult to distinguish one species from another.

How to Use This Book

This book works well both as a reference and as a field guide. Bring it along on camping trips, road trips, work trips, or any other trip that might take you near a wild part of Texas. Or use it in your local parks, urban spaces, and neighborhoods. Wild foods can be found in every habitat in Texas (including cities), so no matter where you are in the Lone Star State, this book can help you find something to eat.

Used as a reference, naturalists and botany enthusiasts who already know how to identify many of the plants in this book can read about the uses of each plant prior to or after going out in the field to gain an understanding of the edible potential of each species and how to harvest it. Used as a field guide, novice foragers can bring this book as a companion with them into the field to aid in identification and harvesting technique. Either way, a thorough understanding of how the book is organized is key to making the most effective and efficient use of it.

We highly recommend reading through the introductory "Foraging Basics" section (with **strong** emphasis on the "Warnings and Safety" and "Most Dangerous Wild Plants in Texas" subsections) before pursuing any kind of wild harvesting. Know the most dangerous plants first, before you move on to the potentially edible species. This will make you much less likely to accidentally eat something dangerous and potentially deadly.

Next, review the "Plant Identification: Basic Botany and How to Identify Plants" section in detail and cross-reference with the "Illustrated Glossary and Botanical Terminology" section (Appendix C) in the back of the book to make sure you understand the basics of plant identification. Crucially, the "Ethics:

Foraging Sustainably" section should also be reviewed prior to your first foraging outing to make sure you responsibly interact with our plant neighbors. The subsequent "Harvesting and Processing Supplies" section describes helpful supplies that you may want to have on hand while foraging or after foraging.

After understanding these foraging basics, read through the "Physical Environment and Ecological Regions" section to gain a better understanding of your local climate, geology, and ecosystem. The plants pay attention to these climatic and geological variables and so should you!

The "Foraging Calendar for Texas" section is a humble attempt to generally group foraging targets for each season. However, because it's such a large state with multiple ecological regions and climates, this will not be 100 percent accurate everywhere in Texas. Instead, think of it as a starting place. You will still have to check the range maps for each species to confirm the plant grows in your area, and you may find that a particular wild edible ripens in a different season or across multiple seasons in your locality. Use this section as a quick reference to what wild foods might be out and then consult the species accounts to get more information.

Once you are up to speed on the foraging basics, the next and main section of the book consists of species accounts for each of the ninety-two covered edible species. The species are grouped into four general categories: Trees, Shrubs/Vines, Herbs/Wildflowers/Forbs, and Aquatics. We find these to be useful groupings as, even if you know almost nothing about botany, it is pretty straightforward to be able to tell a tree from a shrub and an herb from an aquatic plant. However, these groupings are arbitrary in some ways, as the distinction between a tree and a shrub is not always as clear as you would think, and large herbs can sometimes look like shrubs. In fact, some plants can grow as a tree or shrub and vice versa. Note that the Shrubs/Vines section is more or less a catch-all group of everything that is not a tree, herb, or aquatic plant including oddballs as described below.

For the purposes of this book, we have generally defined each grouping accordingly:

- **Trees:** Trees are woody, perennial plants that are larger than a shrub and generally have one main trunk.
- **Shrubs/vines:** Shrubs are woody, perennial plants that are smaller than a tree and have several main stems arising from or near the ground. Vines are trailing or climbing plants that can be woody or non-woody. Other oddballs included in this grouping are the cacti, yuccas, agaves, sotols, and palmettos, as they do not fit well in the other groupings.
- **Herbs/wildflowers/forbs:** Herbs and forbs are herbaceous, non-woody plants and can be annual or perennial. "Wildflower" is not an especially descriptive name, at least botanically, but because it is a

commonly used term, we include it here to refer to wild, often showy flowering herbs/forbs.

- **Aquatics:** Aquatic plants are those that have adapted to living in water and includes obligate wetland species.

The above definitions aside, if you are looking at what you think is a small tree and you think it might have edible fruits but you are not finding it in the Trees section, take a look at the species in the Shrubs/Vines section, as the individual plant you are looking at may just be a large specimen. Again, these groupings are somewhat subjective but are often useful starting places for identification.

Within each grouping, the species accounts are arranged alphabetically by plant family and then by genus (*not* by common name). So, for example, the tree cholla (*Cylindropuntia imbricata*) is listed before the horsecrippler cactus (*Echinocactus texensis*) since *C* comes before *E*. Similarly, all of the Cactaceae species come after the Berberidaceae family (*B* comes before *C*). This alphabetical system makes the book very easy to use once you have a better understanding of plant families, as you can quickly flip to the Cactaceae section of the Shrubs/Vines grouping if you come across an interesting cactus in the field.

This book includes only a small number of the thousands of plant species in Texas, so if you find a plant that is not included, you should first check Appendix A, which contains an abbreviated list of other wild edible plants in Texas (for which you would have to do additional research). If it is not on the Appendix A list, you can consult other helpful references and resources listed in Appendix B or assume it is not edible.

Each species account is titled by one of the species' common names followed by its scientific name in parenthesis and *italicized*. **Note that invasive or otherwise nonnative species have an asterisk (*) in front of the species name.** Within each species account, there are seven sections as described below:

- **Family:** This section simply lists the scientific plant family.
- **Edible part and harvest time:** This section lists the main edible parts of the plant and approximately when each edible part can be harvested. Note that the harvest time is approximate, as the ripening or harvesting season can change drastically among the ecoregions of Texas. The harvest time is a good starting point, but you may need to observe and see if ripening happens earlier or later in your part of Texas.
- **Toxic lookalikes:** This section describes the toxic lookalikes of the edible plant in question. For many plants, there may not be a toxic lookalike. This does not necessarily mean there are no other lookalikes, but it indicates that at least the lookalikes are not especially toxic. We try to list as many toxic lookalikes as can reasonably be encountered in

the plant's particular habitat, but "lookalike" is subjective, and some people may think a yucca is a "lookalike" of a pineapple. The point is, we could not be exhaustive in this section, but it includes the toxic lookalikes that a reasonable person would have difficulty distinguishing from the edible plant. This section also includes key features to look for in order to differentiate the toxic lookalikes from the edible species. It also may include specific cautions for the edible plant itself if there are parts of the plant that are especially toxic or if it is toxic if not prepared in a certain way.

- **Identification:** This section describes the key identifiers of the plant in question. Fair warning, it uses some botanical terms, but we tried to keep them easy and straightforward. If you encounter a word you are not familiar with, refer to the "Common Botanical Terminology" section in Appendix C to understand its meaning. The identification section generally describes the following characteristics for each plant: size, leaf shape and arrangement, flowers, fruits, and seeds. It also notes if the plant is evergreen or deciduous and whether it is an annual or perennial. This section is not intended to be an exhaustive botanical description of each plant but is intended to simplify identification. For each plant, the identification section was adapted from the botanical descriptions in Correll and Johnston's *Manual of the Vascular Plants of Texas* [2]. When helpful, key plant characteristics that are useful identification aids are bolded for convenience and quick reference.

- **Range and habitat:** This section briefly describes the range of the species in Texas and includes a range map that highlights the counties that it grows in or has naturalized in. The maps are based on county records as recorded in the Biota of North America Program's (BONAP) North American Plant Atlas. We have added a county or two to some of the maps based on personal observations of plants in a given county, but the maps generally follow the BONAP records. Note that plants can expand (as with invasive species) or contract (as with rarer species) their ranges, so you may find plants outside of their range or missing from a certain county. The maps are intended as starting points to figure out what can be expected in each area. And make sure to check the "Related edible species" section, as a close relative of the species may be found in your area even if the showcased species is not. Also note that, especially in west Texas, some of the counties are extremely large. Therefore, a particular species may be found in a small part of the county, but it appears that it has a much wider range than it actually does. So, be mindful that the range map is strictly referring to the fact that the plant grows at least somewhere within the county, not necessarily throughout the county. The brief habitat description can help here, as it will narrow down suitable parts of the county that the plant might be found in. Plants can sometimes be found outside of their preferred habitats, but searching for the plants in their preferred or typical habitats is often more fruitful.

- **Related edible species:** This section lists some of the edible species related to the showcased species. Mostly, it includes other species in the same genus, but sometimes species in the same family are discussed. It also briefly describes the range of the related edible species. This section is not an exhaustive list of all the edible relatives in Texas but includes the ones most often encountered or most widespread. Note that abbreviations are often used in this section (and other sections of the book) for the genus name since we're talking about species in the same genus. For example, *Chenopodium album* may be abbreviated as *C. album*.
- **Uses/history/comments:** This section describes the precautions and edible uses of the plant in question and includes the authors' experience harvesting, processing, and preparing the plant. It also sometimes includes ethnobotanical accounts from other authors and sources and can even include interesting historical facts about the plant or other medicinal or utilitarian uses for it. This section also includes a simple recipe that can be used with each edible plant. We tried to include easy, quick recipes when possible to encourage people to try them, but more-involved recipes are sometimes included. That said, the recipes are not the only way to prepare each plant. The text in this section also includes other general options for preparing or cooking the plant.

Each species account has several photos of the plant. We tried to include photos that would both showcase the edible part of the plant and assist with identification, but also included some photos of processing or preparation of the plant.

The back of the book includes helpful appendices that you may want to refer to. The "Abbreviated List of Other Wild Edible Plants of Texas" (Appendix A) lists other edible plants that were considered for inclusion in this book but were ultimately left out to focus on other species. Refer to it, but you will have to do your own research on identification, harvesting, processing, and preparation. "Helpful Resources and Additional Reading" (Appendix B) is an excellent starting point for researching these other edible plants or for learning more about the plants covered in this book. It includes many of the authors' favorite and most frequently used resources for Texas foraging. The "Illustrated Glossary and Botanical Terminology" section (Appendix C) includes basic illustrations of key botanical terms and definitions of other helpful terms. Refer to it frequently when reviewing the identification section of each species account.

FORAGING BASICS

If you read nothing else in this book before foraging for the first time, read and internalize this section. Doing so will provide a solid foraging foundation. You will better understand the importance of foraging, the dangers of foraging, how to identify plants, what supplies you might need, and, importantly, how to forage ethically and sustainably.

Why Forage?

Foraging grounds us. It instantly and directly reconnects us with the natural world and begins melting away the worries and stresses of Western civilization. We forage not because we have to, but because we enjoy it and the profound connection it brings to Mother Earth. It fosters an appreciation for plants and the natural world in general that is sorely missing from our current culture.

Foraging can also be a model of sustainability. As outlined in many studies, books, and documentaries, the intensive agriculture associated with our current food system is unsustainable. Even organic farming can be immensely detrimental to the local ecosystem. Just think of a monocrop (one-species crop) like a field of organic non-GMO corn. How many bird species live in this cornfield? How many insect species? How many amphibians? Are there any mammals there? What about other plant species? While a monocrop may support some life, when compared to what the field of corn displaced (maybe a forest or an intact prairie), the difference in biodiversity is astounding.

Now, there are obviously more holistic and sustainable forms of agriculture, including permaculture, perennial polyculture, and other systems that mimic how the natural world functions (see Joel Salatin's Polyface Farm as a great example), but foraging can sustainably coexist and fill in nutritional gaps in these systems. For instance, learning to find and appreciate the edible "weeds" and invasive species that abound in our urban, suburban, and rural areas can feed people and wildlife from otherwise disturbed or neglected land. Foraged plants, by default, require zero water, fertilizer, transportation, care, or land clearing. And many times, they are more nutritious, delicious, and health-giving than store-bought produce. Is there a grocery store green tastier than wood-sorrel? How does iceberg lettuce compare nutritionally to nettle greens? Try them both and the answer is clear.

Foraging is not only about reconnecting with nature, feeling good about your place in the food system, or just for culinary curiosity. Foraging also provides an extremely practical and valuable skill set that is lacking in the general population. Foraging skills and knowledge are a Swiss army knife against potential disaster scenarios. Foraging knowledge can provide you a sustaining source of medicine, food, and other useful tools and materials. We happen to be writing this part of the book in the midst of the coronavirus (COVID-19) pandemic. As the situation began to unravel in March 2020, one of the first things we noticed was that people began panic-buying canned food, grains, and, yes, toilet paper. While we were not completely immune to some of this panic, we also realized that we had an abundance of food and medicine (and even toilet paper—thank you *Verbascum thapsus* and *Broussonetia papyrifera*) all around us. In fact, we created and perfected many of the recipes described in this book during the spring of 2020 in the early stages of the pandemic. Foraging provides a sense of resiliency and self-sufficiency that builds confidence and reduces stress, even in uncertain times.

Foraging also significantly increases the joy and comfort of hiking, camping, and outdoor adventure in general. Knowing that you can pack in less and never truly run out of food does wonders for your experience in the natural world. It also reduces barriers to just getting outside and *going*. Foraging for your own food increases outdoor time, reduces screen time, and gives you a healthy dose of vitamin D—all things we need in this increasingly developed and digitalized world.

In short, the primary reason for foraging may be different for every individual, but we're sure you can find your own compelling reason in this book. So have fun and stay safe!

Warnings and Safety

Often, the general public is afraid of eating anything that is not purchased in a grocery store. Fear mongering from social media, news outlets, and hearsay do a disservice to the actual dangers of eating wild plants. As with any activity, it is important to understand the true dangers that could be encountered. After all, before getting a driver's license, every sixteen-year-old is (rightly) forced to watch and hear about grisly accidents and deaths from car collisions. Such is the unfortunate risk when it comes to driving a 4,000-pound hunk of metal at 80 mph (this is Texas after all) along with countless other drivers. Though much safer than driving, foraging for wild edible plants comes with its own risks. Below is a list of some of the more serious foraging risks and how to mitigate them. They are generally arranged from highest risk to the lowest risk.

Risk #1: Toxic wild plants

This is the highest risk when foraging. Though there are not that many highly toxic plant species in Texas, it is very important to know them well and avoid them at all costs. Consuming even small amounts can be deadly. Luckily, the following subsection ("Most Dangerous Wild Plants in Texas") covers these plants in detail. *Review this subsection carefully!*

Risk #2: Plant identification error

This is a common risk, especially for new foragers. The excitement of eating something that grows wild for free is exhilarating and can prompt an overconfidence in some foragers. However, it is important to go slow when first starting out and study each plant you are considering eating to make absolutely sure you know which species it is. Learn the basics of botany, and practice your skills before harvesting. As with most skills, it's only after you get proficient at botany that you even know what you don't know. Beginners are often confident about species-level identifications early on, but then, after understanding the intricacies and nuances of botany, know to question themselves more as they gain experience. Be willing to admit to yourself that you may not be able to identify a particular plant yet. Don't needlessly stretch or exaggerate your abilities. It's a good idea to start with the more easily identified plants when beginning. Skip the wild carrot for now and focus on something like pecans or Turk's cap as you ease into plant identification.

Risk #3: Erroneous or incomplete foraging knowledge
This risk is associated with a lack of due diligence on the part of the forager. Some beginner foragers irrationally trust anything they read on the internet or hear about on social media or from others. We once had a friend of a friend tell us about a vast field of nettles (implying the edible *Urtica* spp.) only to later see pictures and realize they had misidentified the toxic Carolina horsenettle (*Solanum carolinense*)—a fairly difficult mistake to make. Don't blindly trust *any* foraging source (this book included). Do your own due diligence and make sure the person or resource you are receiving information from is knowledgeable and that you can verify or cross-reference the claims with other resources and information.

Risk #4: Overconsumption
This risk goes hand-in-hand with Risk #3 and is common for uninformed beginners. It is important to know ahead of time *how* edible a plant is. Many new foragers like to think that edible versus non-edible is a black-and-white distinction but it isn't. Just as with grocery store items, some edible plants should only be eaten in smaller quantities. Most people understand that it would not be a good idea to eat two pounds of raw garlic cloves in one sitting. This does not mean that garlic is necessarily toxic or dangerous, but it must be used in reasonable quantities. Everything in moderation, as the saying goes. Anything can be toxic to the human body in high enough amounts, even water. One concept we find particularly helpful (and first learned about from The Human Path's Sam Coffman) is illustrated by the continuum below:

Poison   **Grocery Store**

On the left side you have "Poison" and on the right side you have "Grocery Store." Imagine that every plant species lies somewhere on this continuum.

There are no black-and-white edible and non-edible plants. Some edible plants (like pokeweed) may be closer to the left, as they require careful harvesting and processing to make them safe for consumption, while other edible plants like hackberries can be eaten raw in quantity with no ill effects. Most of the really dangerous plants are all the way on the left, and most of the edible plants are somewhere on the right half of the continuum. Interestingly, many of the strong medicinal plants are somewhere on the left side, as they are typically taken in small amounts that are anticipated to have a significant effect on your body. We find this continuum concept is helpful in breaking with the edible versus non-edible myth and allows for true understanding of what "edible" means.

Know the particular plant properties and what a reasonable serving looks like for each plant. This is often determined on an individual basis to find out what your body agrees with. Start slow and work your way up as you eat more and more of a particular plant.

Risk #5: Allergic reaction

Every time you eat a new wild plant, it will be the first time your body has encountered this new food. Because you don't know how your body will respond to *any* new food (including new-to-you fruits or veggies from the grocery store), it is best to start slow and in very small amounts. Some people can even have strange allergies to common produce like onions or strawberries. Even well-known wild edible plants like prickly pear have been known to adversely affect certain people. That said, after years of leading edible plant walks, we have not seen or heard of dangerous or life-threatening allergic reactions occurring with the edible plants listed in this book if they are prepared correctly. But as always, be cautious. After correctly identifying the edible plant, take a miniscule nibble and sit with it for an hour or so. Tune in to your body and see if you have any alarming reaction to it, like an itching or burning sensation. If no adverse reaction occurs, try eating a little bit more. It's advisable to wait a day to see if any delayed reaction occurs before eating larger amounts.

In general, it is also not a good idea to introduce more than one new edible plant to your body (at least in large amounts) in a single day. Reason being, if you *do* have a reaction, it will be nearly impossible to tell which plant you are reacting to. We practice this ourselves for new edible plants when traveling and think it is a good rule of thumb. This is especially important if you are far from medical attention. For example, it's not the best idea to experiment with new wild foods on a five-day backpacking trip. It would be preferable to experiment before the trip so you understand how your body will react to the new foods first.

Risk #6: Bioaccumulation of pollutants

This risk is not usually an immediate or short-term risk but can be a long-term risk if contaminated plants are consumed on a regular basis or in large amounts.

Unfortunately, our world is more and more polluted every day. And despite our society's ignorance, the plants are trying to clean it up. Plants and fungi help clean our environment from human-caused toxins and heavy metals. In fact, wetland plants in particular are often important components of wastewater and stormwater treatment in many parts of the world, as they slow down effluent and uptake chemicals and heavy metals. Use extra caution and discernment when harvesting aquatic plants as, ultimately, pollutants flow downhill to water.

Weedy species can tolerate farmlands that may have pesticides or heavy metals sprayed on the fields and can uptake and concentrate (bioaccumulate) some of these chemicals. Other plants near roadsides or other air-pollutant sources may accumulate airborne pollutants on their leaves or fruits. Industrial areas in particular should be avoided when harvesting, and always be skeptical of bare or stained patches of soil, as this could indicate that pollutants are preventing plants from growing in this area. In short, it is important to be aware of potential pollutants that could impact plants that you want to harvest and avoid questionable areas when possible. Let these intrepid plants clean up the environment in peace, free from harvest.

Other potential risks are less common. For instance, some plant species can become infected by toxic fungi that, if consumed, can cause illness. It is a good idea to pay attention to whether a particular plant you want to harvest from is healthy or appears diseased. Does it have leaf spots? Does it have orange fungal "rust" on the leaves? Assess the health of plants before you harvest.

Understanding the above risks is great, but we all make mistakes. Use your instincts: If a plant tastes bad to you, spit it out. Better safe than sorry. Many (but not all) toxic plants don't taste good or trigger an itching or burning sensation in your mouth. Make sure to spit out anything that triggers such a reaction (even if you think you correctly identified it), rinse your mouth with water, and spit again. It is also advisable to collect a leaf or other identifying part of the plant that triggers such a reaction and take it with you in case there is a serious reaction so you or a physician can verify what you actually put in your mouth.

It is also a good idea, especially if you are in a remote area or far from medical attention, to have a safety plan for what to do should you accidentally eat a toxic plant or have an allergic reaction. This does not have to come from a fear-based mindset—think of it more as preparedness. Despite our ample experience with edible plants, we bring a first-aid kit when foraging, which includes an antihistamine such as Benadryl and activated charcoal. Should an allergic reaction occur, taking the Benadryl may delay or eliminate a serious reaction. Should a toxic plant be ingested accidentally, inducing vomiting and/or taking activated charcoal (in pill or powdered form) can help eliminate or absorb some of the toxins. It is also a good idea to forage with at least one other person, especially when new to foraging. If one person makes a mistake, the other can seek help.

Lastly, it's a good idea to have the number of your local Poison Control network just in case. In Texas at least, this number is 1-800-222-1222.

We realize some of this sounds daunting and scary, but if you take the proper precautions and read the subsections below carefully, foraging is a safe and health-giving activity. Much safer than driving a car!

Most Dangerous Wild Plants in Texas

Before you begin foraging from the wild, it's critical to know and be able to confidently identify the most dangerous wild plants in your area. That is, know well the plants that can kill you (even when consumed in small amounts) before you seek out your first harvest. The reason for this is twofold:

1. If you know how to avoid the most dangerous plants in your area, you are acutely safer when foraging for edible species.
2. The number of extremely dangerous plants in Texas is few compared to the number of edible plants, which makes them easy to memorize and become familiar with.

Some of the most dangerous/toxic wild plants you may come across in Texas are **poison ivy, water hemlock, poison hemlock, castor bean, Texas mountain laurel, Nuttall's deathcamas, and moonflower.** Each of these is profiled below with pictures, descriptions, and specific warnings. Note that there are a number of other dangerous/toxic species in Texas, but these seven are among the most dangerous. Following is an abbreviated list of other toxic plants found in Texas that you should also be aware of:

Buckeye (*Aesculus* spp.)
Dogbane (*Apocynum* spp.)
Larkspur (*Delphinium* spp.)
Coral bean (*Erythrina herbacea*)
Bluebonnet (*Lupinus* spp.)
Chinaberry (*Melia azedarach*)
Tree tobacco (*Nicotiana glauca*)
Crow poison (*Nothoscordum bivalve*)
Virginia creeper (*Parthenocissus quinquefolia*)
Mistletoe (*Phoradendron* spp.)
Pigeonberry (*Rivina humilis*)
Silverleaf nightshade (*Solanum elaeagnifolium*)
Jerusalem cherry (*Solanum pseudocapsicum*)
Texas nightshade (*Solanum triquetrum*)
Mexican buckeye (*Ungnadia speciosa*)
Virginia bunchflower (*Veratrum virginicum*)

Potentially toxic/dangerous plants that can be confused with edible plants showcased in this book are noted in the "Toxic lookalikes" section of each species account. It is imperative to pay attention to these toxic lookalikes.

POISON IVY (*Toxicodendron radicans*) AND RELATIVES

Family: Anacardiaceae
Identification: Poison ivy is highly variable in growth form, but typically grows as either a small shrub or large vine with fine, **hairlike aerial rootlets** on the main stem. Leaves are deciduous, alternate, and consist of **three leaflets**. The **two lateral leaflets have "thumbs"** that point downward and are smaller than the terminal leaflet. Leaves often turn bright red in fall. The inflorescence consists of axillary panicles of small white flowers that give way to **yellowish-white fruits** in fall and winter. Poison ivy frequently vines up larger trees and sends out branches that, upon first glance, look like the host tree's branches. Be careful to follow such branches back to the originating central vine to see if it is in fact a poison ivy imposter or a branch of the host tree.

White poison ivy berries in fall and winter

Range and habitat: Common throughout the eastern US, poison ivy is found across much of Texas but is absent in parts of the panhandle, south Texas, and far west Texas. Its habitat is varied, but includes disturbed areas, fencerows, thickets, and riparian areas.

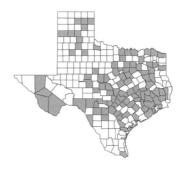

Related toxic species: *T. radicans* is the most common *Toxicodendron* species in Texas, but *T. pubescens* (eastern half of Texas) and *T. rydbergii* (western half of Texas) look similar and come with similar warnings. Poison sumac (*T. vernix*) is found in far east Texas but has very different, pinnate leaves and is reportedly more toxic than the others [3].

Warnings/comments: All parts of poison ivy are potentially dangerous, as they contain a resin called urushiol (which causes contact dermatitis). Not everyone is allergic to the resin in poison ivy (or its relatives), but many people are. Accidental consumption can trigger internal allergic reactions, including constriction of the airway, which could be deadly without swift medical attention. It is also important to be able to identify poison ivy even when not foraging for edible species. Accidentally burning poison ivy in a campfire and inhaling the fumes could constrict an airway or even reach the lungs.

While leading plant walks, we find that a large percentage of the adult population still does not know how to confidently identify poison ivy. Many people bring up sketchy identifying traits such as shiny leaves (many are not) and red stems (often they are green). The best identifying characteristics for spring, summer, and fall are: three leaflets, the two side leaflets with "thumbs" that point downward, and fine aerial rootlets on the main stems. In winter, after the leaves have fallen, the best identifying characteristics are clusters of small yellowish-white fruits arranged at the tip of bare stems, with fine aerial rootlets on the main stems. Note: You can come in contact with urushiol even after the leaves have fallen by brushing up against the bare stem or fruit. If you come in contact with poison ivy or one of its relatives, wash the area with soap and water within 20 minutes of contact to avoid a rash [4].

Notice how the leaves alternate along the stem.

WATER HEMLOCK (*Cicuta maculata*)

Family: Apiaceae

Identification: Water hemlock is an erect perennial herb up to about 6 feet tall. The alternate leaves are **pinnate, bipinnate, or sometimes tripinnate** and up to nearly 1 foot long. The lanceolate leaflets are serrated, and the **leaflet veins run from the middle vein to the notch of the serrations, not the tip of the serrations;** this is a helpful distinguishing feature. The inflorescence is a **compound umbel of small white flowers** that arises from leaf axils and/or from the end of branches. The dry, oval-shaped seeds are ribbed and look somewhat like caraway seeds.

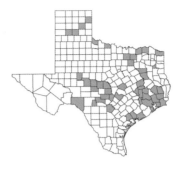

Range and habitat: Water hemlock is found in southeast, central, and north Texas and is always found growing in water or immediately adjacent to water on the banks of streams, lakes, or other bodies of water.

Related toxic species: *C. maculata* is the only *Cicuta* species in Texas, but it is related to our next dangerous plant entry, poison hemlock. There are other dangerous *Cicuta* species around the Great Lakes and on the West Coast.

Warnings/comments: Water hemlock can be fatal even when consumed in very small quantities. The roots and rootstocks contain the highest concentrations of the principle toxin (cicutoxin), but all parts of the plant may contain concentrations of the toxin and

Note the serrated, pinnate leaves with veins that end at the tooth notches, not at the tips of the teeth.

White compound umbels like this should be a red flag for the new forager.

should be avoided. Symptoms can occur quickly and can include stomach pain, nausea, dilated pupils, violent convulsions, and frothing at the mouth. Many experts claim that the *Cicuta* genus contains the most dangerous species in the US. In addition to documented fatal human poisonings, many livestock have died from consuming this species [5]. Therefore, we recommend that first-time foragers do NOT seek out plants in the Apiaceae family (including wild carrots) until they are more experienced with plant identification.

*POISON HEMLOCK (*Conium maculatum*)

Family: Apiaceae

Identification: Poison hemlock is an erect biennial herb up to 10 feet tall. The mature main **stem is green with noticeable purple spots or splotching,** which is an excellent identifying characteristic. The alternate leaves are **bipinnately or tripinnately compound** and are generally triangular in overall outline. The leaflets have a fernlike appearance. The small white flowers are arranged in **compound umbels** and arise from leaf axils and/or the ends of branches. The dry seeds are oval shaped and ribbed, with each rib being somewhat undulating.

Range and habitat: Poison hemlock is an invasive species in Texas and occurs sporadically in moist areas. Most often in Texas, it is found near major rivers and can grow in large colonies.

Related toxic species: No other *Conium* species are found in North America, but it is related to the preceding dangerous plant entry, water hemlock.

Warnings/comments: Poison hemlock is a toxic invasive plant originally from Europe and North Africa. It was allegedly used in ancient Greece to kill Socrates after he was sentenced to death. The fruits and leaves typically contain the highest concentrations of the primary toxin (the alkaloid coniine), but all parts of the plant should be avoided. It is said that young children have been poisoned after playing flutes made from the hollow stalks (mistaking them for elderberry stalks). Small amounts of this plant can cause serious complications or even fatality. Symptoms can come on quickly and include muscular paralysis, blindness, and eventually paralysis of the respiratory muscles. Unlike water hemlock, symptoms do not include

Poison hemlock stems have purple splotches that aid with identification.

convulsions [5]. We recommend that first-time foragers do NOT seek out Apiaceae family plants (including wild carrots) until they are more experienced with plant identification.

Poison hemlock typically grows in colonies and can get quite tall.

*CASTOR BEAN (*Ricinus communis*)

Family: Euphorbiaceae

Identification: Castor bean is a robust non-woody shrub up to 15 feet tall with alternate **large peltate leaves** (up to 2 feet long and wide). Each leaf has serrated palmate lobes. Flowers are arranged in a terminal raceme-like inflorescence of small white flowers. The **spiky seed pods** have three seeds in each and are bright red when new and gradually turn a bluish-green cast before drying to brown. Seeds are shiny and mottled brown and black.

Range and habitat: Castor bean is native to Africa and India but now grows scattered throughout the southeastern half of Texas. It is also commonly found in Central America and the Caribbean. Castor bean is sometimes cultivated but escapes in urban and disturbed areas, frequently near water.

Related toxic species: There are other potentially toxic Euphorbiaceae species in Texas, but castor bean is the most toxic.

Warnings/comments: Castor bean seeds are the source for castor oil, which has many nontoxic uses. However, the leftover raw seed cake after pressing the oils (and the raw seeds in general) contain ricin, a potent toxin. According to some, one seed contains enough ricin to kill an adult. Symptoms from accidental ingestion include nausea, diarrhea, thirst, and convulsions [6]. Luckily, the large compound leaves, robust nature, and overall tropical look make it hard

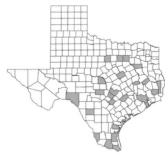

The white flowers give way to spiky seed pods.

Castor bean can grow quite tall and is frequently found near water.

to confuse castor bean with anything else in Texas. It is possible that a young castor bean plant could be mistaken for Texas bull nettle, but the latter is covered in stinging hairs, which makes mistaken identity unlikely. Additionally, the leaves of castor bean have more lobes than bull nettle (castor bean leaves typically have 5–11 lobes, while Texas bull nettle typically has 3–5 lobes).

TEXAS MOUNTAIN LAUREL
(*Dermatophyllum secundiflorum*)

Family: Fabaceae

Identification: Texas mountain laurel (also known as mescalbean) is an **evergreen** shrub or small tree (up to 10 feet tall) with dark green, leathery, **glossy, pinnately compound leaves** (each with 5–13 oval leaflets). The **purple pealike flowers smell like grape bubblegum** and hang in dense clusters in spring. The fruit is a woody pod (silvery gray when new, turning brown) about 4 inches long with **hard, bright red seeds** inside.

Range and habitat: Texas mountain laurel is relatively common in west, central, and south Texas. Habitat includes rocky caliche or limestone soils, often on hillsides.

Related toxic species: Species in the previously broadly defined *Sophora* genus (the former genus of Texas mountain laurel) were reclassified into *Dermatophyllum*, *Sophora*, and *Styphnolobium*. A number of these are reported as toxic, so we avoid them all. In Texas, these include *Sophora nuttalliana* (Trans-Pecos and panhandle), *Sophora tomentosa* (south coastal), and *Styphnolobium affine* (central, east, and north Texas).

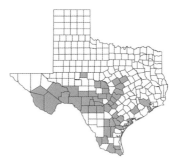

Warnings/comments: Many Texas children come across this plant at an early age for its cruel use as a "burn bean"; if you vigorously rub the red bean on

The irregular pods of Texas mountain laurel arise from the ends of branches.

concrete or rock, it heats up from friction and you can then burn your unsuspecting classmates. It turns out, the Texas mountain laurel bean is quite toxic if consumed. However, because it is so hard, we have heard instances of pets eating it by accident and passing it through their system with no harm done. If it is crushed or abraded, however, that is another story. The seeds contain high concentrations of toxic alkaloids including cytisine, but all parts of the plant should be avoided, even the bubblegum-scented purple flowers. Symptoms of poisoning include dizziness, tremors, nausea, vomiting, and diarrhea [7]. It should also be noted that the beans are commonly used in beadwork. Make sure to be in a well-ventilated area when drilling holes in the beans for beads and avoid inhaling the dust.

The hard red beans inside the pods are especially toxic.

NUTTALL'S DEATHCAMAS (*Toxicoscordion nuttallii*)

Family: Melanthiaceae

Identification: Nuttall's deathcamas is an herbaceous perennial bulb (reminiscent of a large onion) consisting mostly of **basal strap-like leaves** (about 1 foot long and less than 0.5 inch wide) and a 1–2-foot-tall flowering stalk. White flowers (blooming March to May) are arranged as a dense raceme near the top of the flowering stalk, and each has six bright yellow anthers along with a **yellow (sometimes pale yellow) dot at the base of each petal.** Capsules are erect. Note that it **does not have an onion-like odor** when crushed.

Range and habitat: Nuttall's deathcamas occurs primarily in central and north Texas in prairies and calcareous hillsides.

Related toxic species: No other *Toxicoscordion* species occur in Texas, but there are a few others that occur in western

Deathcamas can have stem leaves, unlike its edible lookalikes, which have basal leaves only.

Deathcamas is a more robust, stout plant than our wild onions.

states. A related Melanthiaceae species, Virginia bunch-flower (*Veratrum virginicum*), should also be avoided as it is highly toxic, but only occurs in a few eastern counties in Texas.

Warnings/comments: Nuttall's deathcamas is not especially common in Texas but can grow in locations similar to those of edible lookalikes including wild onions and Atlantic camas, so care should be taken to properly identify those species. Generally, Nuttall's deathcamas is a more robust, larger plant than a wild onion or Atlantic camas. It has a thicker stalk and wider leaves than the aforementioned edibles. Deathcamas also can have stem leaves, unlike its edible lookalikes. It also has bright yellow anthers, unlike the whitish anthers of wild onions. Atlantic camas has yellow anthers as well, but has bluish-purple petals as opposed to the white petals of deathcamas.

MOONFLOWER (*Datura wrightii*) AND RELATIVES

Family: Solanaceae

Identification: Moonflower is a short, widely branched annual shrub (from a perennial root) with a **musky odor.** Leaves are ovate, entire to sinuate margined, velvety, up to 6 inches long, and **asymmetrical at the base.** The large (6 inches long), **white, trumpetlike flowers** bloom April through October, when they open at night. The **nodding fruit is a golf ball–sized green ball covered in dense spikes.** When dry, the brown capsule splits open to reveal many small, flat, brown seeds.

Range and habitat: Moonflower is common in west and central Texas, less common in south and north Texas, and infrequent in east Texas. It is found on roadsides, loose sandy soils, and bottomlands. We also regularly find it in sandy creek beds and gravel bars.

The spiky, round seed capsule is diagnostic.

Datura often grows in clumps like this; note the numerous unopened flowers.

Related toxic species: *D. wrightii* is the most wide-spread/common *Datura* in Texas, but others include *D. quercifolia* in west Texas and the nonnative **D. stramonium*, which has a scattered distribution in Texas.

Warnings/comments: There are many other common names for this plant, including devil's trumpets, jimsonweed, Jamestown-weed, sacred datura, Indian-apple, thorn-apple, and toloache. It has a history of indigenous shamanic use in rituals, but has occasionally been misused by Western youths trying to get high or hallucinate with disastrous and fatal consequences. Do not attempt to use *Datura* internally. All parts of the plant contain highly toxic alkaloids, including scopolamine, hyoscyamine, and atropine [8]. Symptoms of poisoning include headache, nausea, delirium, extreme thirst, loss of sight, burning sensations on the skin, dilated pupils, convulsions, and death [5]. This plant is commonly used in landscaping throughout Texas due to its showy flowers, but respect should be given when encountered.

Plant Identification: Basic Botany and How to Identify Plants

Plant identification is the key skill that you need to develop as a forager. All other aspects of foraging become irrelevant if you cannot reliably distinguish one plant from another. There's no getting around it, so make sure to work on your botany skills before delving into edible plants. And for beginners, walking into a forest or field might just look like a sea of varying shades of green. We get it, it can be overwhelming at first. But, with dedicated practice, we promise that you can learn to distinguish the plants, and the rewards are immense. The forests and fields suddenly pop with diversity as you start to understand and appreciate the sometimes minute differences in that sea of green.

First, some of the most elementary basics seem silly to cover even to the newest naturalist, but they bear repeating because we see questions like these all the time, and it's important to have a baseline understanding of plants in general. So, here it goes:

- Mushrooms are not plants.
- Flowers turn into fruits.
- Fruits come in all shapes and sizes (not always fleshy, juicy, or in any way like grocery store produce).
- Fruits have seeds.
- Seeds grow into new plants under the right conditions.

If you learned something new in the preceding five bullets, that's OK. It just means you might have more to learn. Be patient and read this section carefully. Make sure to put the time in to really understand botany basics. We highly recommend that beginners pick up a copy of Tom Elpel's excellent *Botany in a Day* for a crash course in botany and how to learn the plants by plant family [9].

Plant identification necessitates looking "smaller" than the general public often thinks. We have received numerous identification request from friends, family, and class participants over the years after receiving a photo or two in a text or email. Oftentimes, the photos are from far away or are too blurry to be able to tell what the plant might be. Identifying plants is about examining the leaves, flowers, and fruits in detail and up close. Sure, many plants can be identified at a distance once you are familiar, but to start, it is going to take looking closely at different parts of the plant; "aim small, miss small" as the saying goes.

The reproductive parts of any plant (flower stalks, flowers, fruits, seeds) are often the most distinguishable feature. It is much easier to identify a flowering or fruiting plant than a plant that is dormant or not in season. Leaves are also important distinguishers and can vary in shape, size, arrangement, texture, and margin (leaf edge) characteristics. The bark (for trees and shrubs) or stem texture (for herbs) can also be a helpful distinguisher. It is also important to try to determine if a plant is evergreen or deciduous, if it is woody or herbaceous (non-woody), whether it is a vine or not, and if the plant is annual or perennial. These characteristics will be described in greater detail below. If you understand how to observe and key in on the differences among flowers, fruits, leaves, and other characteristics, you will be well on your way to proficiency with the plant identification process.

And it is important to understand that plant identification is truly a *process*. Especially when beginning, it is not and should not be quick. If you are identifying plants quickly as a beginner, you are most likely not spending the time and doing the due diligence required for accurate identification, and the consequences can be serious. Just because you see a plant and think it looks like a plant you have seen in a book or online that you know is edible does not mean you should eat it. Approach it with the scientific method: formulate a question, form a hypothesis, test the hypothesis, and iterate until you reach a conclusion. The steps should look something like this:

1. **Question:** What is this plant?
2. **Hypothesis:** This plant looks like a plant in a field guide I have. I think it *is* this particular plant.
3. **Testing:** Based on my field guide, are the leaves and leaf arrangement a match? Are the flowers and fruits a match? Is the plant growth habit a match? Is the habitat and range a match? Is it wild (cultivated plants are often more difficult)? Have I checked all the other potential distinguishers for this particular plant as stated in my field guide (evergreen/deciduous, annual/perennial, etc.)? Have I cross-checked against listed lookalike plants? Have I checked other references or resources? If no to any of these, conduct further research or start over with a new hypothesis.
4. **Conclusion:** Because I have checked more than one source and have based my conclusion on several plant characteristics (not just one), I conclude this is the plant in my field guide.

The above steps are valid for the identification of any plant, edible or not. We highly recommend practicing the plant identification process on all types of plants (grocery store produce, garden/landscaping plants, and non-edible wild plants) before applying it to wild edible plants. Consuming a wild plant or using it as medicine necessitates another level of assuredness. Double check your work, consult a third resource, review the "Most Dangerous Wild Plants in Texas" section again, and be absolutely sure you have what you think you have. Below is a list of other good **rules of thumb to consider when identifying edible plants:**

- Do not base your identification on just one or two characteristics. If the plant is not at a growth stage that allows you to look at fruits or flowers and all you have is the leaf, it's better to wait and come back to the same plant throughout the season to make sure you can verify multiple characteristics.

- Do not base your identification solely on photos. Make sure to consult the textual botanical description as well because the botanical terms (when cross-referenced in Appendix C) can back up the photos and, in some cases, are more descriptive than photos.
- Do not base your identification on just one specimen. Seek out other specimens to make sure that the first specimen is not an outlier and to confirm you are looking at consistent plant characteristics.
- Do not eat plants that you need a field guide to identify in the field. This means that you likely do not know the plant well enough to confidently identify it. Only eat edible species after you can consistently identify them without a field guide. The field guide is still important, but do not rely on it solely. *Rely on the knowledge you have learned from it and other sources.*
- Do not taste or eat unidentified plants.

As outlined in the earlier "Warnings and Safety" section, even after you go through the identification process and you are positive you have an edible plant in your hand, make sure you are processing and preparing it correctly before eating it and are starting slowly with small amounts to make sure you don't have an allergy or unexpected reaction to the plant.

Now that you understand the general plant identification process, we will run through some of the specific questions you should be asking yourself when identifying a new plant. Appendix C contains an illustrated glossary and list of botanical terms to refer to while reading this section, but we have attempted to break the characteristics down in simple terms below.

- **Is the plant annual or perennial?** Annual plants reseed each year and then die back, leaving the seeds to reproduce for the following year. Perennial plants persist from year to year either obviously (as with trees and other woody species) or not so obviously (where they may die back to the ground in winter, but a perennial root will send up new shoots in spring).
- **Is the plant woody or herbaceous?** Woody plants like trees and shrubs are often easy to distinguish from herbaceous (non-woody) plants. But the in-between can be tricky for some new foragers. Vines can be either woody or non-woody, and some herbaceous plants (like pokeweed) are quite tall and bushy and look like shrubs but in fact lack woody portions. If it is a tree or woody species, it is good to pay attention to what the bark looks like, as they often have distinctive characteristics.
- **Is the plant evergreen or deciduous?** Evergreen plants maintain their leaves year-round and do not drop them all in winter. Individual leaves may die and fall off to be replaced, but with evergreen plants, this does

not happen all at once. Deciduous plants drop all or most of their leaves cyclically (often in the winter). Some desert plants in Texas drop their leaves in response to drought and then leaf out again as rains come. These plants are known as drought deciduous.

- **How are the leaves arranged?** Refer to Figure 1 in Appendix C. Leaves can be arranged differently in relation to one another. Opposite leaves are arranged directly opposite from each other on either side of the stem. Alternate leaves alternate up either side of the stem. Whorled leaves are kind of like opposite leaves but with more than two; there can be three or more mature leaves coming out of one point on the stem in a circular fashion. Basal rosettes are leaves that only come out of the very base of the plant, as with dandelions. Plants with basal rosettes can be with or without stem leaves depending on the species.
- **What shape is the leaf?** Refer to Figure 2 in Appendix C. Individual leaves come in all kinds of shapes, from long and skinny (linear) to round (orbicular) and everything in between. Note that even on the same individual plant, the leaf shape can change considerably depending on the species. Oak leaves, for example, are notoriously variable.
- **Are the leaves simple or compound?** Refer to Figure 3 in Appendix C. Leaves can be simple or more complex. Simple leaves are leaves that do not have leaflets or other subsections, like an oak leaf. Compound leaves can have multiple subsections or leaflets (like a pecan), which can be arranged in many variations. Common compound leaf types include pinnate (many leaflets arising up both sides of the leaf) and palmately compound (several leaflets radiating from a central location on the leaf). Compound leaves are one of the trickier identification concepts for new foragers to understand, as there can be a wide variety of compound leaves (including trifoliate, bipinnate, tripinnate, etc.). It is important to make a distinction between a leaflet and a leaf. Leaves are attached to the main stems and detach cleanly, often leaving a leaf scar on the stem. Leaflets are part of the leaf itself and do not detach easily or cleanly from the rest of the leaf. This distinction can be difficult at first but gets easier with practice. Pecan leaves make a good, easy example if you want to understand what pinnate leaves look like and how they detach from the main stem. Another good example is poison ivy; people often say it has "leaves of three" but a better description would be "leaflets of three," as the three "leaves" are actually leaflets in a trifoliate compound leaf.
- **What do the margins of the leaf look like?** Refer to Figure 4 in Appendix C. Leaf margins (edges) can be smooth (entire), serrated,

Blackland Prairie

The Blackland Prairie was named for the deep, dark, heavy clay soils that underlie much of this prairie ecosystem, but the region includes several other soil types as well. While much of this region is now under cultivation due to its fertile soils, remnant pockets showcase the various tallgrass prairie ecosystems that once dominated. The region consists of several bands that are separated by bands of Post Oak Savannah and generally stretch from central to northeast Texas. Topography is flat to rolling, elevation ranges from about 250 feet above mean sea level (AMSL) in the south to 800 feet AMSL in the north, and the climate is generally subtropical.

Cross Timbers

The dense woodlands of the Cross Timbers were an impediment to settlers trying to cross from east to west, hence the name. Dominated by oaks, juniper, cedar elm, and hackberry, the woodlands are broken by irregular prairies. Topography is hilly and rolling where elevation ranges from about 400 feet AMSL in the east to about 1,700 feet AMSL in the west. The climate is subtropical and generally wetter than more westerly regions. The rocky upland soils are primarily sands and sandy loams, while the bottomlands consist of sandy or clayey loams and clays. The Cross Timbers region is very similar to the Post Oak Savannah described below but is generally rockier, and the two regions are separated by the Blackland Prairie.

Edwards Plateau

The Edwards Plateau is a land of limestone, caves, cliffs, canyons, aquifers, and springs. This area of central Texas is commonly referred to as the Texas Hill Country, and rightfully so. The dramatic limestone hills and canyons dominate much of the region but are punctuated by nearly flat plateaus, or mesas. While the Edwards Plateau is dominated by juniper and oak woodlands, it is also rich in endemic species found nowhere else in the world, including about sixty endemic plant species [10]. Elevation ranges from about 500 feet AMSL in the east, where the plateau abruptly drops off into the Blackland Prairie at the Balcones Escarpment, to about 2,800 feet AMSL in the west. Shallow, calcareous soils are underlain by limestone almost throughout the region, but the Llano Uplift region, which is sometimes included as a subregion of the Edwards Plateau (although it is geologically distinct), is composed primarily of granite and other volcanic rock. The climate is subtropical steppe with mild winters and hot summers lacking high humidity.

Gulf Prairies

The Texas Gulf Coast consists of coastal beaches, dunes, prairies, barrier islands, and inland woodlands farther from the coast. Topography is generally flat with some rolling plains; elevation throughout is less than 150 feet AMSL. Various wetlands including brackish marshes and lagoons are common as well as isolated freshwater prairie potholes with associated low mounds of sandy soil called "Mima mounds." Woodlands dominate the river bottoms, and oak groves (mottes) are scattered throughout. The climate is humid subtropical with warm to hot temperatures and nearly year-round high humidity. Soils generally consist of sands and sandy loams, with clay deposits along major rivers. The barrier islands support distinct zones of vegetation including beach, dune, coastal, and prairie communities.

High Plains

Together with the Rolling Plains, this region comprises the area known as the Texas panhandle. The High Plains are also known as the Llano Estacado and consist of plains at the top of a nearly flat plateau that is separated from the Rolling Plains by the Caprock Escarpment. Sandy or clayey soils are often underlain by a shallow layer of caliche (a crumbly white soil composed of hardened calcium carbonate) and red sandstone. The land is dominated by mixed prairie and pockmarked with "playa" lakes, which are ephemeral depressions that fill with water only part of the year and attract vast numbers of migrating waterfowl. Many of these playa lakes are small, but some can be quite large, as seen in the below photo from Muleshoe National Wildlife Refuge. Due to elevations ranging from about 2,400 feet AMSL in the south to 4,000 feet AMSL in the north, the climate is cool temperate.

Piney Woods

Pines and oaks dominate the forests and bottomlands of the Piney Woods of east Texas, home to the area known as the Big Thicket. Topography is rolling in the northern portions and flatter in the southern portions. These ecologically diverse pine-hardwood forests extend into Louisiana, Arkansas, and up to Oklahoma. The climate is humid subtropical with higher rainfall than other regions of Texas. Soils are dominated by sands and sandy loams. Elevation ranges from about 25 feet AMSL in the south to about 700 feet AMSL in the north. The native forests are sporadically broken by pastures and cropland. Wetlands and vast floodplains are common.

Post Oak Savannah

The Post Oak Savannah region is very similar to the Cross Timbers described above but is generally less rocky and the two regions are separated by the Blackland Prairie. The Post Oak Savannah, as one could guess, is composed primarily of savannah and grasslands interspersed with oak (primarily post oak) groves. Topography is rolling to flat, and elevation ranges from about 300 feet AMSL in the south to about 800 feet AMSL in the north. The climate is humid subtropical to subtropical, with higher rainfall compared to more westerly regions. The upland soils are primarily sands and sandy loams, while the bottomlands consist of sandy or clayey loams and clays.

Rolling Plains

Together with the High Plains, this region comprises the area known as the Texas panhandle. The rolling, grassy hills of this area are separated from the High Plains plateau by the Caprock Escarpment on its western edge. Shallow sandy and loamy soils are often underlain by limestone or calcareous subsoils, with gypsum layers common. Grasslands and mesquite dominate open areas, while wooded areas are frequently found along streams and drainages. The climate is warm temperate, and elevations range from about 800 feet AMSL in the east to 3,000 feet AMSL in the west near the Caprock Escarpment. The red soils of the Rolling Plains and the High Plains are what give the Red River its name, as sediments from this area are carried downstream to paint the river dividing Oklahoma and Texas.

South Texas Plains

The South Texas Plains are dominated by shrubby, impenetrable thickets of mesquite, yucca, prickly pear, and various other thorny shrubs and mixed with grasslands. It is also the northern extent of the Tamaulipan Thornscrub region, which is more extensive in Mexico. While much of the northern part of this subtropical region is fairly uniform, the very southern tip, known as the Lower Rio Grande Valley, is unique and has a nearly tropical feel to it. The Lower Rio Grande Valley is home to Mexican butterflies, plants, and birds not seen anywhere else in Texas or the US in general. It even includes old-growth palm groves and several resident parrot species. Elevation ranges from sea level at the mouth of the Rio Grande to about 1,000 feet AMSL to the north and west; the topography is nearly level to gently rolling. Note that the boundary between this region and the Gulf Prairies region is not clearly defined, but gradual.

Trans-Pecos

The Trans-Pecos is a highly variable region in far west Texas that generally has the Pecos River as its eastern border, the Rio Grande to the south and west, and New Mexico to the north. This complex region includes "sky islands" (isolated mountains surrounded by lowlands—the Chisos Mountains and Davis Mountains are good examples), the highest point in Texas (Guadalupe Peak), the Chihuahuan Desert, and the canyons of the Rio Grande. The geology is too varied to summarize succinctly, so we won't try. Due to its geologic diversity, the plant diversity of this region is the highest of any other in Texas [10]. Elevation ranges from about 1,100 feet AMSL along the Rio Grande to the south to 8,751 feet AMSL at Guadalupe Peak. Climate similarly varies widely depending on elevation; lowlands are generally subtropical, while mountains can be cool temperate. The low, desertic regions are dominated by creosote bush, cactus species, ocotillo, sotol, and lechuguilla, while higher mountains can be dominated by coniferous forests and oak woodlands.

Foraging Calendar for Texas

As detailed in the preceding "Physical Environment and Ecological Regions" section, Texas is a big and diverse state. Because of the level of variation across the state, creating a foraging calendar that works for the entire state is a challenge, but we humbly submit this section as an attempt.

Table 1 lists wild edibles that can be found nearly year-round depending on your region. Table 2 lists wild edibles by seasonal availability, but note that certain regions in Texas may have an earlier or later season for a given plant food. For example, in northern regions subject to hard freezes, chickweed and other early greens may not be available until early spring, whereas they are present winter through spring in subtropical regions. Table 2 provides a good idea of what may be available in your part of Texas, but specific harvest times may shift earlier or later depending on your location. Use it as a starting place and then consult the species accounts for more information. Some species have multiple edible parts that should be harvested at different times. In these cases, we put the part of the plant (fruit, flower, etc.) in parentheses after the plant name. Remember to refer to the county maps found in the species accounts for each species listed in Table 2 to confirm if it occurs in your area.

Table 1: Year-round wild edibles in Texas

Year-Round Wild Edibles
Barbados cherry, cenizo, dwarf palmetto (heart), lechuguilla (heart), saltwort, sea purslane, searocket, shepherd's purse (root), Texas bull nettle (root), Texas sotol (heart), Texas thistle (root), winecup (root), yaupon

Table 2: Texas foraging calendar for seasonal wild edibles

Season	Wild Edibles
Spring (March–May)	agarita (flower), American pokeweed, Atlantic camas, cheeseweed, cleavers, coma, common chickweed, common dandelion (leaves, flowers), curly dock (leaves), dewberry, elderberry (fruit), greenbriar, heart-leaf nettle, henbit, Japanese honeysuckle, lamb's quarters (greens), lechuguilla (flower stalk), loquat, mulberry, ocotillo (flower), pellitory, pink evening primrose, piñon pine (pollen), plantain (greens), prickly lettuce, prickly sow-thistle, purslane, redbud (flower, pod), retama (flowers), scarlet hedgehog cactus (flower), shepherd's purse (greens, capsules), spiderwort, stork's-bill, Texas ebony, Texas prickly pear (young pads, flowers), Texas sotol (flowering stalk), Texas thistle (stalk), Torrey yucca (flower), watercress, whitemouth dayflower, wild carrot, wild onion, winecup (flower)
Summer (June–August)	agarita (fruit), amaranth (greens), anacua, brasil, buffalo gourd, cattail (pollen, hearts), coma, common dandelion (leaves, flowers), curly dock (seeds), dewberry, eastern black nightshade (young leaves, fruit), elderberry (fruit), golden currant, greenbriar, honey mesquite, honeylocust (green pods), horsecrippler cactus, jujube, lemon beebalm, mayapple, meloncito, mustang grape, plantain (seeds), purslane, redbud (mature bean), retama (young green beans), rose (fruit), Texas bull nettle (seeds), Texas persimmon, Texas prickly pear (fruit), Torrey yucca (fruit), tree cholla (flower), triangle cactus (fruit), watercress
Fall (September–November)	amaranth (seeds), American beautyberry, American beech, American lotus (nuts, tubers), bastard cabbage (greens, flowers), brasil, buffalo gourd, cedar elm, chile pequín, common dandelion (root), common persimmon, common sunflower, desert yaupon, Drummond's wood-sorrel, dwarf palmetto (fruit), eastern black nightshade (fruit), evergreen sumac, farkleberry, firethorn, goldenrod, groundcherry, hawthorn, honey mesquite, honeylocust (mature pods) juniper, lamb's quarters (seeds), live oak (acorns), meloncito, Mexican plum, pawpaw, pecan, peppervine, piñon pine (nuts), purple passionflower (fruit), retama (mature bean), rose (fruit), rusty blackhaw, sugar hackberry, Texas madrone, Texas prickly pear (fruit), tree cholla (fruit), triangle cactus (fruit), Turk's cap (flower, fruit), walnut, whitemouth dayflower
Winter (December–February)	bastard cabbage (greens), cheeseweed, Christmas berry, cleavers, common chickweed, curly dock (leaves), dwarf palmetto (fruit), henbit, pellitory, prickly lettuce, prickly sow-thistle, sugar hackberry

Species Accounts

TREES

For the purposes of this book, trees are generally defined as woody, perennial plants that are larger than a shrub and generally have one main trunk. There are many plants that can grow either as shrubs or trees depending on habitat and growing conditions, so the distinction between tree and shrub is somewhat murky. Additionally, it can be difficult to distinguish a young tree from a shrub, so if you're not sure, check both the Trees and Shrubs/Vines sections in this book.

RUSTY BLACKHAW (*Viburnum rufidulum*)

Family: Adoxaceae
Edible part and harvest time: Fruits ripen in late fall.
Toxic lookalikes: None in Texas
Identification: This small deciduous tree (or large shrub) can reach 30 feet tall but is typically smaller. The **bumpy, checkered bark** of mature specimens is prominent and distinct. Leaf shape ranges from elliptic to oblanceolate. The **opposite leaves** are **glossy above and below with finely serrated edges.** Fine rusty hairs cover winter buds and the central vein on the underside of the leaf. Small white flowers form dense clusters in spring. The **elliptic, raisin-sized**

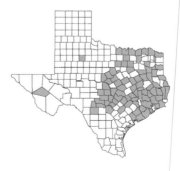

Rusty blackhaw flowers in early spring; note the opposite leaf arrangement.

Distinctive checkered bark

fruits (drupes) start out pinkish but turn bluish black and slightly wrinkled when ripe. Each drupe has one large, **flat seed** surrounded by sweet pulp.

Range and habitat: Rusty blackhaw is found in east Texas and much of central Texas. We usually find it near creeks in sandy or rocky soils in central Texas, but it can be found in thickets and forest edges throughout much of east Texas.

RECIPE

Blackhaw Juice

Place ¼ cup ripe blackhaw fruits in a pot with 1½ cups water and bring to a simmer. Remove the pot from the stove and mash the berries with the back of a fork to remove the skin and pulp from the large seed inside each fruit. Strain the dark purplish-brown juice through a fine stainless-steel mesh strainer to remove the seeds and collect the liquid. Add the liquid back to the pot with ½ tsp. sugar and ½ tsp. cinnamon and bring to a simmer. Stir until the sugar is dissolved, then remove and let cool. The resulting juice is best cold and can be further strained to remove any remaining bits of skin or pulp.

Related edible species: Other edible *Viburnum* species in Texas include *V. nudum* and *V. recognitum* (both found in east Texas). Another, *V. prunifolium,* is fairly uncommon in Texas and has a limited distribution in central Texas and far east Texas.

Uses/history/comments: Rusty blackhaw fruits ripen in November and December, when they are dark bluish black and slightly wrinkled. Usually the leaves have already turned red when the fruits are ready, which makes locating a potentially ripe tree easier.

There are many *Viburnum* species throughout the US but only a handful in Texas, many of them only found in east Texas. Many of the *Viburnum* species found in east Texas bear fruits that are not especially tasty. Rusty blackhaw, however, has delicious fruits. The fruits are analogous to mealy, less-sweet raisins, with a large flat seed inside each. Very tasty, but hard to gather in quantity. Birds and other animals love them, so they are usually hard to find in abundance.

Rusty blackhaw (and other *Viburnum* species) has also been used medicinally for abdominal and menstrual cramps (another common name for many *Viburnum* species is crampbark). Typically, a simple alcohol tincture is made out of the spring leaves and stems [11].

PAWPAW (*Asimina triloba*)

Family: Annonaceae

Edible part and harvest time: Fruits ripen from late summer to early fall (usually early August through September in Texas).

Toxic lookalikes: None in Texas. CAUTION: Some people develop a mild dermatitis when handling the pawpaw fruit skin and leaves, so use caution when harvesting.

Identification: In Texas, pawpaw is a small to medium-sized deciduous tree with fairly smooth, gray bark. The **large obovate leaves** are acuminate and up to 1 foot long at maturity. The **maroon-colored flowers** appear in spring at around the same time as the leaves and consist of three smaller inner petals nested within three larger outer petals. The **irregularly shaped green fruits** can be up to 6 inches long and 4 inches thick and look like a strangely shaped mango. The large fruits get brown spots on their thin skin as they ripen before turning yellowish brown. Each fruit has a yellowish pulp inside surrounding several large, flat, dark seeds.

Range and habitat: Pawpaw grows in far east Texas and is primarily found in the undergrowth of floodplains and bottomlands. In Texas, one of the best areas to find pawpaws is the area around Nacogdoches.

Related edible species: There is one other native *Asimina* in Texas. Smallflower pawpaw (*A. parviflora*) can be found in southeast Texas, but the range extends into pockets of central Texas. Pawpaws are in the same family as cherished fruits from tropical America such as cherimoya (*Annona cherimola*) and soursop (*Annona muricata*).

Uses/history/comments: Pawpaws are legendary in the foraging scene and are rightfully prized. Along with the mayapple (*Podophyllum peltatum*) and purple passionflower (*Passiflora incarnata*), pawpaws are one of the most distinctly tropical-tasting fruits native to Texas. The large, ripe pawpaw fruit is similar in flavor and texture to its tropical cousins (cherimoya and soursop), but pawpaw is cold-hardy and can grow as far north as Michigan and New York. This large range has led to some fun common names,

Maroon pawpaw flower in early spring.

Ripe pawpaws after peeling off the skin and cutting in half

"hillbilly mango" being our favorite. Though more common in the midwestern and eastern US, pawpaw can be found fairly easily in parts of east Texas.

The regal, maroon-colored flowers can give off a funky smell but are often odorless. Although a single tree may produce many flowers, they are finicky about fruiting, as only a handful of the flowers typically set fruit. Once pollinated, the fruit grows through the summer and ripens into an irregularly shaped green fruit that is typically growing in clusters of three, but we have seen up to nine fruits growing in a bundle. The fruit looks kind of like a curvy mango; each fruit, even on the same tree, is a slightly different shape. Fruits are green and nearly the same color as the leaves, so it can be somewhat difficult to pick them out, as they can grow pretty high up in a mature pawpaw tree. We try to key in on sagging branches that may indicate a heavy load of fruit. If you're planning a pawpaw foraging outing, we recommend bringing either a ladder or a long pole with a hook on the end to assist with harvesting.

In Texas, fruit harvest can begin in early August once the fruit is full-sized, but harvesting this early may require further ripening in a paper bag before eating. The best-tasting fruits will be harvested in early fall but this is risky, as other animals and birds tend to get to them. The best fruits we've found will have started to develop black dots on the skin and will feel soft when lightly squeezed, like a peach. The delightful tropical smell also gives away that the fruit is ready and ripe. Once harvested, peel off the thin skin and eat as is while spitting out the large seeds (and planting them nearby for posterity). The texture is somewhere between a ripe banana and a mango, smooth and creamy.

Ripe pawpaws can be used in many dessert recipes including ice creams, pies, and baked goods. Our favorite way to eat them is raw after letting them ripen off the tree for a few days until they look almost rotten, but they also pair really well with cinnamon and yogurt.

RECIPE

Pawpaw + Yogurt + Cinnamon

Obtain your favorite plain (no sugars or flavors added) yogurt and dice ripe pawpaw into it. Add a pinch or two of cinnamon and mix well. If you don't like yogurt, just sprinkling cinnamon on each bite of pawpaw sans yogurt is excellent, too.

The other native *Asimina* species (*A. parviflora*) is like a miniature version of the common pawpaw. More of a shrub than a tree, with similar but smaller leaves, flowers, and fruits, it can be used the same way as *A. triloba*.

ANACUA (*Ehretia anacua*)

Family: Boraginaceae

Edible part and harvest time: Fruits ripen from summer to fall.

Toxic lookalikes: None in Texas

Identification: Anacua (or knock-away, as it is sometimes called) is a medium-sized subtropical tree 15–30 feet tall **often with multiple or split trunks.** The bark is gray and furrowed, while the leaves are simple, alternate, and ovate with an extremely rough texture reminiscent of sandpaper. Leaf margins are usually entire (untoothed) but can be coarsely toothed as well. The top of the leaf is darker green than the paler underside. Terminal clusters of fragrant **white flowers** are borne in spring. Approximately 0.25-inch fruits follow in summer and into fall and ripen from yellow to dark orange. Each fruit contains two hemispheric seeds (technically stones).

Range and habitat: Anacua occurs along the southern Gulf Coast and ranges up to the Colorado River in Travis County. It is found in many types of soils but grows largest along river bottoms with good drainage [12]. It can also be found in thickets, brushland, and forests.

Related edible species: There are no other *Ehretia* species in Texas, but Texas wild olive (*Cordia boissieri*) is also in the Boraginaceae family and has edible fruits (when cooked) that are typically made into jelly or jam. Texas wild olive is found in south Texas along the Rio Grande.

Anacua flowers and close-up of the rough, sandpapery leaves

Furrowed anacua bark and split trunk

Uses/history/comments: Anacua is an interesting subtropical tree with extremely rough leaves, which make identification easy. The leaves are remarkably similar to sandpaper; another common name for anacua is sandpaper tree. Once you feel the leaves, you should easily be able to identify anacua based on touch alone. Anacua wood is also very hard and dense, and has been used to make fence posts, tool handles, axles, and wheel spokes [12].

We often find anacua near major rivers, where it can fruit prolifically. It approaches its northern range limit around the Colorado River in Austin, but look for it farther south along major rivers. Large populations can be found around Ottine, Texas, along the San Marcos River.

The ripe fruits are orange and sweet and have two large edible seeds inside. We enjoy eating them straight off the tree, but they can also be made into an excellent jam. The flavor of the raw fruit is somewhat tart, but distinctly pleasant when ripe. The flesh is somewhat mealy, but most foragers enjoy it. You can also eat the fruits when yellow, but the taste is better as they mature to orange or orange-red.

RECIPE

Anacua Jam

Blend 5 cups ripe anacaua in a Vitamix on high until the fruit and seeds are broken up. Put the anacua mash into a pot and cover with filtered water (just enough to cover the mash). Cook the mixture on low-medium heat for about 20 minutes while stirring occasionally. Remove from heat and let cool, then strain through a cheesecloth. You should get about 2 cups of liquid. Pour the liquid back into the pot along with 2 tbsp. lime juice and 1 cup sugar. Bring the mixture to a boil and simmer until it congeals into a jam consistency (about 10–15 minutes). Scoop the jam into a jar and keep refrigerated for up to 3 weeks.

SUGAR HACKBERRY (*Celtis laevigata*)

Family: Cannabaceae

Edible part and harvest time: Fruits are available in fall through early spring.

Toxic lookalikes: None in Texas

Identification: Sugar hackberry is a broad-crowned, medium-sized tree (up to 30 feet tall) easily recognized by prominent, **warty, gray bark.** Leaves are simple, alternate, **asymmetrical,** and lanceolate. The small red hackberries (**about the size of a BB**) form during late summer and ripen in fall. Each hackberry has a single large stone inside surrounded by thin, sugary flesh. Hackberries do not fall off the tree like many other ripe fruits but persist through winter and into spring.

Distinctive, warty hackberry bark

Range and habitat: *C. laevigata* is common in thickets, woodlands, and bottomlands throughout most of Texas, although it is not found in the Trans-Pecos. However, every ecoregion in Texas has at least one native hackberry species.

Related edible species: *C. reticulata* (scattered throughout Texas) and *C. ehrenbergiana* (south and west Texas) are regionally common species.

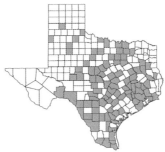

Hackberry flowers and new leaves in spring

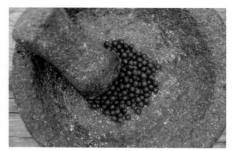
Hackberries can be ground into an orange paste.

C. occidentalis and *C. tenuifolia* are less common in Texas. *C. ehrenbergiana* is the only *Celtis* species in Texas with a soft, fleshy, orange fruit; the others produce hard drupes surrounded by a thin, reddish, sugary skin.

Uses/history/comments: Hackberries ripen from October to January and can stay on the tree into spring. Hackberry fruits are one of the oldest known human plant foods in North America [13]. The berries can be eaten raw straight off the tree, but they have a hard seed in the center that should be avoided if you have sensitive or brittle teeth. Alternatively, the fruits can be collected and then ground using a metate or other grinding method. The resulting orange paste can be formed into a sort of quick energy bar (complete with sugars, fats, and protein) and dried for later use. Native Americans also molded the hackberry paste to the end of a stick and then roasted it over a fire [13]; we have found this method is fun for kids and gives them a good reason to help you collect hackberries. Hackberry "milk" is also a worthy pursuit.

Hackberries are a favorite of many resident and migrant birds in Texas and therefore frequently sprout up along fencerows and in vacant lots. Although much maligned in Texas due to its brittle tendencies (more than one fence or roof has been destroyed by a fallen hackberry tree), hackberry also produces a worthy bow wood.

RECIPE

Hackberry Milk

Add 1 cup ripe hackberries and 2 cups water to a Vitamix blender. Blend on the highest setting until the hackberries are pulverized and the liquid turns an orangey color. Then squeeze the liquid through a cheesecloth or strainer to remove the remaining hard bits of the shell. Drink this "milk" (hot or cold) as is or use in place of your favorite nut milk. Hackberry milk is sweeter than most nut milks because it also contains the sugars from the thin flesh.

JUNIPER (*Juniperus* spp.)

Juniperus ashei

Family: Cupressaceae

Edible part and harvest time: For most species, berries ripen in summer or fall.

Toxic lookalikes: There are no other evergreen conifers in Texas with fleshy "berries" other than the *Juniperus* species. However, one species of juniper, *J. virginiana*, which is often called eastern redcedar, contains thujone in its leaves (and to a lesser extent in its berries) and should not be used in large quantities, although its berries are edible in smaller amounts [14]. *J. virginiana* is easily distinguished from the other smaller junipers in Texas, as it typically is a taller tree with one central trunk, whereas the other junipers that overlap in range are often shrubby with multiple trunks. There are other junipers in west Texas that have single trunks, but their ranges do not overlap with *J. virginiana*. There are also some European juniper species used in landscaping that should be avoided due to potential toxicity.

Identification: Junipers are small, aromatic **evergreen conifers,** often with shredded or furrowed bark and one to several trunks depending on species. The **leaves are small and scalelike** and do not resemble traditional leaves. Junipers are often dioecious (having male and female flowers on separate individuals) and have clusters of small, inconspicuous flowers at the ends of branches. Male plants produce clouds of yellow pollen, which pollinates the female cone-bearing trees. The modified cones found on female trees consist of **fleshy blue or reddish "berries"** (depending on the species) with one to several seeds inside. Most juniper species have two different types of leaves. Young leaves are typically

Juniperus pinchotii, one of the red-fruited juniper species in Texas

larger, pointed, and needlelike, whereas older, mature leaves are small and scalelike. This can cause confusion for many new foragers who might think a pine tree is sprouting up when it is actually a juvenile juniper.

Range and habitat: *Juniperus* species are common in much of Texas except for the South Texas Plains. Habitats for many of the western species include caliche, rocky limestone soils, and other rocky, dry areas, but *J. virginiana* can also be found in the sandy and loamy soils of east Texas.

Related edible species: All of the juniper species in Texas are edible in some form, but some are tastier than others and *J. virginiana* should be consumed sparingly, as mentioned above. Junipers in Texas include *J. ashei* (Edwards Plateau and north-central Texas, blue berries), *J. coahuilensis* (Trans-Pecos, red berries), *J. deppeana* (Trans-Pecos, bluish berries), *J. flaccida* (Chisos Mountains, bluish-green berries), *J. monosperma* (Trans-Pecos and panhandle, blue berries), *J. pinchotii* (west Texas, red berries), *J. scopulorum* (Trans-Pecos and panhandle, bluish berries), and *J. virginiana* (primarily eastern half of Texas, bluish berries).

Uses/history/comments: "Are cedar berries edible?" This is invariably one of the first questions we get asked when leading plant walks in central Texas. The answer is yes, but with caveats. First, the common name "cedar" is confusing since that is applied to many other genera including the *Cedrus* species of the Mediterranean and Middle East and the *Thuja* and *Chamaecyparis* species of the eastern and western US. These other species have

Juniperus virginiana, the most common juniper species in east Texas

woody cones, whereas *Juniperus* species have fleshy "berries" that are actually highly modified seed cones. Additionally, we think of juniper berries more as a flavoring or spice than a staple food, since it is hard to eat more than a few berries at a time due to the pungency and astringency of some species. However, some of the west Texas species of junipers are juicier, sweeter, and quite enjoyable. Alligator juniper (*J. deppeana*), oneseed juniper (*J. monosperma*), and redberry juniper (*J. pinchotii*), in particular, are enjoyable raw straight

RECIPE

Juniper Pork Chops

In a mixing bowl, combine 2 tbsp. crushed juniper berries, 2 minced garlic cloves, 3 bay leaves, 3 tbsp. brown sugar, zest from half an orange, ½ cup port wine, and a dash of salt and black pepper. Mix well until the sugar dissolves into the mixture. Pour the mixture into a ziplock bag along with 4 pork chops and let marinate for at least an hour in the fridge. Once marinated, preheat oven to 375°F. Heat a well-oiled cast-iron pan on high heat and sear the pork chops for 2 minutes on each side. Then place the pork chops in a baking dish and bake in the oven for about 15 minutes or until cooked through. While the pork chops are cooking, heat the remaining marinade in the cast-iron pan and pour this sauce over the pork chops when done.

off the tree when ripe. But the more common and widespread species in Texas, Ashe juniper (*J. ashei*) and eastern redcedar (*Juniperus virginiana*), are generally not very tasty unless used sparingly as a spice or additive.

Juniper berries can be harvested at different times of the year depending on species but are available in summer or fall for most species. Harvesting is straightforward and involves picking each berry one by one, as they do not tend to drop if you try shaking them off the branch. The leaves of some species can be prickly, so be cautious when harvesting. The berries of the juicier, better-tasting species can be mashed and dried into cakes for later use or used in various meat/game dishes. The less-tasty species are best used as a flavoring for spirits (after all, *J. communis*—a northern juniper species not found in Texas—is the flavoring used in gin) and vinegars. The berries can also be eaten in small quantities as a wilderness breath freshener. Furthermore, the leaves can be used as a tea for coughs and colds and are also commonly bound, dried, and burned as incense [15].

TEXAS PERSIMMON (*Diospyros texana*)

Family: Ebenaceae
Edible part and harvest time: Fruits ripen in late summer (usually August).
Toxic lookalikes: None in Texas
Identification: Texas persimmon is a small tree or shrub 10 to 20 feet tall. The gray bark is distinct: **smooth with thin, peeling outer layers** similar to crepe myrtle bark. Leaves are small (1–1.5 inches), semievergreen, alternate, pubescent, and ovate to obovate. The leaf margins are entire but **roll slightly under (revolute)**; many leaves on a tree will have

small wart-like growths formed by a gall wasp. This is so common on Texas persimmon that we have not actually seen a gall-free tree, although some individual leaves will have them and some won't. Flowers are small, **bell-like, and white,** while the fruit starts out green and **ripens to black** (round and about 1 inch in diameter, with several large, flattish seeds inside).

Range and habitat: Texas persimmon is abundant in central and south Texas and extends west into the Trans-Pecos. It is not as common in counties around Houston. Its habitat consists of open woodlands and thickets in rocky soil and rocky outcrops and hillsides.

Related edible species: In Texas, *D. virginiana* (eastern half of Texas) is the only other persimmon. It's a taller tree with larger, orange, delicious fruits. Other edible *Diospyros* species can be found in temperate to tropical regions around the world.

Uses/history/comments: The jet-black fruit of the Texas persimmon is one of our most abundant and tasty wild fruits. They ripen in late summer, when the skin is black (with no hint of green) and soft when lightly squeezed. Our favorite way to harvest them is to find a fruiting tree and lightly shake the branches or main trunk. The ripe fruits will fall, as they are precariously attached to the stem when fully ripe. You can also find ripe fruits on

Texas persimmon's bell-shaped flowers

Smooth, gray bark of Texas persimmon

the ground under fruiting trees, but you have to beat the ants, birds, and other wildlife to them. We have noticed that many birds like to just peck at or eat half of a fruit, so look out for half-eaten ones still on the tree and try to avoid them. The fruits can be eaten raw (our favorite) or used in jams, pies, wine, etc.

Fair warning: Eating Texas persimmons with a friend makes for great memories of black-stained smiles. The fruits temporarily stain your mouth and teeth when eaten, but a quick swig of water does the trick. They will stain clothing more persistently, though.

TEXAS MADRONE (*Arbutus xalapensis*)

Family: Ericaceae

Edible part and harvest time: Fruits ripen in fall.

Toxic lookalikes: None in Texas

Identification: Texas madrone is a relatively uncommon small evergreen tree throughout much of its range but is frequent and more robust in Big Bend National Park. It has **prominent, smooth, reddish bark** with an outer layer sometimes peeling into thin, papery flakes (similar to crepe myrtle). Leaves are alternate, leathery, ovate, and 2–5 inches long. Leaf margins are entire or, more often, serrated. The white flowers are small, **urn shaped,** and arranged in clustered panicles. The **round, textured fruits are red when ripe** and about 0.5 inch in diameter.

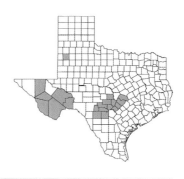

Range and habitat: Texas has two disjointed populations of Texas madrone: the Trans-Pecos and the Edwards Plateau. Habitat consists of dry, rocky limestone outcrops, hills, and canyon slopes.

Related edible species: There are no other madrone species in Texas, but the Pacific Northwest and California have the Pacific madrone (*Arbutus menziesii*), which has similarly edible fruits.

Uses/history/comments: The taste of the fruit of the European relative, strawberry tree (*A. unedo*), is somewhat overexaggerated, but our Texas species is decently

Smooth red bark of Texas madrone

RECIPE

Madrone Berry Mash

Obtain 1 cup of ripe madrone fruits and add to a mixing bowl along with ½ cup fresh strawberries and ½ cup fresh blueberries. Mash all the fruits together with a potato masher or similar utensil until well smooshed and integrated. Add the mix to a pot and cook on low heat while stirring for about 3 minutes, until the fruits have mixed well. Serve over ice cream or yogurt.

sweet when ripe, though dry. When encountered, it rarely fruits as prolifically as in the first photo here but can occasionally bear large numbers of fruits under the right conditions. More often, you may find a handful of fruits on any one tree. Madrone is often a small, shrubby tree and is not especially common in the Edwards Plateau. However, it is much more common in the mountains of the Trans-Pecos, where it can grow into a quite tall tree. The

Texas madrone leaves showing serrated margins

strikingly distinctive reddish bark is smooth and flaky like crepe myrtle bark.

Please harvest madrone fruits responsibly in the Edwards Plateau, where it is not as common. In the dry, rocky habitat they prefer, they make a good trail nibble, but only harvest larger amounts when abundant.

REDBUD (*Cercis canadensis*)

Family: Fabaceae

Edible part and harvest time: Flowers are available in early spring; young pods after flowers; mature beans through winter.

Toxic lookalikes: Mexican buckeye (*Ungnadia speciosa*) is an unrelated tree that superficially resembles redbud, as it is covered with pink flowers around the same time as redbud (early spring). However, Mexican buckeye leaves are pinnately compound, the pink flowers are not pealike, and the fruits are not bean-like (Mexican buckeye has three-lobed capsules with large, black, round seeds).

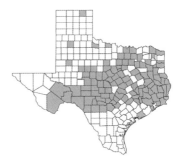

Identification: Redbud is a small deciduous tree with alternate, simple, **heart-shaped leaves**. Flowers are **pink with typical pealike blossoms** and **arise in clusters directly off the branch**. The pealike pods are bright green when young and then turn dry and brown and about 2–4 inches long when mature. The bark is smooth and reddish brown when young and turns to gray and somewhat flaky with age.

Range and habitat: Redbud can be found in many ecoregions in Texas, but generally is not found in the South Texas Plains or much of the northern panhandle. Preferred habitat includes calcareous soils in the Trans-Pecos and Edwards Plateau and forested sandy areas farther east.

Related edible species: There are no other redbud species in Texas (although there are multiple subspecies), but there are other edible *Cercis* species in Asia and Europe.

Uses/history/comments: Redbud produces an abundance of bright pink flowers in early spring (usually in March before or as the leaves emerge) that can be added raw to salads or used as a garnish. The flavor of the flowers is fairly neutral but has a slight sweetness to it. The flowers are easy to pick, as they grow in clusters directly off the branch.

Young, green redbud pods are good eating until they get too fibrous.

Mature redbud pods with small, dried beans

After the flowers are pollinated, small, green, pealike pods form later in spring. When young and tender, these are a poor man's version of snap peas, albeit nearly paper thin. They can be eaten raw straight off the tree, but we prefer them in stir-fries. Make sure to harvest them when very young and tender (1–2 inches long or less), as they get tough and fibrous quickly after developing. While not nearly as juicy as a good snap pea, they are more than adequate in a stir-fry or as a quick trail nibble.

The mature dried beans are also edible, but not choice. The dried pods are easy to collect en masse, as they are clustered in groups along the branches and stay on the tree into winter. You can either crush up pod and all and then winnow out the small, black, flat beans or individually open the pods and dump the beans into a container. We prefer the latter, but it is not a fast method. Once collected, the beans must be soaked overnight (as with store-bought dried beans) and then cooked in fresh water to make them edible.

RECIPE

Redbud Pod Stir-Fry

Harvest 3 cups of young, tender redbud pods. In a cast-iron pan, heat 1 tbsp. sesame oil on medium heat while adding 1 minced garlic clove and a dash of red pepper flakes. Cook this for 1 minute, then add the redbud pods and cook for an additional 2–3 minutes while stirring. Turn off the heat and toss with black sesame seeds, salt, and pepper to taste. This makes an excellent Asian-influenced side dish. Add rice and/or chicken to make it a main dish.

TEXAS EBONY (*Ebenopsis ebano*)

Family: Fabaceae

Edible part and harvest time: Beans from green pods can be found in spring and into summer.

Toxic lookalikes: While there are a number of potentially toxic Fabaceae species that grow in the same habitats, the hard, dense, woody pods of *Ebenopsis* are unique. For an inexperienced forager, Texas mountain laurel (*Dermatophyllum secundiflorum*) could be misidentified, but the larger leaves, lack of thorns, and bright red seeds easily distinguish this toxic plant from Texas ebony.

Identification: Texas ebony is an evergreen small tree or large shrub with **alternate bipin-nate leaves**. Each leaf has three to six pairs of pinnae, with two or three pairs of leaflets. Its **branches are zigzagged**, with thorns protruding at the angles along with the leaves. The flowers are dense white spikes, which look like puffballs. The **pods (6 inches long) are woody and thick walled** and turn from green when young to brown when mature. Each pod has about 10 tightly packed beans inside. The ground under each mature Texas ebony tree will be littered with old, brown, dried pods, which aids in identification.

Range and habitat: Texas ebony is found in the South Texas Plains and thornscrub, where it is one of the dominant evergreen trees. It can be found along the south Texas coast and farther inland as well.

Related edible species: None in Texas

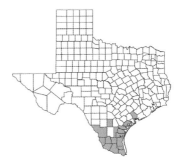

Uses/history/comments: Texas ebony, also known as ébano, is an amazing plant. It produces an abundant crop of food even during the worst droughts south Texas can muster. The dense, hard, woody bean pods are ubiquitous under and around each tree—so hard and dense that many people would not even consider trying to eat them. Prepared correctly, however, they are one of south Texas's most delicious and abundant wild foods. Harvesting the pods at the correct stage is critical. You want to find pods that are still green but fully developed other-wise. These green pods will be vigorously attached to the branch, so you may need to use shears to cut them off.

Texas ebony leaves

Once gathered, the green pods will need to be split along the seam between both halves to remove the edible beans inside. Even though the pods are still green, they are still hard and difficult to open. It's possible to cut them open with a knife, but it's difficult and somewhat dangerous due to the amount of pres-sure you need. In our experience, a better, safer method is to first boil the pods for 5 to 10 minutes. Once boiled, the pod halves may have already separated or just pushing a knife between the two halves at the seam will open it easily. Once the

Shelled ebony pods; the green beans on the top left are edible, the tan coatings on the top right are not.

RECIPE

Crispy Roasted Texas Ebony

After separating the inner "meat" of the ebony beans from the outer coating, add 1 cup of them to a parchment-lined baking sheet and toss with 1–2 tbsp. olive oil and a pinch of salt. Spread the beans evenly and roast at 400°F for 15 minutes, until the beans are browned but not burnt. You can eat as is or mix in some of your favorite spices (a pinch of garlic powder is our favorite here).

pod is open, remove the thick, rubbery, pale yellowish outer coating from each bean. If you open the pod and the beans are black or reddish and hard, the pods you picked were too mature. If you've harvested correctly, the inner "meat" of the bean will be a light green; this is the edible part.

Ebony beans are versatile but are best dry-roasted prior to eating. They taste like a cross between corn and peanuts, with the texture of a chickpea. After roasting, eat them salted as is, sprinkled on salads, ground into flour, or any other way you might incorporate chickpeas into your meals. Overall, a very tasty, protein-rich wild food, even in drought.

We have also heard that a traditional practice in northern Mexico is to use the mature black Texas ebony beans as a substitute for coffee, but we have not experimented with this yet. Additionally, the dense, reddish heartwood is prized for wood carvings and furniture [12].

HONEYLOCUST (*Gleditsia triacanthos*)

Family: Fabaceae
Edible part and harvest time: Unripe green pods are available in summer, while ripe brown pods are available in fall.
Toxic lookalikes: The branched thorns that come off the trunk of honeylocust are distinct, and there are no toxic lookalikes in Texas with such thorns. However, many people confuse black locust (*Robinia pseudoacacia*, another pea family tree) with honeylocust. Some authors claim that black locust is toxic, which is probably true for the roots and leaves. However, the white flowers and new green pods (cooked) of black locust are edible.

Bipinnate honeylocust leaves

Imposing, branched thorns coming directly off the main trunk

Honeylocust flowers   SAM KIESCHNICK

Nonetheless, it is important to know the difference between these two species. Black locust has much smaller (4 inches) flaky pods, non-branched axillary thorns, and pinnate leaves, as opposed to bipinnate for honeylocust. Also, black locust leaflets are rounder than the narrower leaflets of honeylocust, and black locust flowers are much larger and pealike compared to the smaller cream-colored flowers of honeylocust.

Identification: Honeylocust is a deciduous tree up to 100 feet tall. The alternate leaves are **bipinnate (sometimes pinnate)** with narrow elliptic leaflets. The small cream-colored flowers hang in dense axillary racemes. The large, flattened **pods are sometimes over 1 foot long and often twisted. The seeds are arranged closer to the convex side of the**

pod, which is fairly distinguishing. The most distinguishing feature on honeylocust trees are the devilishly large, **branched thorns that adorn the trunk and branches**. When present, these branched thorns make identification easy. When thorns are not present (as in cultivated varieties used in landscaping), identification is trickier but the size of the pods and bipinnate leaves help.

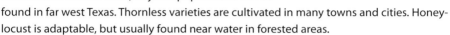

Range and habitat: Honeylocust is scattered throughout east and central Texas; disjunct populations can be found in far west Texas. Thornless varieties are cultivated in many towns and cities. Honeylocust is adaptable, but usually found near water in forested areas.

Related edible species: We have not found evidence confirming that the pods are edible in the same way as honeylocust, but the related water locust (*Gleditsia aquatica*) is found scattered in east Texas. That said, they would not be worth the effort anyways, as they are much smaller (less than 2 inches).

Uses/history/comments: Honeylocust has the most imposing, devilish thorns in Texas. The branched thorns (up to 5 inches long) that arise directly from the trunk are unique identifiers, as nothing else in the state possesses this characteristic. The prize of honeylocust is the sweet, gooey, orange pulp inside the long, often twisted pods; the pulp can be found in young green pods and mature brown pods. Green pods (which can be steamed like green beans) have a more liquidy, gooey pulp, whereas the mature brown pods may have gooey pulp when they first ripen, but the pulp then dries and hardens. You can soak dried, matured pods in water overnight to loosen them up and extract the pulp more easily. If you find a honeylocust tree in fall, look on the ground, where many of the pods will have fallen. Fallen pods are still worth harvesting, as you can still scrape out the hardened pulp after soaking. As the name implies, the pulp tastes like honey and is excellent raw straight from the pod or used in place of honey in most recipes.

The seeds of honeylocust are also edible and can be ground into a powder. We have also ground whole pods into a coarse powder that ends up being fairly sweet due to the pulp. It's no replacement for honey mesquite flour but can be useful if that's all you have to work with.

RECIPE

Charcuterie with Honeylocust

Harvest a few green or newly ripened (brown) honeylocust pods when the orange gooey pulp is present. Split the pods in half and scrape out the sticky pulp with a spoon. Use the scraped pulp on a cheese board or charcuterie board in place of honeycomb. The honeylocust pulp goes great with most hard cheeses.

RETAMA (*Parkinsonia aculeata*)

Family: Fabaceae

Edible part and harvest time: Flowers are found spring through summer; green pods in summer and mature pods in fall and into winter.

Toxic lookalikes: None in Texas

Identification: Retama is a small, weedy tree with a diffuse, feathery appearance. The branches are green and the **long, alternate leaves** are twice pinnate. Each leaf has one or two pairs of long pinnae with numerous tiny leaflets. **Sharp but short spines arise from the base of the leaves.** The showy **yellow flowers** hang in clusters among the leaves, and each has a **reddish spot on one of the five petals**. The pods (up to 4 inches long) are **constricted and flattened between each bean** and start out green and pliable and mature to dry, fibrous, and brown. There are one to eight small beans in each pod. Retama often retains the previous year's old, dry pods on the tree into the following season, although the beans inside are usually rotten or desiccated by then.

Range and habitat: Retama is found throughout much of the southern half of Texas in dry fields and low drainage areas. It is so common in some areas that many consider it a noxious weedy tree. It's commonly used in xeriscaping so may be found planted outside of its normal range.

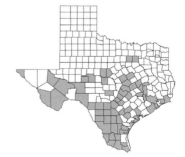

Related edible species: There is one other *Parkinsonia* species in Texas (*P. texana*, which grows in south Texas and along the Rio Grande), but we have not tried eating this species or know anyone who has. For that reason, we can't recommend it.

Uses/history/comments: Retama is an interesting, drought-tolerant pea family tree with edible flowers and beans. It is not an especially well-known edible, but is actually one of the most abundant wild plant food sources in many drier parts of Texas and was a staple for the Seri tribe of Mexico [16]. The bright yellow flowers in spring and summer are edible, though bitter. We use them more as a garnish.

Retama flowers in spring

The real gems, though, are the green pods in spring and summer. The beans can be removed and eaten raw when green and young or steamed or boiled. The pod itself is usually too fibrous and tough to eat unless very young, so we typically just eat the beans inside. The green beans taste like soybeans. Cooked like edamame, they are excellent. Once the pods dry and turn brown in fall and winter, the beans can still be harvested, separated from the pods, and then soaked and cooked as with other beans. To harvest, pick the pods one by one off the tree; the pods don't fall to the ground as easily as mesquite pods and are typically found hanging on

Mature, dried retama beans

the tree well into winter. Retama is abundant, the beans are available nearly year-round, and the flavor is superb; these characteristics make for an excellent wild food.

RECIPE

Retamame

Green retama pods are excellent prepared and eaten like edamame. Boil pods in salted water for 5 minutes or steam them for about 5–10 minutes. After straining the cooked pods, toss with salt to taste and add spices if you wish. Our favorite spices to use for this are garlic powder, ginger powder, and/or crushed red pepper. After seasoning, eat the beans out of the pod and discard the pod as you would edamame. The pods themselves are bitter, so seasoning helps.

HONEY MESQUITE (*Prosopis glandulosa*)

Family: Fabaceae

Edible part and harvest time: Mature pods can be found from late summer to early fall.

Toxic lookalikes: There are several *Vachellia* and *Senegalia* (formerly included in the *Acacia* genus and commonly called acacias) species with feathery compound leaves that could be mistaken for honey mesquite and are potentially toxic. However, the acacia species generally have rounded inflorescences as opposed to the elongated spikes of mesquite. Most of the acacias in Texas have tiny leaflets, much smaller and arranged more compactly than those of mesquite. Acacias can have hooked or straight thorns depending on the species, while mesquite always has straight thorns. And lastly, acacia pods are smaller, darker, and woodier than mesquite pods.

Identification: Honey mesquite is a small, open tree with rough grayish bark and **large thorns** (sometimes over 2 inches) at the leaf bases.

The alternate leaves are **doubly compound; each leaf is split into two pinnae,** which each have 6–15 pairs of leaflets. The leaflets are larger and more spread out than many other legumes in Texas. White flowers are arranged in compact spikes giving way to 4–10-inch-long straight or curved pods. Pods start out green but **mature to a light tan color, sometimes with purple streaks**. Mature pods are hard but have a somewhat spongy, sugary pulp surrounding the seeds.

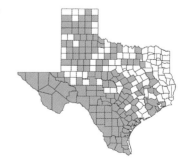

Range and habitat: Honey mesquite is common in south, west, and central Texas as well as most of the panhandle. It is less common farther east. Honey mesquite is sometimes considered a "native invasive," as it can take over pastureland, vacant lots, and other opportunistic areas. Habitat preference skews toward disturbed or open grasslands, but large specimens can be found closer to bottomlands or streams.

Related edible species: Honey mesquite is the most common *Prosopis* in Texas, but there are others. Tornillo (*Prosopis reptans*) is a smaller shrubby *Prosopis* found in south Texas, with tightly corkscrewed pods that are not as pleasant to eat as honey mesquite. Screwbean mesquite (*Prosopis pubescens*) is found in the Trans-Pecos.

Uses/history/comments: Mesquite is ubiquitous in many parts of Texas. The mature

Ripe mesquite pods

dried pods are typically abundant in late summer and into early fall and can be gathered en masse. The young green pods in summer are also edible, but we rarely harvest these,

Fallen but perfectly ripe mesquite pods littering the ground

preferring to wait for the mature pods. The mature pods are tan and dry when ripe and can be found on the tree or on the ground under the tree. After they drop, as long as it doesn't rain significantly, the dried pods can be found well into fall and are edible as long as the insects or mold haven't gotten to them. Insect infestations will be evident by small circular holes in the sides of the pods where the seeds are located. We still eat these pods

Mesquite flower

sometimes, but if you're going to store them, the infested pods will get further eaten. So, if you're going to store them long-term, it's best to kill off any insects by baking/drying in the oven for a few hours.

Mesquite pod flavor can vary widely from tree to tree. Some trees produce sour flavors, while others are sweet and caramel-like. Make note of the better-tasting trees, as these are typically reliable in flavor from year to year. Take care to watch where you step and wear thick-soled shoes when harvesting mesquite, as the large thorns from downed branches can go right through tennis shoes or sandals.

You can either eat the pods on their own (where we typically spit out the hard seeds while chewing up the surrounding sugary pulp) or grind them into a flour to use in various recipes. When making mesquite flour, make sure the pods are bone-dry, as they otherwise tend to gum up blenders. Dry thoroughly in a dehydrator or oven, then grind with a Vitamix, metate, or other manual grinding method. The whole pods can be ground into flour; you don't have to remove the seeds. Then run the flour through a fine-mesh strainer to make for a better texture and flavor when used in recipes. We use mesquite flour in baked goods and smoothies, and to make mesquite butter. Mesquite butter (mesquite flour mixed into melted butter at about a 1:3 ratio) is a trick we learned from our friend and fellow mesquite aficionado Sandeep Gyawali. It's great on toast as is or can be used in any baking recipe to impart the rich mesquite flavor. Cheers, Sandeep!

RECIPE

Mesquite Cookies

Preheat oven to 350°F. In a large mixing bowl, combine 1½ cups almond flour, ¼ cup maple syrup, ¼ cup melted coconut oil, ¼ cup mesquite flour, ⅓ cup shredded coconut, and a dash of salt and cinnamon. Mix well. Scoop out the dough, form small balls, and flatten them on a parchment-lined cookie sheet. Bake for about 8 minutes, until slightly browned on the edges.

ESCARPMENT LIVE OAK (*Quercus fusiformis*)

Family: Fagaceae

Edible part and harvest time: Acorns ripen late fall to early winter.

Toxic lookalikes: None in Texas

Identification: Escarpment live oak is an evergreen small to medium-sized tree or large shrub with a **spreading crown**. The thick, simple, alternate leaves are 1–3 inches long, **dark green, and often glossy above and paler below**. The variable leaves are usually oblong or elliptic with entire, sometimes revolute, margins or with a few pointed teeth scattered along the edge. Some of the leaves drop off in spring just before new leaves start to bud. The non-showy flowers bloom in spring and on the male and female catkins. Oak pollen often coats cars, driveways, and other surfaces below and causes significant allergies in central Texas. The **acorns are about 1 inch long** and fairly slender and smooth, with yellowish nut meat inside.

Range and habitat: Escarpment live oak (also known as plateau live oak) occurs throughout central Texas and extends into north and south Texas and the eastern edge of the Trans-Pecos. Found in rocky uplands and usually associated with calcareous soils, it is the most common oak found on the Edwards Plateau.

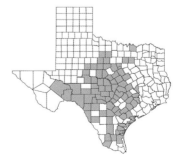

Related edible species: All *Quercus* species native to the US have edible acorns when processed correctly. In Texas, there are approximately 48 species total

Perfectly ripe live oak acorns

throughout the state, with at least a few species native to each ecoregion. Oaks are closely related to beech (*Fagus grandifolia*) and American chinquapin (*Castanea pumila*), which are found in east Texas and also have edible nuts.

Uses/history/comments: There are a whopping number of *Quercus* species in Texas. All have edible acorns, but they require processing and cannot be eaten raw in quantity. Acorns drop to the ground when ripe, so acorns still on the tree are not ready. Escarpment live oak acorns usually have a purplish cast to them when ripe and weevil-free; green acorns on the ground are almost always infested or rotten. Inspect acorns for tiny holes, which could indicate a weevil larva is inside. Side note: The weevil larvae are edible and generally good (see photo on page 85). Only harvest clean-looking acorns. We have found that when you find a ripe, clean acorn, the tree you're under typically has dropped many more ripe ones in the same area.

Processing acorns is necessary to remove the bitter tannins found in varying concentrations depending on the oak species. There are two simple ways to process acorns: hot

RECIPE

Acorn-Battered Catfish

Mix 1 cup leached acorn flour with 1 tsp. black pepper and a dash of salt in a mixing bowl. Use this to coat about 1–2 lbs. of catfish. Fry in oil on high for a few minutes on each side until the fish is cooked through.

leaching and cold leaching. Hot leaching is faster; while cold leaching takes longer, it leaves more nutritional value and flavor. To hot leach ripe acorns, remove the shells and add to a pot of filtered or spring water, then bring to a boil. The water will turn a dark brown from the high tannin content. Pour off (decant) this brown water and add another round of fresh water, and repeat the boiling and decanting process until the acorns no longer taste bitter. This usually takes

A shelled acorn and an escaping acorn weevil larva

about eight rounds of boiling and decanting but can vary widely and is faster if you break the acorns into halves. They'll be soft, darker brown, and non-bitter when done.

Cold leaching is a similar process, but you use cold water and grind the acorns as finely as possible prior to leaching. It's easiest to shell and grind the acorns after drying them in the sun or a dehydrator. This lets the acorn nut meat inside shrink so the shells are easier to crack. Grind the dried and shelled acorns in a metate or Vitamix; the finer the grind, the quicker it will leach. Then soak the acorn meal in a large container filled with cold filtered or spring water (if you use chlorinated water, the flavor will be awful). We typically fill the container ¼ with acorn meal and ¾ with water. Let sit overnight in the refrigerator and then decant the leaching water in the morning. Add clean water and repeat the process daily until the acorn meal is no longer bitter. Sometimes this takes a week or so but can be faster depending on the species. There is also a fast cold-leaching method that involves percolating clean water through a thin layer of acorn meal. We recommend Ortiz and Parker's *It Will Live Forever: Traditional Yosemite Indian Acorn Preparation*, which delves into this method in detail.

Once leached, pour the acorn meal onto a layered cheesecloth and dehydrate. Then run the dried meal through a blender once more to produce a fine acorn flour. Acorn flour can be used for porridge, baking, or as a batter for frying. Cold-leached live oak acorn flour has a pleasant caramel note to it that works well in baked goods and pancakes.

Our favorites of the Texas acorn species we've tried are *Q. fusiformis* and *Q. macrocarpa* (bur oak) due to flavor, abundance, and ease of harvesting/processing. These two species belong to the white oak group, which are generally easier to process. The red oak group (which includes *Q. shumardii* and *Q. buckleyi*, among others in Texas) are more time-consuming to process due to a skin (called the testa) that adheres to the nut meat even after drying. The testa is papery and bitter so should be removed. For an in-depth account of processing and using various acorns from other oak groups, see Samuel Thayer's *Nature's Garden*.

PECAN (*Carya illinoiensis*)

Family: Juglandaceae
Edible part and harvest time: Pecans ripen October to November.
Toxic lookalikes: None in Texas
Identification: Pecan trees are large, deciduous, usually straight-trunked trees up to 160 feet tall. The massive trunks can approach 6 feet in diameter and have gray-brown bark with scales and ridges. The alternate, **pinnately compound leaves have 9–17 asymmetrical and serrated leaflets**, including opposite pairs of leaflets and a terminal leaflet. Male and female flowers form catkins that hang in clusters much like oak catkins. Fruits form clusters of usually three or more; each fruit consists of an **oval-shaped, smooth nut** 1–2.5 inches long that is pointed at the apex and rounded at the base. The nut is surrounded by a **green husk that splits open**, dries to black, and often stays on the tree even after the nuts have fallen. Contrast this with the related walnuts in the next species account, which have husks that do not split open to release the nut.

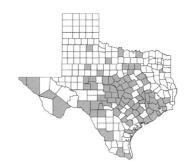

Range and habitat: Cultivated pecans are planted in urban and rural areas throughout Texas, but wild native pecans (which have smaller nuts and thicker shells) can be found throughout central and southeast Texas and range into south and west Texas when habitat is suitable. They grow wild along creeks and rivers and in rich bottomlands.

Related edible species: Pecans belong to the *Carya* genus, which includes the hickories. Texas has eight other hickory species that primarily grow in the eastern half of the state. *C. aquatica*, *C. texana*, and *C. tomentosa* are the most widespread hickory species in Texas, and all have edible nuts that look like fatter pecans and can be used the same way. Distinguishing the numerous hickories can be challenging.

Uses/history/comments: The pecan is the state tree of Texas, and its nuts are likely the most commonly harvested wild food in the state. It's always heartening to see young and old alike filling up their bags during the fall haul. Interestingly, pecan harvests vary year to year depending on drought and other factors. Some years will produce bumper crops, while other years will be light. Many times, it alternates between the two extremes from year to year.

Pecan catkins

RECIPE

Candied Pecans

Harvest 3–4 cups of wild pecans and preheat oven to 325°F. In a mixing bowl, add 2 egg whites and ⅛ tsp. salt and whisk vigorously for about 30 seconds, until it starts to foam. Next add 4–5 tbsp. melted coconut oil to the egg white mixture along with ¼ cup coconut sugar (or similar), ⅛ tsp. nutmeg, and ½ tsp. cinnamon. Mix well. Add the pecans and mix until they are completely coated. Spread the coated pecans evenly on a parchment-lined baking sheet and bake for about 12 minutes. Then remove the pan, stir the pecans a bit with a spatula, and bake for another 12 minutes. Watch the pecans closely, as you don't want them to burn. Serve while warm or let them cool so the sugar crystallizes.

Texan "York" Nut Sheller at work

While native pecan trees are abundant in areas where they occur in Texas, almost every region in the state has cultivated pecans in and around settlements. The cultivated varieties typically have much larger, thinner, easy-to-crack shells and larger nuts that are easier to pick out. It is significantly more difficult to harvest substantial amounts of pecan nut meat from the smaller native pecans. That said, we think it's well worth the effort, as the flavor is superior. We highly recommend getting a pair of the Texan "York" Nut Shellers, which are inexpensive and make shelling the small, hard native pecans much easier. Instead of cracking the nut, this type of sheller essentially shears off the two ends of the nut, which makes extracting the nut meat much easier. There are also large manual or automated nut crackers that can be purchased for cracking large batches, but remember to save some for the squirrels.

For a long time, we had assumed that the leaves of pecans would be bitter and unpalatable. But then Ginger Webb from the Sacred Journey School of Herbalism in Austin showed us that the leaves can be brewed into a surprisingly flavorful tea. It's somewhat astringent, but decidedly tasty. Cheers, Ginger!

WALNUT (*Juglans* spp.)

Family: Juglandaceae

Edible part and harvest time: Walnuts ripen in fall.

Toxic lookalikes: None in Texas

Identification: Our native walnut species range from large (*J. nigra*) to small (*J. microcarpa*) trees but all have deciduous, **pinnate leaves with serrated leaflets** and **spherical fruits/nuts**. The bark is often furrowed or scaly. The pinnate leaves have 9–23 serrated leaflets depending on the species, and flowers are arranged in catkins like pecan. The nuts have indehiscent husks, meaning the **husks do not split open** and release the nuts as with pecans and hickories. The hard nutshells are **furrowed on the exterior** unlike pecans and hickories, which are smooth. The nuts, sans husk, range from 2.5 inches (*J. nigra*) to 0.5 inch (*J. microcarpa*) in diameter.

Range and habitat: The three walnut species in Texas are generally found in an east–west band across the central portion of the state. The two western species are often found along wet-weather drainages, creek beds, and canyons. The eastern species is found in rich woodlands and fields.

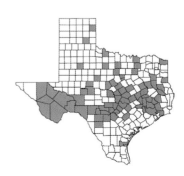

Related edible species: Three native walnuts can be found in Texas: *J. major* and *J. microcarpa* (both in the Trans-Pecos and central Texas) and *J. nigra* (central and east Texas). *J. nigra* has larger nuts, while *J. major* and *J.*

Ripe walnut in fall

microcarpa have nuts often less than half the size. In many respects, *J. major* has intermediate characteristics between the other two species.

Uses/history/comments: First things first: Finding a fat, whole walnut like those you buy at the store is not going to happen on your next foraging adventure. Our native walnut species have smaller nuts with incredibly hard and thick shells, making it impossible to extract an intact walnut. More likely, you will be picking small pieces of walnut meat out of the shell after smashing it open. You'll first have to remove the exterior green or brown hull from the shell, which does not simply separate and fall off like with pecans and hickories. And fair warning: The hulls stain *everything* including hands, fingernails, clothes, etc., so be careful or use gloves. Some people peel the hull from the shell, but we usually just smash the walnut (hull and all) with a rock or hammer against a concrete or rock anvil. If done with sufficient force, this will crack the nut *and* the hull will split away from the shell.

RECIPE

Nocino

In early summer, harvest about 20–30 young, green walnuts that are still easy to cut through because their hard shells have not developed. Using your least favorite cutting board and gloves (due to staining), quarter them using a sharp knife. Add the pieces to a large glass jar (that has a lid or cap) with 2 cinnamon sticks, 5 cloves, 1-inch vanilla bean, zest from 1 lemon, and 2 cups sugar. Then pour 4 cups (or enough to cover the walnuts) of pure, unflavored vodka into the jar. Cap the jar and shake, then leave this mixture at room temperature for around 6 weeks, shaking daily. It will turn black over time. Carefully strain the liquid into bottles through a cheesecloth or similar material to remove the solids. Tightly capped bottles will have a long shelf life (years) if stored in a cool, dry, dark place. The flavor is fairly bitter after bottling but mellows over time. We have also made nocino using the older green hulls after the nut has matured inside with similar results. Nocino is great drizzled over ice cream or in coffee.

After cracking, use a pick or pocketknife to remove small pieces of walnut. You will likely have to continue smashing the shell to get the small morsels out. Note that ripe walnuts will fall to the ground, so you won't need to reach high into the trees to harvest. Look for green or brown walnuts on the ground in fall and then dehull after harvesting.

Juglans microcarpa leaflets

The flavor of our native walnuts is excellent, but the difficulty in getting a substantial amount to eat makes them less sought after than the more abundant and easier to obtain pecan. However, there's another use for our native walnuts. Herbalist Ginger Webb from the Sacred Journey School of Herbalism in Austin let us know about an amazing, easy recipe using whole young walnuts: nocino, a traditional walnut liqueur from Italy. Nocino is essentially an alcohol extract of young green walnuts (in early to midsummer before the shells have hardened) with a few variable additives. On the previous page is a recipe adapted from Ginger's recommendations.

Walnut hulls also have a long history of medicinal use. They are primarily used as antihelminthics to help expel parasites from the body. Tinctures or powders of the hull are used for this purpose, but a strong nocino will likely have a similar (but tastier) effect.

Cracked walnut showing nut meat pieces and black-staining husk

MULBERRY (*Morus* spp.)

Family: Moraceae
Edible part and harvest time: Mulberries ripen in spring (usually April).
Toxic lookalikes: None in Texas
Identification: Mulberry trees are deciduous medium to large trees up to around 40 feet tall. The bark is gray to gray-brown and smooth or scaly. The alternate, simple, broadly ovate (when mature), and **serrated leaves** have a smooth to rough texture above (depending on species) and softer texture below. Note that young mulberry leaf shapes can vary wildly from trilobed to two uneven lobes to quasi palmate; identifying young mulberries can be tricky. The male and female flowers are inconspicuous and form catkins. The catkins give way to the **fruits that look like smaller, skinny blackberries when ripe.** Ripe fruits are usually dark red or purplish.
Range and habitat: Mulberries can be found throughout almost the entire eastern US. In Texas, they are most common in southeast Texas but are also found in central Texas and to a lesser extent south and north Texas. Habitat includes riparian areas, river bottoms, and moist woods.

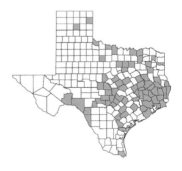

Related edible species: There are three *Morus* species found in Texas. The nonnative *white mulberry (Morus alba)* has a scattered irregular distribution in Texas. White mulberry is similar to our more common native

White mulberries at various stages of ripeness and mature leaves

Young mulberry sapling; note how different the young leaves look compared to mature leaves.

red mulberry (*Morus rubra*), which is found most commonly in southeast and central Texas; white mulberry can be distinguished from red mulberry by its larger serrations on the leaf margins and shiny, smooth upper leaf surface. Surprisingly, white mulberry fruits are not always white and can often look like red mulberries. There is one other native edible mulberry in Texas: Texas mulberry (*Morus microphylla*). This is a less common species but can be found in central Texas, the Trans-Pecos, and parts of the panhandle. It is a shrub or small tree with smaller leaves than the other two *Morus* species.

RECIPE

Mulberry Crumble

Preheat oven to 375°F. In a small baking dish, mix 4 cups ripe mulberries with juice from 1 lemon and spread evenly on the bottom of a dish. In a separate mixing bowl, mix 1 cup almond flour, ¼ cup chopped pecans, ¼ cup melted butter, 2 tbsp. maple syrup, ¼ tsp. cinnamon, and a pinch of salt. Then lather this mixture over the top of the mulberries (don't worry, you won't cover it completely). Bake for about 35 minutes. This quick recipe goes great with ice cream or fresh whipped cream!

Uses/history/comments: Mulberries are prolific in spring. They seem to rain down on whatever lies below, causing some unenlightened landowners to cut them down for fear of coating a car, driveway, or house in rotten fruit. However, they are one of our favorite wild edible treats in spring. Mulberries can be gathered right off the tree in spring when the fruits turn a dark red or purple. Ripe fruits may fall to the ground but rot quickly, so if you harvest them off the ground, be picky with which ones you eat. The taste of ripe mulberries is great, but not especially sweet unless very ripe. We like adding fresh ripe mulberries to salads, as the fruits are not overbearingly sweet. However, if dehydrated, they transform into a distinctly sweet treat. These are great added to granola and trail mix. Mulberries are also great in baked goods.

PIÑON PINE (*Pinus* spp.)

Family: Pinaceae
Edible part and harvest time: Pollen is available late spring to early summer, while nuts are available in early to mid-fall.
Toxic lookalikes: None in Texas
Identification: Piñon pines are relatively short **evergreen conifers** up to 30 feet tall with scaly brown or gray bark. The **needles are short (less than 1.75 inches)** and grouped in **bundles of two or three** depending on the species. The **round or ovoid cones** are less than 2 inches long and start out green and turn brown as they ripen and dry out. As the **blunt cone scales** open, a dark ovoid nut less than 0.5 inch long is exposed at the base of each scale. The hard nutshells contain **oily, cream-colored nuts** inside.

Range and habitat: Piñon pines grow in the mountainous and rocky areas of the Trans-Pecos, but one species ranges into the southwestern Edwards Plateau on rocky limestone outcrops. They are also planted in rural towns and villages for shade in the Trans-Pecos and parts of the panhandle. Note that this range map only shows the range of the three related piñon pine species, not the range of all pines in Texas.

Related edible species: There are three piñon pine species in Texas that all have large, delicious pine nuts: *P. cembroides* and *P. edulis* (both in the Trans-Pecos) and *P. remota* (Trans-Pecos and western Edwards Plateau). Other pine species don't have easily edible pine nuts but do have pollen that can be collected. Other common pines in Texas include *P. echinata* and *P. taeda* (both from east Texas).

Uses/history/comments: Piñon pines are a group of several desert- and mountain-dwelling pine species that are often shorter than other pines and have short needles and a similar, smallish, ball-shaped cone. The main distinguisher from other pines, though, is that they contain numerous large pine nuts within each cone. These pine nuts are much like store-bought pine nuts but even tastier in our opinion. They are sweet and oily, and almost every other animal in the canyons and mountains where piñon pines grow gorge on the nuts when they produce an abundant crop. Unfortunately, they don't always produce every year, so you may have to wait one or two years between harvests. But, when they do produce, you'll want to be ready in early fall. And because piñon pines are often

Pinus cembroides from left to right: ripe cone, shelled nut, unshelled nut

Ripe *Pinus cembroides* cones and needles

planted for shade in rural towns in west Texas, you may not have to hike up a mountain to find them.

Piñon nuts are found at the base of most cone scales and are enveloped in a hard, brown shell that must be cracked to get to the rich nut. The shells are very hard, so don't crack them in your teeth; better to use a rock, hammer, or nutcracker to shell them. We have noticed that piñons (at least in Texas) can be fairly hit or miss, as sometimes you'll find a tree that produces many perfect nuts, while an adjacent tree may produce aborted nuts that look good until you crack them open to reveal an empty shell or a shriveled nut. Be persistent if you run into one bad tree and move on to the next. We also keep an eye out for large piles of shells left by squirrels, as they usually know where the good trees are. Use them as you would store-bought pine nuts in salads, desserts, pesto, etc.

Another enjoyable edible part of any pine tree species (not just the piñons) is the pollen in late spring and early summer and the green needles year-round. The male cones produce a prodigious amount of yellow pollen that can be collected in plastic bags by covering the cone with the bag and shaking to release the pollen. In windy conditions, you can see yellowish plumes of pollen streaming off the pines, so it's best to collect before windy weather to maximize the harvest. Pine pollen can be added to almost any dish: soups, stews, flours, smoothies, etc. It doesn't taste like much but is excellent nutritionally and has more protein per pound than most meats and high amounts of beta-carotene and iron. In fact, it is often referred to as a "complete food" [17]. Green pine needles brew up nicely as a pleasant tea wherever you find them.

RECIPE

Toasted Piñon Salad

Sauté 3 cups chopped kale leaf (with central stem removed) in a well-oiled pan over medium heat until soft. Add 2 minced garlic cloves and a dash of black pepper and salt to taste. Continue sautéing for a few minutes while mixing the spices in well. In a separate pan, toast ¼ cup pine nuts over low heat for a few minutes, making sure they don't burn. Toss the kale and toasted pine nuts together and serve.

*JUJUBE (*Ziziphus jujuba*)

Family: Rhamnaceae

Edible part and harvest time: Fruits ripen in late summer and early fall.

Toxic lookalikes: None in Texas

Identification: Jujube is a small, nonnative deciduous tree with **zigzagging branches** and furrowed bark. Jujube leaves are 1–2 inches long, **glossy, dark green**, and simple, with scalloped margins and **three prominent veins**. There are typically two spines at the base of the leaves, but this is not consistent. Some branches will have the spines, others will not. Small yellowish flowers arise from the leaf bases either singly or in small clusters, and each has five small petals. The fruits are about the **size and shape of a date fruit** and have a similarly sized, **elongated pit**. Jujube fruits start out green on the tree, with a crisp, apple-like flesh consistency, and ripen to brown, when they have a softer, spongier, and sweeter flesh.

Range and habitat: The nonnative jujube is most often found in and around human settlements, where it was formerly planted for its delicious fruits. It has since escaped into the wild around many cities in Texas and can be found in urban parks, dry woodlands, and thickets.

Related edible species: The related lotebush (*Z. obtusifolia*) is a smaller thorny shrub that grows through much of the western half of Texas. It has large thorns, smaller leaves, and a smaller, bluish-purple fruit that is edible though not as tasty as the jujube.

Jujube leaves and bark

Ripe jujubes; the riper, browner one will be sweeter.

Uses/history/comments: Originally from China, jujube has been planted in many dry parts of the world for its abundant fruits, which are available even during hot, dry summers. In Texas, it was planted in many settlements and has since escaped into the wild surrounding towns and cities. Though it is not highly invasive, it can grow into large patches around older trees and crowd out other vegetation. Due to its nonnative status, feel free to harvest liberally (assuming you are harvesting ethically and legally). Harvesting the fruits can be tricky, as they do not tend to fall easily from the tree. We usually bring a ladder or climb the tree (watch out for the thorns) to pick the fruits, but sometimes the loaded fruiting branches hang low enough that you can harvest from ground level. Some orchards still grow jujube trees and harvest and sell the fruits at farmers' markets around Texas.

The date-sized fruits ripen in late summer but are edible in two distinct phases of ripeness. When fully formed but still green, you can eat the crisp, crunchy fruits like an apple (but watch out for the large pit). After this green phase, the fruits turn brown and start to wrinkle as they dry out, becoming sweeter and softer. Though not related, these very ripe (brown and wrinkled) jujube fruits are often compared to dates due to their sweet, sugary nature, their size, and their large pit.

RECIPE

Chocolate Jujube Jewels

Harvest ripe, brown jujubes and allow to further ripen for a week or so in a paper bag until they are a bit shriveled. Cut each jujube in half lengthwise and remove the pit. Fill the center of each halved and pitted jujube with your favorite nut butter (pecan, cashew, peanut, etc.). Then stick each half back together to create whole, nut-butter-filled jujubes and set these aside. Melt a small pot of your favorite dark chocolate chips or bars over low to medium heat. Dip each stuffed jujube into the chocolate to cover thoroughly and place these on a parchment-lined dish so that they are not touching each other. Sprinkle with some coarse sea salt and place in the fridge overnight or in the freezer for 20 minutes to set.

*LOQUAT (*Eriobotrya japonica*)

Family: Rosaceae

Edible part and harvest time: Fruits ripen in April.

Toxic lookalikes: None in Texas

Identification: Loquat is a small **evergreen** tree up to 30 feet tall with relatively smooth, gray bark. The **large stiff leaves** are 6–12 inches long, 3–5 inches wide, and **tomentose on the underside**. **White flowers** bloom in clusters in fall and winter and give way to green **fruits that ripen to orange** in spring. Ripe fruits have a fuzzy coating that can be rubbed off with your finger and are somewhat pear shaped, ranging from 1–3 inches wide. The flesh inside is lighter orange or whitish in color depending on ripeness. Each fruit has one to five large, hard, ovoid seeds inside.

Range and habitat: Native to East Asia, loquats are commonly used in landscaping and have escaped in and around urban areas including Austin, Dallas, Houston, San Antonio, and the Lower Rio Grande Valley.

Related edible species: None in Texas

Uses/history/comments: While not native, loquats are one of the most abundantly fruiting trees in many urban areas of Texas. Branches can get so weighted by ripe fruits that they hang down to the ground. Loquats are commonly grown in warm temperate to subtropical regions around the globe and are highly prized in

Loquat flowers

Loquat harvest; note the varying sizes.

Japan, where they are relatively expensive at local markets. Luckily for Texans, loquats are free for the picking in many cities and are absolutely delicious.

Loquats are ripe when orange with no hint of green remaining. Flavor varies from tree to tree, so if you aren't impressed with one tree, move on to another. The best ones taste somewhat like a watery apricot. We've found that smaller loquats are usually sweeter but have a high ratio of seed to flesh, whereas large loquats typically aren't as sweet. The large, smooth seeds inside are easily removed prior to eating or simply spit out. Loquats are excellent raw but are also used to make wines, jams, and various desserts. We also like to dry loquats, as this accentuates the flavor immensely and offers a unique tanginess somewhat akin to dried goldenberries.

MEXICAN PLUM (*Prunus mexicana*)

Mexican plum flowers in February

Family: Rosaceae

Edible part and harvest time: Fruits ripen in late summer and early fall.

Toxic lookalikes: There are no toxic lookalikes in Texas, but the leaves and seeds of *Prunus* species themselves contain varying levels of amygdalin, which breaks down to form hydrocyanic acid. Avoid consuming the seeds or leaves.

Identification: Mexican plum is a small deciduous tree with **cherry-like, striped bark**. Its leaves are 2.5–5 inches long, obovate, and softly pubescent. As with many other *Prunus* species, the petiole (leafstalk) often has **two glands near the base of the leaf**. These glands, along with the striped cherry-like bark and plum- or cherry-like fruits, are strong indicators of the *Prunus* genus. The glands are not present on every leaf, but if you check a few leaves, you'll often find them. The **white flowers arrive in late winter or early spring before the leaves emerge**. Flowers are arranged in groups of two to four and have five petals each. The red to purple ripe fruits are globose and 0.5–1 inch in diameter. Unripe fruits are green or yellowish. Each fruit has one hard pit inside, similar to a store-bought plum or cherry.

Range and habitat: Mexican plum is scattered throughout north, central, and parts of east Texas in deep, rich soils of open woods and prairies or near rivers and creeks. It can grow in full sun (where it produces more fruit) or as an understory tree. It is also frequently used in landscaping, so look for it in urban areas.

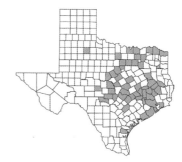

Dried cedar elm samaras that can be picked off the ground; the dried seeds inside taste like sunflower seeds.

Winnowing can be time-consuming, but it can also be meditative and relaxing. Keep winnowing until you have mostly just the small flat seeds left in the bowl. These seeds can be eaten raw or ground into a flour. The taste and texture remind us of a drier sunflower seed. We like to sprinkle them on salads.

Note that other native elm species like *U. americana* produce samaras in spring instead of fall. So, depending on where you are, you may have a fall *and* spring harvest of different elm species.

SHRUBS/VINES

For the purposes of this book, shrubs are generally defined as woody, perennial plants that are smaller than a tree and have several main stems arising from or near the ground. Some plants can grow either as shrubs or trees depending on habitat and growing conditions, so the distinction between tree and shrub is somewhat murky, especially for young plants. Vines are generally defined as trailing or climbing plants that can be woody or non-woody. This section also includes other non-arborescent and non-herbaceous plants like yuccas, sotols, agaves, palmettos, and cactus species, although they do not necessarily meet the shrub definition above.

ELDERBERRY (*Sambucus nigra*)

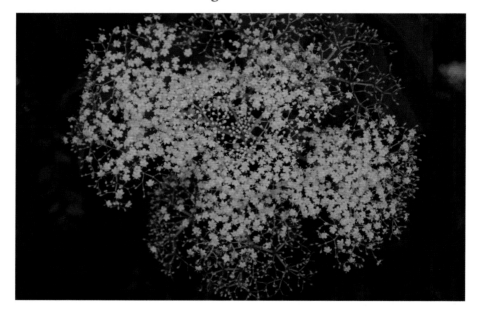

Family: Adoxaceae

Edible part and harvest time: Flowers are available in late spring through midsummer; berries ripen later in summer. Flowers and fruits should be cooked, not eaten raw.

Toxic lookalikes: CAUTION: Inexperienced foragers can mistake two of the most toxic plants in the US for elderberry. Poison hemlock (*Conium maculatum*) and water hemlock (*Cicuta maculata*) are both in a different plant family (Apiaceae), but their flowers and hollow stems look similar to elderberry. The leaves of water hemlock even look somewhat like elderberry, and all three can grow in similar wet habitats. Elderberry is a perennial shrub with brown, woody main branches leading to green stems, while poison hemlock and

Ripe elderberries in summer; birds get to them quickly.

water hemlock are non-woody and herbaceous. Elderberry leaves are opposite and once pinnate, while water hemlock leaves are alternate pinnate (divided two or three times) and poison hemlock leaves are alternate and finely pinnate (divided two to four times). Poison hemlock also has purple splotches dotting the main stem, which elderberry lacks. Elderberry flowers are arranged in a compound cyme, while the hemlocks are compound umbels. Water hemlock is a smaller plant (3–4 feet tall) than elderberry, although poison hemlock can approach the height of elderberry, but at that height the purple splotchy stems distinguish it from the brown, woody main branches of elderberry. Elderberry produces a fleshy fruit, while the hemlocks produce dry seeds, so picking elderberries is not as potentially dangerous as picking the flowers. Also note that raw elderberries are potentially toxic and should be cooked prior to consumption to render them safe to eat. See further discussion below in the "Uses/history/comments" section.

Identification: Elderberry is a deciduous, partially woody shrub up to 13 feet tall. It often has numerous **slender branches that are hollow inside except for a soft white pith**. Mature branches and stems are smooth, brown, and woody, while younger branches are green. Leaves are **opposite and pinnately compound**, with each leaf having 5–11 leaflets including one at the tip. Each leaf is up to 1 foot long and each leaflet is 2–5 inches

One elderberry leaf with nine leaflets

long, lanceolate, glabrous, and serrated. The small white flowers are arranged in a flat cluster (technically a **cyme**) that can be about 1 foot in diameter. Each flower has five petals. Fruits are **small and dark purple or black when ripe** and have three or four small yellow seeds inside.

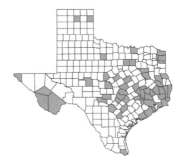

Range and habitat: Elderberry can be found scattered throughout central, north, and east Texas in moist soils near creeks, rivers, and lakes. It can also be found in the cooler mountain habitats of west Texas near springs.

Related edible species: While there are no other *Sambucus* species in Texas, two very similar-looking subspecies of *S. nigra* in Texas are sometimes classified as their own species. *S. nigra* ssp. *canadensis* (also known as *S. canadensis*) is found in the eastern half of Texas, while *S. nigra* ssp. *caerulea* (also known as *S. mexicana* or *S. cerulea*) is found in the mountains of west Texas.

Uses/history/comments: Elderberry has a long history of use as a medicine in North America and the Old World. It is frequently used as a cold/flu remedy or as a general immunity booster; syrups are made with the berries and tinctures are made with the flowers. Herbalist Sam Coffman from the Human Path in Bulverde, Texas, maintains that the flower is the most medicinally potent part of elderberry and uses this extensively for colds and flus [18]. However, the flower is also very similar to some of the most toxic plants in Texas, so extreme caution is advised if you are going to harvest elderberry flowers. Please refer to the "Toxic lookalikes" section above to make sure you are comfortable distinguishing elderberry from the deadly toxic poison hemlock and water hemlock. The elderberry fruits, on the other hand, are not easily confused with those two very toxic plants, as elderberries are, well, bluish-black berries, whereas poison hemlock and water hemlock have dry, oval-shaped, ribbed seeds. Elderberry flowers are also edible when cooked, and are commonly dipped in batter and fried as fritters.

In addition to the stellar properties of the flowers, the fruits are excellent in syrups, jams, pies, and even wine. When harvesting (typically in mid- to late summer in Texas),

---

RECIPE

Wild Elderberry Syrup

Mash 1 cup ripe elderberries in a pot and bring to a boil with about 4 cups water, ½ tsp. cinnamon, and ¼ tsp. powdered ginger. After it starts boiling, reduce the heat, cover, and simmer for about 45 minutes or until the liquid has reduced by about half. Strain through a fine stainless-steel mesh and press to make sure you get all the liquid. While still hot, add 1 cup liquid raw honey, mix thoroughly, and pour into a jar. This syrup should be stored in the refrigerator and used within a month or two.

we usually remove the whole fruiting inflorescence to collect in our basket or bag rather than picking the fruits one by one. Then it is easy to process out the stems from the fruits back at home or camp. Syrups are our favorite use for elderberries, but however you plan to use them, make sure to cook them before consumption. The raw berries contain toxic cyanide-containing compounds. These potentially dangerous compounds are negated by cooking and to a lesser extent by drying. Some foragers insist that elderberries are edible raw when: (1) completely ripe, (2) if only eaten in small quantities, or (3) after dehydrating. We have no reason to dispute these accounts (we have eaten dried elderberries in small quantities on numerous occasions), but it's worthwhile cooking them to be safe, especially when you are starting out, to see how your body reacts. If you want to get adventurous and try raw or dried elderberries, be our guest, but do so in small doses to see how you feel before eating larger amounts.

LECHUGUILLA (*Agave lechuguilla*)

Family: Agavaceae
Edible part and harvest time: Hearts can be harvested year-round, while flower stalks are found spring through summer (both must be cooked).
Toxic lookalikes: While not known to be toxic, there is a lechuguilla lookalike that grows in similar habitats in west Texas: Texas false agave (*Hechtia texensis*). *Hechtia* can easily be distinguished from lechuguilla by its leaves, which are thinner, less fleshy, and curve outward or down to the ground. By contrast, lechuguilla leaves are thick, fleshy, and generally curve upward toward the sky. The flowering stalks are also different, as lechuguillas are

Lechuguilla flowers at the top of the tall flowering spike

much taller (up to 13 feet) while *Hechtia* stalks are only up to 2 feet tall. *Hechtia* leaves also tend to turn reddish or have reddish spots on the leaves, unlike lechuguilla. False aloes (*Manfreda* spp.) somewhat resemble lechuguilla but they lack large downcurved spines and their ranges hardly overlap. Lechuguilla itself (along with other *Agave* species) should not be consumed raw and the raw juice can cause contact dermatitis in some people, so handle the raw plant with care.

Identification: Lechuguilla is a small agave consisting of a rosette of **yellowish-green, succulent leaves** about 1 foot long. Each leaf (1 inch wide) curves a bit and points upward at the tip, while the base is attached to the heart of the plant at ground level. Leaf edges have **sharply down-curved teeth** and a **strong terminal spine. Tall, plume-like flower spikes** reach up to 13 feet in the air, with numerous individual flowers blooming closely off the sides of the spike. The flowers look **reddish, yellowish, or purplish (or a mix of those).** Fruits are brown, woody capsules that open to release black, flattish seeds. Lechuguilla is colony forming, so single lechuguillas are not common.

Range and habitat: Lechuguilla is exceedingly common in the Trans-Pecos, where it can be found in habitats including flat desert expanses, limestone outcrops, and dry mountainous areas. While most common in the Trans-Pecos, it can also be found in a few spots in the western Hill Country.

Related edible species: There are several other wild and naturalized *Agave* species in Texas that are also edible, but none of them are as common in the wild. Some of the more common species include *A. americana* (west and south Texas but more common in landscaping) and *A. gracilipes* and *A. havardiana* (both in the Trans-Pecos).

Uses/history/comments: Lechuguilla and other *Agave* species have a long history of edible and utilitarian use in Texas and across the southwestern US and Mexico. This book highlights lechuguilla, as it is by far the most common wild *Agave* species in Texas, but it is also the smallest. There are actually a number of edible uses for this ubiquitous desert plant. The most sought after is the heart; hearts of *Agave* species can be pit roasted in earthen fire pits and yield an aromatic, sweet pulp that can be eaten immediately after roasting or mashed

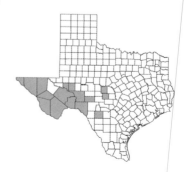

Lechuguilla rosettes showing the down-curved marginal teeth

and dried into cakes for storage. Note that harvesting the heart kills the plant, so only harvest lechuguilla (which is abundant) or cultivated/landscaped larger *Agave* species.

When harvesting and processing, take care not to get raw juice from the plant on your skin, as some people get contact dermatitis from the juice. Gloves and a machete are recommended for removing the spiny outer leaves after dislodging the plant right around ground level using a sharpshooter shovel, rock bar, or fire-hardened digging stick. Even in its rocky habitat, dislodging the plant at the base requires less effort than you'd think. Then use a machete to cut the leaves off, leaving just the central heart.

Once harvested, pit baking is the preferred method. This method takes skill, time, and effort. Start by digging a 2–3-foot-deep fire pit (easiest in sandy soils) and line with rock. Build a large fire over the rocks and let it burn down to coals, then add more rocks on top of the coals. Be careful when the rocks are heating up, as they may pop and send shards flying. Place the hearts on top of the rocks. Lay the leftover *Agave* leaves and other available greenery over top and cover the entire pile with the dirt left over from digging the pit. Let cook for at least 24–36 hours. When you uncover the pit, the hearts should have turned a reddish color if ready. After baking, the central portions of the hearts can be pounded and flattened into cakes for storage, or the pulp can be extracted from the heart by scraping the pulp from the leaf bases.

Well-cooked lechuguilla pulp ranges from sweet to slightly bitter depending on the plant, harvest time, and cooking time and temperature. Playing around with these variables can create excellent results. The pulp has a sticky texture, caramel color, and flavor reminiscent of cooked sweet potato. For a more modern method using a conventional oven, the recipe described in the Texas sotol account that follows works for lechuguilla

Cut lechuguilla hearts ready for roasting

(and to a lesser extent larger *Agave* species due to their size). Because lechuguilla is small, each plant does not render a ton of edible pulp, so you may want to harvest and process 5–10 at a time to get a decent amount.

The young flowering stalks of *Agave* species (while they are still 1–2 feet tall) can also be roasted and eaten in a similar manner to that described above, or they can be roasted over coals. The sweetish inner stalk takes on the consistency of a banana when cooked properly.

Additionally, while not especially fruitful for the diminutive lechuguilla, other larger *Agave* species can produce a nutritious, sweet liquid called aguamiel (which translates to "honey water"). Harvesting aguamiel the "right" way is a prescriptive process, but it essentially involves decapitating the emerging flowering stalk before it grows beyond the outer leaves. After leaving the cut for a period of time (up to six months), a divot is created at the base where the stalk was removed to form a bowl where aguamiel collects. New aguamiel can be collected nearly every day for up to six months or so [1]. Aguamiel is the precursor to the fermented alcoholic beverage pulque, which is common in rural Mexico.

Lastly, lechuguilla often has a fairly large skipper (a type of butterfly) larva lodged near the base of the plant. The larvae are edible, nutritious, and similar to the tequila "worm" that is found at the base of many agave species and added to tequila in Mexico [19].

RECIPE

Dried Lechuguilla Cakes

After either pit cooking or using a conventional oven to obtain the pulp from several lechuguillas, scrape the inner leaf bases and central heart with a spoon to separate the pulp from the fibrous parts. Taking the pulp from 3–4 lechuguillas, flatten the sticky mass into a thin pancake form with your hands. Dry the cakes in the sun or with a dehydrator on the lowest setting until completely dry. They will be leathery and chewy, but sweet and stable if kept dry. If they are bitter, it means you likely did not cook them long enough. More of a survival food than a delicacy, these rudimentary patties can be spruced up before drying by adding cinnamon or other spices to the pulp.

TEXAS SOTOL (*Dasylirion texanum*)

Family: Agavaceae

Edible part and harvest time: Hearts can be harvested year-round, and young stalks can be found in spring (both must be cooked).

Toxic lookalikes: Beargrass (*Nolina*) species are said to be toxic but are easily distinguished from sotols by their lack of leaf spines.

Identification: Texas sotol forms a dense cluster of **long, flexible, narrow leaves** (up to 3 feet long) with **hooked spines** (directed outward) on both edges of the leaf. The inflorescence consists of a 6–15-foot flowering stem with dense, tan clusters of tiny flowers. Don't confuse sotol with yuccas (which do not have spines on the leaf edges) or agaves (which have fleshier leaves with stiff, sharply pointed tips).

Range and habitat: Texas sotol is found in the Trans-Pecos and portions of the Edwards Plateau. In the Trans-Pecos, look for sotol in dry, rocky, or sandy slopes and flats. You can also frequently find sotols in xeriscaping throughout much of Texas.

Related edible species: *D. leiophyllum* (leaf spines recurved toward the heart) and *D. wheeleri* (bluish cast to leaves) look very similar to *D. texanum* and have similar edible hearts.

Uses/history/comments: While these spiky relatives of yuccas and agaves do not look especially edible, they are one of the more reliable and abundant plant foods

Sotol has a tall flowering stalk.

Close-up of the sotol heart at the base of the spiny leaves

in west Texas. The heart of the sotol is much like an artichoke heart, but getting to it and making it edible is appreciably more challenging. You will want gloves and a machete to remove the long outer leaves. Then dislodge the heart from the top of the root around ground level using a sharpshooter shovel, rock bar, or fire-hardened digging stick.

Traditionally, sotol hearts were baked in earthen fire pits using the same method described in the preceding lechuguilla species account. When you dig up and remove the sotol hearts, you will need to remove some of the remaining outer leaf bases until you get to the artichoke-like center. The leaf bases can be eaten just as with artichoke. If you only bake for 24 hours, it is similar to artichoke in flavor and consistency. If you bake longer, more of the starches are broken down into sugars and you get a gooier consistency that can be formed into cakes and dried for later use. Note that the young, green flower stalks can also be baked and eaten in a similar manner. Additionally, baked or steamed sotol hearts can be fermented and distilled to make an alcoholic spirit (known simply as sotol) that is similar to tequila.

Dried sotol stalks are also one of the best woods to use for friction fires in Texas, as they make excellent spindles for bow-drill kits. The leaves are also a good source of fibers for cordage.

RECIPE

Easy Sotol Hearts and Butter

While it doesn't produce the exact same result, we have approximated the earthen baking method in a traditional stove. Take the sotol hearts and wrap in two layers of aluminum foil, then place on a baking pan. Put in a 350°F oven for 12 hours, then reduce to around 285°F for another 12 hours. Remove the leaf bases and dip in melted butter.

TORREY YUCCA (*Yucca torreyi*)

Family: Agavaceae

Edible part and harvest time: Flowers are available in spring; fruits ripen in summer.

Toxic lookalikes: Beargrass (*Nolina*) species are said to be toxic but are easily distinguished from yuccas, as they have long, flexible, grasslike leaves that do not end in a sharp point, whereas yucca species' leaves are stiff and sharply pointed at the tip.

Identification: Torrey yucca is a treelike plant up to 14 feet tall. It typically has one or two main trunks that are **covered with dead, hanging, old leaves that give it a shaggy appearance**. The green, leafy heads at the top of the trunk have many broad, sharply pointed, **swordlike leaves up to 3 feet long and 2 inches wide**. The leaves are thick and rigid, but not fleshy like an agave and lack leaf margin spines like agave and sotol. The margins of the leaf also have **curly or straight fibers** that peel off. The erect flower stalk rises from the center of the leaves and reaches up to 2 feet tall, with numerous **cream-colored, hanging, bell-shaped flowers** in a large cluster along the flower stalk. The fruit is a **green capsule up to 4 inches long that ripens to brown**. The fruit is gummy when ripe, similar to a date fruit. Each fruit has numerous flat, black seeds inside.

Range and habitat: Torrey yucca grows in dry, rocky grasslands, mesas, and slopes throughout the Trans-Pecos and into the Edwards Plateau and even ranges down along the Gulf Coast.

Green unripe fruit from *Yucca treculeana*, a close relative of *Yucca torreyi*

Related edible species: Many other *Yucca* species in Texas are edible in some form. There are two general groups of species: those with woody fruits (and often thinner leaves) and those with non-woody fruits (and often wider, longer, stiffer leaves). *Y. torreyi* is in the latter group. Common woody-fruited species include *Y. arkansana* (eastern half of Texas), *Y. campestris* (panhandle), *Y. constricta* (central and south Texas), *Y. glauca* (panhandle), *Y. elata* (Trans-Pecos), and *Y. rupicola* (central Texas). Common non-woody-fruited species include *Y. baccata* (Trans-Pecos) and *Y. treculeana* (central and south Texas).

Uses/history/comments: Torrey yucca is one of the non-woody-fruited yucca species in Texas and is often confused with *Y. treculeana*. They can be eaten the same way, so the edible points brought up below apply to *Y. treculeana* (and *Y. baccata*) as well. Torrey yucca has a triple threat of edibility: flowers, fruits, and young stalks. The woody-fruited species mentioned in the "Related edible species" section above only have two edible uses: flowers and young stalks. The somewhat fleshy fruit is the key difference maker here for Torrey yucca. The green fruits ripen to brown and gummy, similar to a date fruit in texture. Many indigenous tribes ate the fruits of this species and other non-woody-fruited yuccas after roasting the ripe fruits over a fire and removing the flat, black seeds. Many people also enjoy eating the ripe fruits raw, but the raw fruits tend to upset one of the author's stomach, so we prefer to cook them first. Baked or roasted, the fruits are sweeter and tastier. Be cautious when harvesting the fruits, as the tips of the swordlike leaves are often right around eye level; to be safe, it's a good idea to wear some eye protection.

RECIPE

Roasted Yucca Fruit + Yogurt

Roast ripe yucca fruits on a baking sheet at 400°F for 25 minutes. Allow the fruits to cool enough so that you can split them open with your hands (they split into three different sections, each with two rows of flat, black seeds). Remove and discard the seeds and stiffer fibers around the seeds. Dip the baked pulp into your favorite yogurt. The sweetness blends well with the creaminess of the yogurt.

Yucca species in Texas, regardless of fruit type, have edible flowers that can be eaten raw or cooked (be cautious with the raw flowers, as they can cause stomach upset in some people). Raw, the flowers are somewhat bitter, but they are excellent sautéed with onions. The young flower stalks of many yucca species are also edible when cooked but should be harvested when young and still flexible.

Note that many people conflate yucca with yuca. These are completely unrelated plants with different edible parts and uses. Yuca is one of the common names for the cultivated cassava (*Manihot esculenta*), which has a root that is edible when cooked and can often be found in Mexican grocery stores. Please don't try to harvest yucca roots thinking you can eat them like yuca roots. In fact, yucca roots are high in saponins and can be used as a soap substitute—not good eating.

Bell-shaped flowers of Torrey yucca

EVERGREEN SUMAC (*Rhus virens*)

Evergreen sumac flowers in fall

Family: Anacardiaceae

Edible part and harvest time: Fruits ripen in fall and stick around into early winter.

Toxic lookalikes: CAUTION: *Rhus* species are in the same family as poison ivy, mango, and cashew. If you are highly allergic to any of these, it is best to avoid *Rhus* species out of an abundance of caution. Poison sumac (*Toxicodendron vernix*) has pinnate leaves like evergreen sumac and other *Rhus* species, but the fruits can easily be distinguished. *Rhus* species have red pubescent berries when ripe, whereas poison sumac (and other *Toxicodendron* species) have white or pale yellowish fruits that lack hairs. Therefore, mistaking the ripe fruits is not likely. Other mildly toxic or otherwise unpalatable lookalikes include the *Peruvian peppertree (*Schinus molle*), the *Brazilian peppertree (*Schinus terebinthifolius*), and *Chinese pistache (*Pistacia chinensis*). These nonnative species can be found in south Texas and in some urban areas around the state. They are most easily distinguished from *Rhus* species by their smooth, red fruits in contrast to the hairy, pubescent fruits of *Rhus* species.

Identification: Evergreen sumac is an evergreen shrub up to 10 feet tall. The alternate, **pinnately compound leaves** have five to nine dark **green, shiny, leathery leaflets**. The small **white flowers** appear in summer and early fall in terminal panicles at the ends of branches. Unripe green fruits ripen into **large reddish fruits** (compared to other sumac species) up to 0.25 inch that are **flattened and orbicular** in shape. Each fruit is **covered with hairs** and often has a coating of a **whitish, sticky substance** that looks kind of like moist white sugar. Each fruit has one large seed inside and a thin rind with no flesh to speak of.

Range and habitat: Evergreen sumac can be found throughout much of the Hill Country and Trans-Pecos in a variety of rocky habitats. Rocky slopes, canyons, and limestone-rich woodlands are common habitats. It's also increasingly used in landscaping.

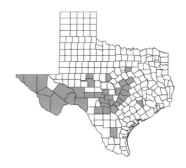

Related edible species: There are several other edible *Rhus* species in Texas including *R. aromatica* (much of Texas except coastal and southern counties), *R. copallinum* (eastern half of Texas), *R. glabra* (eastern half of Texas), *R. lanceolata* (central and west Texas), and *R. microphylla* (western half of Texas). Leaf shape varies considerably among these species, but all have fuzzy red fruits when ripe.

Uses/history/comments: Evergreen sumac is one of the easiest wild foods to enjoy right off the bat, but caution is advised. Sumacs are in the Anacardiaceae family, which includes poison ivy, mangoes, and cashews. If you are highly allergic to any of these, it is best to avoid *Rhus* species out of an abundance of caution. If you are only allergic to poison ivy, but not mangoes or cashews, you should be OK, but proceed with caution and start with a very small amount to see how you react.

Assuming you are not in that category, first-time foragers love the instant sour kick the fruit delivers the moment it hits the tongue, even before chewing. It is also one of the easier plants to identify, even given that it has a few toxic lookalikes. The flattened red fruits are in a terminal cluster and are covered in short hairs; the ripe fruits can also have a distinctive, visible, whitish coating of a sticky, tangy substance. These characteristics make evergreen sumac easy to identify. The whitish sticky substance (which studies on related *Rhus* species indicate has a high malic acid content [20]) is responsible for the unexpected flavor. We have tried all the native *Rhus* species in Texas and evergreen sumac is our favorite, as it tends to pack more of a punch. However, other species like *R. glabra* are easier to harvest en masse because they grow in larger clusters.

Fruits from the related *Rhus lanceolata*

Regardless of which *Rhus* species you harvest, because the flavor-carrying substance is found on the outside of the fruit, chewing the tough fruit imparts almost no additional flavor. Some people just suck on the fruits to get the flavor and then spit them out. We normally chew up the fruits but admit it does not add much to the experience. However, the whole fruits are useful if you want to use sumac as a spice or flavoring, as is traditional in Middle Eastern cuisine with Syrian sumac (*R. coriaria*). The whole dried fruit can be powdered and imparts a pleasant sour flavor to hummus, kebabs, falafels, etc. A consequence of having the flavor-carrying substance on the outside of the fruit is that rain washes away much of the tang. Therefore, it's best to harvest before heavy rains.

Sumac is especially tasty in beverages. Countless long, hot hikes have been improved by adding a few ripe sumac berries to our water bottles to quench our thirst and add a bit of sweetness and tang. Upping the ante, try adding a lot of sumac berries to water to make a lemonade-like replacement affectionately referred to in foraging circles as "sumac-ade" or "rhus juice."

RECIPE

Sumac-ade

Add 2 cups whole, ripe sumac fruits (preferably with heavy coatings of the exterior malic-acid-containing substance) to about ½ to 1 gallon (depending on how strong you like it) filtered water in a glass bowl or pitcher. Agitate with a spoon for a minute to dissolve the exterior coating into the water. Let this mixture sit at room temperature or in the refrigerator for a couple hours. Agitate again and then strain to remove the fruits. This can be drunk as is for a sour, refreshing drink, or you can sweeten with honey. Perfect on a hot Texas afternoon!

YAUPON (*Ilex vomitoria*)

Family: Aquifoliaceae

Edible part and harvest time: Leaves are available year-round for tea.

Toxic lookalikes: The berries of yaupon itself are toxic and should be avoided. There are also other *Ilex* species that are not considered fit for consumption (leaves or berries). These include *I. coriacea* (which has black fruits), *I. decidua* (which is deciduous and has leaves that are narrowly tapered at the base), *I. longipes* (which has long, pedicelled fruits), and *I. opaca* (which has thick, spiny leaves). Out of these, *I. decidua* (possumhaw) looks most like yaupon. The leaves are the easiest distinguishers: Yaupon has thick evergreen leaves that are more or less oval shaped, while possumhaw has longer leaves that are noticeably narrowed at the base compared to the apex. Also, if you bend a mature yaupon leaf slowly between two fingers, it will eventually snap in half, as it is a fairly thick, stiff leaf. If you bend a mature possumhaw leaf like this, it will just keep bending and will eventually crease. This is because possumhaw leaves are much thinner and more flexible. Another potential lookalike is the invasive *Chinese privet (Ligustrum sinense)*, but this is easily distinguished since Chinese privet has opposite leaves while yaupon has alternate leaves.

Identification: Yaupon is an **evergreen** shrub or small tree up to 25 feet tall. It has smooth, light gray-brown bark that is often **mottled and spotted with lichen**. The simple, **alternate**, dark green, elliptic, **leathery leaves** have rounded teeth and are typically 1–2 inches. The plant is dioecious (male and female flowers on separate plants), and the small **white flowers** arise in clusters from the leaf axils in late spring. Each flower has four petals.

The red berries of yaupon are toxic.

The **bright red fruits** (about the size of a BB) appear on the female plants in fall and winter and are shiny and fleshy with four seeds inside.

Range and habitat: Yaupon is abundant in the southeast Texas Piney Woods and along the Gulf Coast but can also be found in central Texas and parts of north Texas. It is usually found near creeks in central Texas but can be found almost anywhere in southeast Texas. Soils range from rocky limestone to deep sands and loamy soils. Yaupon is also one of the most commonly used evergreen shrubs in Texas landscaping, but landscaped varieties have much smaller leaves that are typically not worth harvesting.

Related edible species: There are no other consumable *Ilex* species in Texas, although yaupon is closely related to yerba mate (*Ilex paraguariensis*) and guayusa (*Ilex guayusa*), both of which grow in South America and also contain caffeine and theobromine.

Uses/history/comments: If you noticed that the name at the top of this species account contained *vomitoria* and skipped this plant, we would not blame you. Fortunately, the species name is a misnomer. There are a few different explanations for why yaupon was given such an unfortunate scientific name. The most plausible, in our view, is that early European settlers observed Native Americans drinking yaupon ritualistically and then vomiting. The Europeans assumed the vomiting was due to some toxic quality in the leaves themselves. However, a closer reading of firsthand accounts indicates *how* yaupon was consumed in these rituals. According to Cabeza de Vaca's accounts of the Karankawa tribe, it was typically drunk after or during fasting, while still very hot, and in very large quantities (around four gallons in a day) [13]. Imagine drinking four gallons of any piping hot beverage on an empty stomach. You could probably replicate the vomiting aspect using four gallons of plain hot water, but imagine it being four gallons of hot coffee and you can easily understand how vomiting could be induced. On top of this, other plant species were sometimes added to the ritual brews, which could have increased the emetic properties of the drink.

Small white yaupon flowers among the alternate, evergreen leaves

Yaupon is the only native plant species in Texas (and the US for that matter) that naturally contains substantial amounts of caffeine. It was commonly consumed for its energizing effects by settlers and Native Americans alike and was actually exported to Europe for a period before coffee took its place. Also known as cassine or black drink, yaupon was a popular

RECIPE

Cold-Brew Yaupon

Toast fresh yaupon leaves in a cast-iron pan on low to medium heat while constantly stirring until the leaves are dry and brittle, but not burnt. Alternatively, you can roast the leaves in a 350°F oven for 30–45 minutes until dry and brittle. You can also alter this process to use a lower temperature and longer roasting time so that you get more of a green tea than a black tea result. Once you have your dried leaves, crush them and add approximately 3–4 tbsp. to a cloth tea bag and submerge in a 16 oz. glass jar full of cold water. Then let it cold-steep in the fridge to your desired strength (typically 5–10 hours). At the start, you can see the cold steep in action, as the dark yaupon constituents will sink away from the tea bag toward the bottom of the jar. After steeping, you should have a dark, caffeinated beverage that is excellent as is or with your favorite milk and/or sweetener.

everyday beverage. It is unfortunate that imported coffee, Japanese and Chinese teas, and other caffeinated beverages displaced this abundant native caffeine source. Fast-forward to today, and a number of small businesses are bringing yaupon back into the mainstream as a local caffeine alternative. In fact, we founded a company called Local Leaf (www.local-leaf.com) to do just that. Local Leaf wild-harvests and sells yaupon products including cold-brew yaupon and yaupon matcha (yaupon leaf powder). We are also founding members of the American Yaupon Association.

Regarding its health-promoting properties, yaupon contains theobromine (a mood-boosting alkaloid related to caffeine and found in high concentrations in chocolate) and is very high in antioxidants and polyphenols [21]. Because of yaupon's theobromine content, the lift it provides is more gentle, smooth, and sustained than the harsh ups and downs associated with coffee.

Fortunately, yaupon is evergreen, so the leaves can be harvested year-round. We recommend avoiding harvesting from plants that are flowering or fruiting, as it can be difficult to avoid accidentally picking some of the berries or flowers. Find a yaupon bush with full, dense, green leaves and simply strip the leaves from the ends of the branches and stems. You can either dry the leaves green or roast them to get a bolder flavor. Use as you would green tea or yerba mate. We find that cold-brewing yaupon works very well and results in a less bitter and more enjoyable brew compared to hot-brewing.

DWARF PALMETTO (*Sabal minor*)

Family: Arecaceae
Edible part and harvest time: Fruits ripen in fall and winter; heart is available year-round.

Toxic lookalikes: There are no toxic native or naturalized members of the palm family (Arecaceae) in Texas, but palms from all over the world can be cultivated in parts of Texas (especially along the coast and in south Texas), so be careful around cultivated palms with unknown origins. One unrelated but similar-looking plant to avoid is the *sago palm (*Cycas revoluta*), which is not actually a palm but a member of the cycad family. This is widely used in landscaping and has apparently escaped cultivation in Harris and Cameron Counties. The seeds of sago palm are particularly toxic, but the entire plant should be avoided. While somewhat similar to coconut palm leaves, the leaves of *Cycas* are very easy to distinguish from *Sabal*: *Cycas* leaves are long and feather-like, while *Sabal* species have fanlike leaves.

Ripe dwarf palmetto fruits in winter

Identification: Dwarf palmetto is a short, shrubby palm that usually **lacks any recognizable trunk**. The aboveground portion consists primarily of **evergreen fan-shaped leaves**, leafstalks, and a flowering stalk. The large leaves can be **up to 4 feet across**; leaf stems are long and rigid and extend on the underside of the leaf as a midrib. Each leaf stem appears to sprout straight out of the ground but actually arises from the terminal bud (heart) right around ground level. The flowering stalk is tall and usually reaches to or beyond the leaves. The flower stalk has numerous clusters of tiny white flowers in summer, which ripen into **spherical, black-blue fruits 0.5 inch in diameter**. Each fruit has a thin, sweet rind surrounding a hard, spherical seed.

Range and habitat: Dwarf palmetto is found scattered throughout the eastern half of Texas in low, moist areas like swamps and floodplains. It is almost always found in wetlands or rich alluvial soils near creeks and rivers.

Related edible species: There are two other much less common *Sabal* species in the Lower Rio Grande Valley: *S. mexicana* (synonymous with *S. texana*) and *S. palmetto*. These species are taller trees and have edible fruits and hearts, but we do not recommend eating them (unless cultivated) due to their relative scarcity compared to *S. minor*.

Uses/history/comments: Dwarf palmetto is the most common native palm species in Texas and has multiple uses, which make it an excellent foraging target. The most commonly eaten part of the dwarf palmetto is the fruit. While related to the popular and commercially available date fruits (from *Phoenix dactylifera*), dwarf palmetto fruits are not nearly as substantial. The fruit consists of a large spherical seed surrounded by a very thin coating of sweet, bluish to black flesh. We have read that some people disagree with the flavor, but we find it pleasantly date-like though not as sweet. We usually eat the skin off the large seed and spit the seed out, as it is extremely hard. However, the seed can be ground up with considerable effort to make a very crude and rough "flour." But because it is difficult to get the hard seed into fine enough of a powder, we would leave this for emergency use only. Boiling the "flour" after grinding helps soften the seed, but it is still unenjoyably hard to chew. Another option for the fruit is a syrup.

Flowering stalk of dwarf palmetto in summer

The other edible part of dwarf palmetto is the heart of the terminal bud. Note that removing the terminal bud kills the plant, so only do this if you are harvesting from a cultivated plant, from a large patch, or from an area that has already been slated for development or clearing. You will want to dislodge the heart right at the root crown (ground level) with a sharpshooter shovel or similar tool. You can also use a machete to hack the heart

RECIPE

Palmetto Syrup

Harvest 1 cup of ripe dwarf palmetto fruits and place into a pot with 2 cups water. Bring to a simmer on medium heat for about 3 minutes before mashing up the fruits with a potato masher or similar utensil to remove the skin and thin pulp from the hard seed. Strain the seeds out and add the liquid back to the pot. Add 2 tsp. maple syrup and a dash of cinnamon and simmer until all ingredients are integrated and the liquid turns viscous and syrupy (about 5 minutes). This rich syrup is good on pancakes and French toast.

from the base of the plant, but this is much easier if you first remove most of the leaves and leafstalks from the plant. After harvesting and trimming away the outer leafstalks, the whitish terminal bud can be eaten raw or baked and tastes kind of like the more traditional heart of palm. You'll know once you've gotten to the edible part, as it will not be fibrous and will be white and crunchy.

SALTWORT (*Batis maritima*)

Family: Bataceae

Edible part and harvest time: Leaves and stems can be harvested year-round.

Toxic lookalikes: None in Texas

Identification: Saltwort is a **light green to yellowish, succulent**, spreading or prostrate shrub with a semi-woody base. Creeping stems can be up to 6 feet long, but the plant rarely reaches more than 2 feet off the ground. Stems root at the nodes and form large, spreading colonies. The cylindrical, succulent leaves (1 inch long) are **opposite and often curve upward**. The inconspicuous flowers and fruits are arranged in **cone-like spikes arising from the leaf axils**.

Range and habitat: Saltwort is common along the Gulf Coast in saline soils near water. It is often found on the shores of lagoons on the bay side of barrier islands.

Cone-like, yellowish saltwort fruits

Low-growth habit showing upward-curving, succulent leaves

Related edible species: There are no other *Batis* species in Texas, but a few other edible plants grow in similar habitats and look similar but belong to different plant families. These include silverhead (*Blutaparon vermiculare*) and glasswort (*Salicornia* spp.). Both of these plants are succulents that have similar low-growing, sprawling habits and also grow in saline soils along the Gulf Coast. They can be used in much the same way as *Batis*.

Uses/history/comments: Saltwort is a common plant along the shores of lagoons and bays in coastal Texas. It's known by a few other common names including vidrillos, beach-wort, and pickleweed. Due to its preference for brackish and salty habitats, the succulent leaves and stems are predictably salty, much like other succulent edible species along the coast. The leaves and stems are variable in their juiciness and saltiness depending on habitat and rainfall but are usually tasty. That said, we have run into some stands that are too salty to eat in larger amounts.

Harvesting is straightforward: Snap off the younger, succulent tips of the plant. Take care to avoid or wash off plants that have had sand blown onto them. Saltwort is excellent raw in salads, in stews, as a potherb, or pickled.

According to one account, the Seri tribe along the Gulf of California used the roots of saltwort as a source of sugar after peeling away the outer skin [16].

RECIPE

Saltwort Salad

Bring a pot of water to a boil, then add a handful or two of young saltwort leaves and stems and boil for 1 minute. Strain the saltwort through a colander and cool quickly in an ice bath to preserve the color. Refrigerate the boiled saltwort leaves so that they are cold before proceeding to the next step. Place the cold saltwort leaves in a salad bowl and drizzle juice from ½ lemon and 2 tbsp. olive oil on top, then add grated Parmesan and black pepper to taste and toss well to combine. This is a great side salad to grilled fish.

AGARITA (*Mahonia trifoliolata*)

Family: Berberidaceae

Edible part and harvest time: Flowers are available in early spring, while fruits ripen in late spring and early summer.

Toxic lookalikes: Do not confuse agarita with one of the ornamental holly species like American holly (*Ilex opaca*) or Chinese holly (*Ilex cornuta*), both of which have sharply pointed leaves somewhat similar to agarita and toxic, spherical red fruits. It's easy to distinguish agarita from these hollies: agarita is trifoliate (three leaflets per leaf), whereas the hollies have simple leaves. Also, the inner bark of agarita is bright yellow, which is not the case with the hollies.

Identification: Agarita is a common evergreen shrub up to 6 feet tall. The bark is brown but the **inner bark, when cut, is bright yellow**. Each leaf is **trifoliate with three stiff, spiny leaflets** that join together at one point. The leaflets can range from dark green to bluish gray and have three to seven points each. The **flowers are yellow** and grow in clusters in spring. The ripe fruits in early summer are strikingly **bright pink or orange** and elliptic, with small seeds inside.

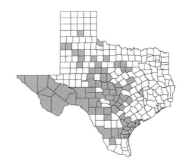

Range and habitat: Agarita is most abundant in central and west Texas but is also found in parts of south and north Texas. Habitat includes dry limestone soils, fencerows, and juniper-dominated woodlands.

Spiny, trifoliate leaves of agarita

Related edible species: *M. haematocarpa* is a related desert species ranging from the Trans-Pecos to the deserts of California. *M. swaysei* is found in limited portions of the Edwards Plateau but is much rarer than agarita. For this reason, we never harvest *M. swaysei* fruits and advise you not to as well. The well-known Oregon grape (*M. aquifolium*) is also related but is found in the Pacific Northwest.

Uses/history/comments: Agarita (or algarita to some) has a botanical synonym, *Berberis trifoliolata*, and is one of the hardiest edible plants in Texas. The yellow flowers that first appear in early spring make for a somewhat bitter addition to salads. We prefer, however, to leave the flowers and wait until the fruits develop. As they ripen, they can turn hot pink, bright orange, or bright red and are best in early summer. We usually try one or two from an individual plant to gauge the ripeness, as the ones that are not ready will be fairly bitter, whereas ripe ones are pleasantly sweet with only a hint of bitterness. Be careful when harvesting the fruits, as the leaves are very prickly. We recommend wearing leather gloves *or* using this simple technique: Place a shirt, blanket, sheet, or similar material under the bush as best you can and then beat the bush with a stick so the fruits fall onto the cloth. An improvement on this method was offered to us by a Hill Country winemaker who suggested swapping the sheet for an upside-down umbrella. The fruits fall into the umbrella and can then be poured into a container or bag.

RECIPE

Agarita Jam

Use a food processor or blender to blend 1 cup ripe agarita berries into a chunky consistency; you may need to add water if the fruits are fairly dry in order for it to mix well. Mix the blended agarita berries with 2 tbsp. sugar, 2 tbsp. lemon juice, and a pinch of salt in a small pot. Bring to a boil over medium heat for about 3 minutes while stirring constantly. Depending on how juicy your agarita berries were and how much water you had to add at the start, it may take a bit longer to get to a jam-like consistency. Then let cool, scoop into a glass jar, and keep the jam in the fridge for up to 3 weeks or so.

Agarita fruits can be enjoyed raw straight off the bush or made into various jams, jellies, pies, and even wine.

Agarita is also an excellent medicine with uses similar to goldenseal (*Hydrastis canadensis*). Goldenseal, which is not native to Texas, has been overharvested in the eastern US and should only be used when cultivated, but agarita is an abundant substitute in Texas. The bark and root contain berberine, which is a

Yellow agarita flowers in early spring

bright yellow alkaloid known to be strongly antibacterial and antiviral and is useful for nearly any type of gastroenteritis [18]. Sam Coffman from the Human Path in Bulverde, Texas, is a huge proponent of agarita and has used it extensively to treat clinical patients.

TRIANGLE CACTUS (*Acanthocereus tetragonus*)

Family: Cactaceae

Edible part and harvest time: Young stems and ripe fruits can be found nearly year-round in the Lower Rio Grande Valley, but fruits are most common in summer and fall.

Toxic lookalikes: None in Texas

Identification: Triangle cactus is a **large, upright, arching, or sometimes climbing cactus** species up to 10 feet tall when standing on its own but can climb higher when

Messy habit typical of triangle cactus

Triangle cactus spines and three-angled stem

supported by adjacent trees. A single plant often has multiple stems, each of which are a few inches wide with **three (and sometimes four or five) prominent ribs**. Areoles containing **seven or eight spines** each are arranged along the ribs. Spines are about 1.5 inches long and areoles **lack glochids** (hairlike bristles at the base of spines, fruits, and flowers in many cacti). The **large white flowers** (8 inches wide with numerous petals) bloom at night. The fleshy fruit (similar to a prickly pear) is ripe when **red and has many spines, but no glochids**. Each fruit has red pulp with numerous small black seeds.

Range and habitat: Triangle cactus is found in thickets and thornscrub in the Lower Rio Grande Valley, where it typically grows in dry soils. However, it has also been cultivated up to Corpus Christi and San Antonio, although it is sensitive to freezes so dies back farther north.

Related edible species: There are no other *Acanthocereus* species growing wild in Texas, but a few similar tall, thin cacti are sometimes planted in the Lower Rio Grande Valley. Luckily for us, these cultivated species from South America also have edible fruits. An example is *Cereus repandus*, which grows straight up and down, unlike *Acanthocereus*.

Uses/history/comments: Triangle cactus is a distinctive large cactus found growing wild in Texas only in the Lower Rio Grande Valley. It was formerly known as *Cereus pentagonus* and then *Acanthocereus pentagonus* but is currently known as *A. tetragonus*. It's an imposing cactus that clambers through larger trees or forms massive clumps. We've seen some larger stems reaching up to 25 feet into treetops, where it depends on its neighboring tree for structural support. Interestingly, it is the fastest-growing cactus species in the US, with growth spurts of 5–6 feet in a single season [22]. It also has dangerous spines to beware of, which explains its other name: barbed-wire cactus. However, this species lacks the hairlike glochids present in many other cactus species, so as long as you avoid the spines (either by cutting them out or burning them off), you don't need to worry about cleaning the fruits or stems as much as with prickly pears, for example. The stem spines are more spaced out than many other cactus species, which makes it easier to grab the stem with two carefully placed fingers in order to cut and remove a succulent stem or fruit.

The young, green stems are edible and taste similar to young prickly pear pads but get stringy and fibrous with age. Fruits grow directly off the side of the stem, usually toward the end of a branch. The fruits are often too high to be able to safely reach them unless you bring a ladder. Additionally, the fruits are eaten quickly by birds and rodents, so it is probable that you will find fruits with holes eaten through them during your search. The bright red/pink fruits are gently sweet and overall similar to other cactus fruits, but the flesh separates into strands. Because the fruits have spines on them, it's best to peel them or at least cut the spines off before eating either raw or cooked into a jam or other recipe. The black seeds can be ground into flour or swallowed while eating the fruit.

RECIPE

Triangle Cactus Sorbet

Harvest about 10 triangle cactus fruits and thoroughly de-spine them, cut them in halves, and freeze them (seeds and all). Add the frozen fruits to a Vitamix or similar blender along with 2 tbsp. raw honey and 1 tbsp. lemon juice. Add a little warm water if they're too frozen and blend until smooth. Eat the sorbet immediately if you want a softer texture or refreeze for a firmer texture.

TREE CHOLLA (*Cylindropuntia imbricata*)

Family: Cactaceae

Edible part and harvest time: Flowers are available in summer; fruits ripen in late summer and into fall.

Toxic lookalikes: There are no toxic lookalikes in Texas, although the fruits of the related tasajillo (*C. leptocaulis*) have been noted as having possible hallucinogenic effects. We had eaten tasajillo fruits on a number of occasions before we heard about the possible side effects and never experienced anything out of the ordinary. That said, tasajillo fruits are very small and spiny so not worth it in our opinion. Tasajillo stems are very thin (it's also called pencil cactus due to the small diameter) with red fruits, while tree cholla and other chollas in Texas have thicker stems and yellow fruits when ripe.

Identification: Tree cholla is a shrub or small tree (3–8 feet tall) with a single trunk that branches out with **numerous spiny joints**. Each joint or section is cylindrical, 1 inch in diameter, and 2–6 inches long, with elongated, raised tubercles throughout. Tubercles each have one areole with 10–30 variably colored spines and few glochids. **Purplish to hot pink flowers** are up to 3 inches wide, with fleshy petals. The spherical to hemispherical fruits are **yellow when ripe** and covered in tubercles with glochids. Fruits **often hang in clusters at the ends of terminal joints**. Each fruit is spongy and white inside and contains small seeds in a central cavity.

Range and habitat: Tree cholla grows through much of the Trans-Pecos and panhandle. It can be found in sandy or gravelly dry soils and is easily seen along west Texas roadsides. Tree cholla (or one of its relatives) is also frequently planted in xeriscaping in Texas.

Related edible species: There are a few other edible *Cylindropuntia* species in Texas including *C. davisii* (Trans-Pecos, western Edwards Plateau, and panhandle), *C. kleiniae* (Trans-Pecos and northern edge of Edwards Plateau), and *C. leptocaulis* (western two-thirds of Texas; see caution in "Toxic lookalikes" section above).

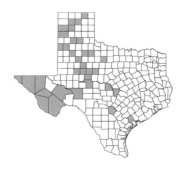

Uses/history/comments: Tree cholla and other cholla species are closely related to the flat-pad prickly pear (*Opuntia*) cacti. In fact, they used to be lumped into the same genus, but cholla species are less commonly eaten. One reason for this is that the cholla stems are not easily edible like the *Opuntia* species. So, right off the bat, you are realistically limited to the flowers, buds, and fruits. However, the Seri tribe does eat the young stems of some *Cylindropuntia* species after burning off the spines and roasting [16]. Cholla flowers and buds are more or less equivalent from an edibility and taste perspective to *Opuntia* flowers and buds. *C. imbricata* in particular has hot pink flowers in summer that can brighten up salads instantly. Where the main edibility difference lies, however, is the fruits. Cholla fruits are overall less exciting compared to *Opuntia* fruits; they lack the sweetness, bright color, and high water content. However, they have a blander flavor that works well in fermented or pickled foods. We've made tasty pickles with them that had a great flavor, but the consistency was a bit slimy so maybe not for everyone.

To harvest cholla fruits or buds, we first like to take a leafy branch of a nearby shrub and brush it over the fruits or buds while they're still attached to remove some of the spines and glochids. This will not remove all the glochids, but many. Next, use a pair of tongs or wilderness chopsticks (read: two straight sticks) to pluck the yellow fruits. Harvest the fruits when they no longer have a hint of green and are starting to shrivel. Buds can be harvested the same way but in spring. Process either buds or fruits by rubbing them between two gloved hands and carefully removing all spines and glochids. Alternatively, you can burn off the glochids and spines over a fire. After you think you've removed all the glochids, roll the fruits around using your bare hands;

Pink tree cholla flowers in summer

Upright habit; note the hanging clusters of yellow fruits.

glochids are less painful and easier to remove from your skin than your mouth or throat. We find cholla fruits and buds more time-consuming to de-spine than *Opuntia* species, but your mileage may vary.

Thoroughly de-spined buds can be used in sautés, soups, and stir-fries. The fruits are kind of spongy inside and have a few hard seeds in the center, which can be removed easily. As mentioned above, the flavor of the fruits by themselves is not especially exciting, but they take on pretty much any flavor. Below is one of our favorite uses for the fruits.

RECIPE

Dried Cholla "Chips"

Obtain a handful of ripe yellow cholla fruits and thoroughly de-spine, making sure to remove *all* of the tiny glochids. Cut each fruit into ¼-inch slices and remove the seeds. Then make a simple syrup by mixing ½ cup water, ½ cup sugar, and a dash of salt in a pot and bringing it to a boil. Turn off the stove and add the sliced cholla fruits to the simple syrup and let marinate for at least 30 minutes. Remove each fruit with a slotted spoon and dehydrate completely in the sun or a dehydrator until crispy. These little snacks have an interesting texture and remind us of dried apple rings, though not as sweet. Tajín (a Mexican blend of chili peppers, lime, and salt) is an excellent addition before dehydrating.

HORSECRIPPLER CACTUS (*Echinocactus texensiS*)

Family: Cactaceae
Edible part and harvest time: Fruits ripen in early summer.
Toxic lookalikes: Many fruits from plants in the Cactaceae family are either edible or at least not toxic in reasonable quantities. However, peyote (*Lophophora williamsii*) is one to avoid (both for the potentially undesirable hallucinogenic side effects and from a conservation perspective). It is easy to distinguish from horsecrippler cactus, though, as it has no large spines.
Identification: Horsecrippler cactus is a short (2–8 inches tall), **dome-shaped cactus** that is **often nearly flush with the ground**. They often grow in loose clusters near each other, with each stem or plant up to 1 foot wide with 13–27 ribs. Areoles are arranged on the ribs, have a whitish wool at the base, and have **one stout central spine that curves downward surrounded by usually six radial spines**. Each spine is **angular in cross section**. The small flowers are variably colored, with numerous petals. The

Ripe horsecrippler fruit cut in half to reveal the bright pulp and small black seeds

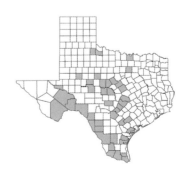

Small horsecrippler flowers can vary in color.

1-inch-diameter fruits are **bright red**, nearly spherical when ripe, and unarmed. Fleshy fruits have hot pink pulp and numerous small black seeds.

Range and habitat: Horsecrippler cactus is found along the counties that border Mexico and in central, south, and parts of north Texas. It can be found in dry, flat desert areas, limestone mesas, thornscrub, and grasslands.

Related edible species: There is one other *Echinocactus* in the Trans-Pecos that is apparently edible: *E. horizonthalonius* [23]. Though uncommon in Texas, there are two barrel cactus species (*Ferocactus* spp.) that have edible fruits, although these are easy to distinguish from *Echinocactus* given their yellow fruits. Nipple cactus (*Mammillaria* spp.) could also be confused with horsecrippler cactus, as they have edible red fruits and are about the same overall shape, but if you look closely, they lack distinct ribs and instead have "nipple" protrusions (tubercles) with spines at the tip.

RECIPE

Horsecrippler + Spoon

Because we caution you not to overharvest from this slow-growing cactus, we don't have an elaborate recipe that might require dozens of horsecrippler fruits. Simply cut the fruit in half, add a squeeze of honey or lime, and scoop out the pulp, seeds and all, with a spoon.

Uses/history/comments:
Horsecrippler cactus (also known as devil's head) has surely been cursed throughout Texas history by unsuspecting passersby. Stepping on one of these half-buried, stout cacti with bare feet or even regular tennis shoes can become a hospital-worthy ordeal. And, as the name suggests, horsecrippler has also injured its share of domesticated animals. Horsecrippler cacti can be very difficult to see before it's too late when not flowering or fruiting, as they blend in amazingly well with surrounding grasses and herbs (see photo).

Horsecrippler is redeemed by its juicy red fruit that can be found even during droughts in the hot summer months. While only a few fruits can be found on any single plant, horsecrippler cactus often grows in

In grassy or weedy areas, horsecrippler is extremely difficult to spot. There are six horsecrippler cacti in this photo.

colonies. However, because it is a slow-growing cactus, we only take one fruit from each to ensure that the future of the colony is safe. Please harvest responsibly! Unlike the glochid-ridden fruits of other cactus species, horsecrippler fruits are unarmed, with only a few prickly bits left over from flowering. We usually pick these fruits barehanded without much concern and brush off the chaff and hairy parts before eating.

Once harvested, cut in half to expose the bright pink flesh. It looks and tastes much like the exotic dragonfruit (which is also in the Cactaceae family), although not as sweet. Unlike prickly pear cactus (*Opuntia* spp.) fruits, the seeds of horsecrippler are delightfully crunchable and can be eaten raw with the pulp.

SCARLET HEDGEHOG CACTUS
(*Echinocereus coccineus*)

Family: Cactaceae

Edible part and harvest time: Flowers are available in spring, and fruits ripen in summer.

Toxic lookalikes: Many fruits from plants in the Cactaceae family are either edible or at least not toxic in reasonable quantities. That said, use caution when identifying edible cacti; we do not recommend eating just any cactus you come across.

Identification: Scarlet hedgehog cactus is a short, **clumping cactus with tightly packed stems** that form 1–6-foot-diameter masses. Each stem is about 2.5 inches in diameter with 8–11 ribs. The areoles are arranged along the ribs, each with 8–12 radial and 1–4 central, straight spines (0.5–1.75 inches). The 1–2-inch-diameter flowers are **bright red** with fleshy petals. The fruits are much like prickly pears but have deciduous bristles and are **bright red** when ripe, with small black seeds inside.

Range and habitat: Scarlet hedgehog cactus can be found in the Trans-Pecos and Edwards Plateau in dry grasslands, scrublands, and limestone outcrops. It frequently grows in clumps and colonies in partial shade of other shrubs.

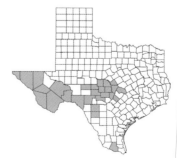

Related edible species: There are a number of other *Echinocereus* species in Texas, but many have unverified edibility and/or fruits that are too small or unpalatable to be worth eating anyways. However, three other clump-forming *Echinocereus* species in Texas are very similar to *E. coccineus* and are also edible and tasty: *E. enneacanthus* (along the border from west Texas to the Gulf of Mexico), *E. mojavensis* (Trans-Pecos and into central Texas), and *E. stramineus* (Trans-Pecos and adjacent counties to the east). These are sometimes collectively referred to as strawberry cacti and look almost the same to the untrained eye.

Uses/history/comments: Scarlet hedgehog cactus (also known as strawberry cactus or pitahaya in some areas) provides a splash of color to the landscape in spring with its bright red flowers. Other closely related species have hot pink flowers that are equally stunning. The flower petals of the strawberry cactus and its close relatives are edible and can be plucked and added to salads, used as a

Bright red flowers bloom in spring.

Red fruits ripen in summer.

Cactus Cooler

Obtain 3 scarlet hedgehog cactus fruits and thoroughly de-spine and rinse them. Blend (seeds and all) with 1 tbsp. lime juice, 2 tbsp. water, and 1 tsp. raw honey until smooth. Strain the resulting juice through a fine stainless-steel mesh and pour the strained juice into ice cube trays to freeze overnight. The next day, put the frozen cubes back into the blender and blend on high until smooth (if too chunky, add a bit of water). Add a splash of vodka if you are so inclined or drink on its own as a cold summertime refreshment.

garnish, or eaten raw on the trail. While they don't add much in the way of flavor, they are mucilaginous and add an interesting texture.

But the real show stoppers come later in summer when the bright red fruits ripen. The fruits are well protected by spines, so pick these carefully, preferably with gloves. It is also best to have a hard-sided collection bucket or jug to keep from getting stuck on the hike back. Sometimes you can remove the spines by brushing them off with a gloved hand, as they fall off easier than with other cacti. The flesh is usually hot pink with tiny black seeds, but some related species have white flesh and this may be variable. The flesh and tiny, crunchable seeds are edible raw and taste a lot like a strawberry. The fruit can be used to make jams, jellies, candies, etc. Scarlet hedgehog cactus usually grows in large clumps, so there may be a number of fruits available at one time. That said, make sure to only harvest a few at each cactus clump since the desert-dwelling animals that typically live around this cactus depend on it for food and water. The more abundant prickly pear fruits (see next species account) are better candidates for larger harvests.

TEXAS PRICKLY PEAR (*Opuntia engelmannii*)

Family: Cactaceae

Edible part and harvest time: De-spined young pads are available spring to summer, while flowers can be found in spring and fruits (tunas) ripen summer to fall.

Toxic lookalikes: None in Texas

Identification: Texas prickly pear is a shrub 3–9 feet tall with **flattened, circular or obovate pads** (joints) 8 to 14 inches long. Each pad has areoles both on the flattened portions of the pad and the edges of the pad, where they are more numerous. Each areole has 1–5 yellowish spines (0.75–2.5 inches) when young and up to 12 spines per areole on older pads (note that the lower areoles are often spineless). Areoles also have coarse glochids that look like smaller spines in some cases. The **bright yellow, orange, or reddish flowers** are 3–4 inches wide, with fleshy petals. The **pear-shaped fruits** are often **dark red or burgundy** when ripe, 2–3 inches long, and have glochids in regularly spaced areoles. The **top of the fruit is usually brown or grayish and flat or concave** and can become convex when plump and ripe for picking. The **flesh is hot pink**, with small dark seeds inside.

Range and habitat: Texas prickly pear grows in a variety of habitats including grasslands, pasturelands, dry woods, and limestone outcrops. It grows throughout most of Texas except the panhandle, east Texas, and much of north Texas. At least one species of *Opuntia* grows in nearly every corner of Texas.

Ripe tunas in late summer

Sliced tunas reveal bright flesh and many small seeds.

Related edible species: Note that this account of *O. engelmannii* includes what some botanists call *O. lindheimeri*, which is either a subspecies of *O. engelmannii* or a distinct separate species depending on who you ask. Either way, they are similar enough for our purposes. The other flat-pad *Opuntia* species in Texas are also edible, although their small size or abundance of spines makes some species impractical to harvest. There are many species but some of the more common include *O. humifusa* (eastern half of Texas), *O. macrocentra* (Trans-Pecos), *O. macrorhiza* (scattered throughout much of Texas), and *O. phaecantha* (western two-thirds of Texas).

Uses/history/comments: Prickly pear cactus provides numerous edible and medicinal opportunities despite its spiny appearance. In all cases, however, care should be taken to avoid the long spines and especially the smaller glochids. Glochids are the most difficult to see and to remove, so it is best to harvest using gloves and make sure to remove all glochids prior to eating. Glochids are annoying when you accidentally get them on your skin but can be dangerous if you accidentally swallow them. One trick to help remove glochids and spines is to take a leafy branch of a nearby shrub and brush it over the fruits, buds, or pads while they are still attached. This won't remove all spines and glochids but goes a long way and makes the rest of the spine/glochid removal process easier.

Nopales (cooked strips of young green pads) are common in Mexican cuisine and taste like a slimy green bean. Our native species of *Opuntia* can be used in the same way once spines and glochids are removed (we usually cut out spines and glochids, but some people burn them off). Note that many of the pad spines are concentrated along the edge of the pad; cutting around the edge with a knife removes most spines, but others in the middle of the pad will have to be removed individually. For nopales, only young green pads should be used, as older pads get fibrous and tough. You can eat nopales raw or cooked (steamed is usually best). Pads cut in half longitudinally (i.e., cutting between the two sides of the pad) to reveal the inner flesh can also be used as a great first aid for cleaning and covering cuts, scrapes, burns, and sunburns while promoting healing.

The mucilaginous flower petals of *Opuntia* species are also edible and can be carefully plucked when in bloom. We usually eat these in situ but have also used them in salads. After the flowers come the prickly pear fruits themselves (often called tunas). The texture of a fully ripe prickly pear is similar to kiwi, but the flavor and color is more similar to dragonfruit (another fruit from the cactus family in the *Hylocereus* genus). Prickly pears are ripe when dark red or burgundy and plump, not shriveled. No hint of green should be visible on the fruits.

The young pads of this *Opuntia* spp. would make excellent nopales.

One other trick is that fruits that are not yet fully ripe normally have a divot or depression on the top, but this becomes convex in fully ripe fruits. When you slice open the fruit, it should be hot pink inside with no hint of green. Note that the fruits have glochids (but no long spines), so it is best to rub them off with gloves or roll them around in grass, rinse under water, then peel the skin in order to eat raw. Only if we're extremely confident that we've removed *all* glochids will we eat the fruits skin-on. The seeds are small and hard (not especially chewable), but we usually just swallow them. Seeds can also be removed prior to eating the fruits and then dried and ground to make a usable flour.

RECIPE

Prickly Pear Instant Smoothie

Take 4–5 fully ripe prickly pear fruits and thoroughly remove *all* glochids. Add them (skin, seeds, and all) to a strong blender and blend on high for 30–60 seconds. It's best to use a Vitamix or similar blender so that the small, hard seeds get pulverized as well. This results in a hot pink smoothie complete with sugars and fiber from the flesh and protein and fats from the seeds. If the fruits are sweet, no additions are needed, but if lacking in flavor, you can add honey or cinnamon to spice it up.

*JAPANESE HONEYSUCKLE (*Lonicera japonica*)

Family: Caprifoliaceae

Edible part and harvest time: Flowers/nectar are available in spring, while leaves are available for tea in spring, summer, and fall.

Toxic lookalikes: The *Lonicera* genus contains a number of potentially toxic species, so it is best to be sure you have the vining *L. japonica* as opposed to some of the more shrubby invasive *Lonicera* species in Texas, which have little evidence of edibility. CAUTION: Many species of *Lonicera* have toxic fruits (including *L. japonica*), so avoid eating honeysuckle berries.

Identification: Japanese honeysuckle is an **evergreen** trailing or climbing vine that often grows over lower shrubs. The pubescent stems are green when young but turn brown or reddish with age. The simple, **opposite, ovate leaves** are up to 1.5 inches long, rounded or cuneate at the base, with smooth margins (although young leaves may be lobed). The **tubular flowers** are fragrant, 1.5 inches long, and **white when new but turn yellowish with age**. The fruits are black and 0.25 inch wide.

Range and habitat: Japanese honeysuckle is found in much of the eastern half of Texas and is most common in disturbed areas and urban settings including roadsides, thickets, and open woods. It's an invasive rampant weed in Texas.

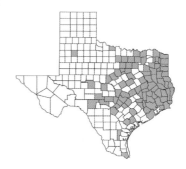

Japanese honeysuckle outcompeting other plants; note the older yellow flowers near the bottom right.

Related edible species: There are several native and invasive *Lonicera* species in Texas but little information regarding many of the other species' edibility. *Lonicera* is one of the genera that contains both toxic and edible species, so other species are best avoided. *L. japonica* is by far the most common, so seeking out other species is not necessary. One exception we make is with *L. sempervirens* (eastern half of Texas), which has bright red flowers that produce excellent nectar.

Uses/history/comments: The honeysuckle name matches our experience with the species. As kids, we both can remember sucking the honey-like nectar out of the flowers (probably one of many Texans' first forays into wild edibles). The nectar is easily enjoyed and brings back fond memories to many. Just pluck a flower and bite off the very tip of the back end, and then suck out the nectar.

Note the variable leaf margins; most are entire, but some are lobed.

Simple Honeysuckle Tea

Gather ½–1 cup of honeysuckle flowers and add to a steeping pot. Pour about 1 cup boiling water over the flowers and steep for several hours or overnight. Drink this refreshing, naturally sweetened tea as is or refrigerate for a refreshing iced tea.

Alternatively, you can soak the fresh flowers in cold water for a few hours for a refreshing beverage. The whole white flowers of *L. japonica* are also edible raw and can add a nice touch to salads.

However, honeysuckles (*L. japonica* in particular) have a dark side. The *Lonicera* genus makes up one of the most prolific and destructive group of invasive plants in the country. In Texas alone, we have at least four species of nonnative invasive *Lonicera* species. *L. japonica* is by far the worst culprit, as its vining habit can smother smaller, less vigorous native plants. But, when we see a plant that is invasive and edible, we get a little excited. You now have carte blanche to harvest as much as your heart desires. And on top of the edible uses for the flowers, the leaves and stems have been used as a tea in traditional Chinese medicine for viral infections and fever [11]. We typically steep a handful of leaves when we feel a cold or sore throat coming on during flu season.

BUFFALO GOURD (*Cucurbita foetidissima*)

Family: Cucurbitaceae

Edible part and harvest time: Seeds from ripe fruits are available in late summer and early fall.

Toxic lookalikes: There are no toxic lookalikes in Texas, but care should be taken to process buffalo gourd seeds to remove pulp before eating, as the pulp can cause stomach upset.

Identification: Buffalo gourd is a **prostrate**, non-woody vine with a perennial rootstock and stems up to 20 feet long running in all directions from the root. The root is massive and reaches deep into the ground. The **large grayish-green leaves** are up to 1 foot long, **rough textured, and arrow shaped**, with a rounded or cordate base. Most people consider the smell of the bruised leaves to be unpleasant. The large, **yellow, squash-like flowers** are up to 4 inches long and flared. The

Large, squash-blossom-like flowers

Cut buffalo gourds reveal many seeds reminiscent of miniature pumpkin seeds.

gourds are 3–4 inches in diameter, nearly spherical, and **green and striped when young but turn yellow with maturity**. The flesh inside is light green to yellowish, with numerous small light-colored seeds that look like mini pumpkin seeds. By the end of summer, the green stems will usually be dried and shriveled, leaving yellow balls of gourds strewn around the root.

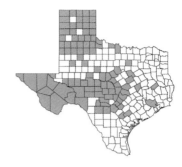

Range and habitat: Buffalo gourd is common in the Trans-Pecos, the panhandle, and central Texas along roadsides and in other dry, sandy or gravelly soils.

Related edible species: Many cultivated squashes are derived from *C. melopepo* (also known as *C. pepo* and *C. texana*, among others), which was cultivated by indigenous peoples for thousands of years. Current cultivars include acorn squash, pumpkin, zucchini, and summer squash. Wild varieties of *C. melopepo* can still be found scattered throughout the southeastern half of Texas.

Uses/history/comments: Buffalo gourd, also known as stinking gourd, is not well known as an edible, but it furnishes one of the most consistent and abundant crops in many of the drier parts of Texas, as it is sufficiently immune to drought. But this is not your standard gourd; the pulp inside each mature fruit has a high saponin content, which makes it more of a soap than a food. In fact, the pulp of buffalo gourd makes a serviceable wilderness soap when mixed with water and even suds up if rubbed between hands vigorously. Useful in a pinch when out in the woods or on a backpacking trip.

But the mature seeds in late summer and early fall are the real prizes. Once separated from the soapy, bitter pulp, the seeds can be roasted like pumpkin seeds to good effect. The trick is separating the pulp from the seeds. This is not as easy to do as it is with pumpkins or other squashes, as the pulp is rather slippery and tenacious. We have found that the following method (though time-consuming) works well. First, cut the gourd in half and scrape/comb out the seeds as much as possible with a spork or similar utensil. This will leave most of the pulp attached to the inside of the gourd, but some of the pulp will come out with the seeds. Put this mass of seeds and pulp in a colander or strainer and set it under a running faucet of hot water while rubbing the pulp between your hands or against the sides of the strainer to loosen up and detach the pulp from the seeds. Repeat this for a while until most of the pulp has detached from the seeds. Then pour this into a pot and fill with hot water. Decant the water slowly so that the floating immature seeds and pulp pour off while the heavier seeds remain at the bottom. Repeat this a few times until you have mostly seeds. Then dry the seeds and minimal remaining pulp in a dehydrator until completely dry. Take the dry seeds and winnow them (rub between your hands) in front of a fan or outside in a light breeze to get the remaining pulp to blow away, leaving you with just the seeds. Alternatively, just pick out the remaining dry pulp, as there should not be much left. We know this sounds like a lot, but it only takes about five minutes to get from intact gourd to the dehydrator step, and the rest is easy.

Buffalo Gourd Pepitas

After removing seeds from pulp as described above, toss them with olive oil and salt in a bowl at a ratio of about 1 cup seeds to 1 tsp. olive oil and ½ tsp. salt. Then spread the coated seeds on a baking sheet and bake at 350°F for 15 minutes, until browned but not burnt. Eat these crunchy snacks as is or toss in other herbs and spices before or after baking. We like them with garlic and cayenne powder added before baking.

Once you have the clean, pulp-free seeds, roast them or toast them as you would pumpkin seeds. We do not recommend eating them raw since there may be some residual bitter pulp, which can cause stomach upset. The seeds are about half the size of pumpkin seeds but are quite tasty. They are high in protein and oils and are under investigation as a potential arid land crop.

The flowers are also edible and can be used similar to squash blossoms, but they are bitter and have an unpleasant odor, so we don't use them much. If you do use them, we recommend frying with other better-tasting ingredients in a squash blossom recipe. Interestingly, the root system is massive; the taproot of one specimen was recorded at over 8 feet long and weighed over 150 pounds [24].

MELONCITO (*Melothria pendula*)

Small yellow meloncito flowers in summer

Family: Cucurbitaceae

Edible part and harvest time: Unripe green fruits are available sporadically from spring to fall.

Toxic lookalikes: The ripe (purplish-black) fruits of meloncito itself are considered toxic by some, as they can induce a strong laxative or purgative effect. Look-alikes to avoid include balsam gourds (*Ibervillea* spp., which have bright orange/red fruits and dissected leaves), milkweed vines (*Matelea* spp., which have long, pointed, and spiky fruits and milky sap), and snailseeds (*Cocculus* spp., which have clusters of small, round fruits that turn from green to red). Another uncommon and potentially toxic vine from southeast Texas, *Cayaponia quinqueloba*, looks very similar but has white flowers and green fruits that don't have whitish/yellowish spotting or reticulations on the skin.

Identification: Meloncito is a **non-woody**, climbing vine from a perennial root. The vine stems are **thin and delicate** and have tendrils at their ends. The alternate leaves (2.5 inches long) are nearly heart shaped, but often have three to five shallow lobes. The small **yellow flowers** are solitary or clustered with five petals each. The fruits look like **miniature, short and squat watermelons** and are less than 1 inch long. Fruits are **green and mottled when young** and turn black at maturity with many small seeds inside, much like a cucumber.

Range and habitat: Meloncito can be found in the southeastern two-thirds of Texas. It is frequently found in relatively moist, sandy soils growing in and among other shrubs in shaded areas.

Related edible species: There are no other *Melothria* species in Texas, but a related species (*Melothria scabra*) from Mexico and Central America is cultivated for its cucumber-like fruits.

Uses/history/comments: Meloncito (also known as creeping cucumber) is a fairly common vine that is often overlooked because it tends to grow in and among bushes and shrubs and has very thin, delicate stems. We used to think the green fruits were infrequent, but we came to find that the fruits are just a little hard to see, as they are often obscured by the meloncito leaves or by the shrub it's growing in. So,

Green fruits look like miniature watermelons, but the insides look more like a cucumber.

if you find a meloncito vine, look diligently and poke around until you find a green fruit—sometimes they are not obvious at first look.

Meloncito is in the same family as the domesticated cucumber and watermelon, and the unripe, green, grape-sized fruits look like a tiny version of both. It's important to note that only the *unripe* green fruits are edible. The fully ripe fruits turn purple to black and apparently have a strong laxative and/or purgative effect when eaten. Avoid the ripe black fruits. The unripe green fruits can be eaten as you would normally eat a cucumber: raw, pickled, added to salads, etc. The flavor is similar to a cucumber but a little sweeter and you don't need to peel them—just eat the skin, seeds, and all.

RECIPE

Tiny Quick Pickles

Gather a handful of unripe, green meloncito fruits and cut them in half and set aside. Prepare a quick pickling brine that is equal parts filtered water and apple cider vinegar; add a pinch of salt and mix well. Then put the meloncito halves in a clean glass jar and pour enough brine over the top to cover all the fruits. Screw the cap tightly onto the jar and set it in the fridge for 3–4 days. The results are tiny, delicious quick pickles! You can also add other spices and flavorings to the brine. Some good additions include fresh garlic, black peppercorns, coriander, and mustard seeds.

FARKLEBERRY (*Vaccinium arboreum*)

Family: Ericaceae

Edible part and harvest time: Berries ripen in fall but can stay on the tree into winter.

Toxic lookalikes: None in Texas

Identification: Farkleberry is a shrub (or rarely a small tree) with **smooth to flaky, brown to orangish bark**. The alternate leaves are obovate, leathery, dark glossy green above, and deciduous (although nearly evergreen in coastal Texas). The **leaves turn**

Fruits are like smaller, drier blueberries.

red in fall around the time the fruit matures. The small, **white, urn-shaped flowers** (typical of many Ericaceae species) are arranged in loose racemes. The ripe **black fruits** are a bit larger than a BB and somewhat dry, with many small seeds inside.

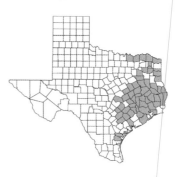

Range and habitat: Farkleberry is found most commonly in the sandy soils of east Texas but approaches

Ripe farkleberries in fall

the eastern edge of central Texas as well. Habitat includes thickets, mixed woods, pine-lands, and along wooded streams.

Related edible species: Farkleberry is the most widespread and common *Vaccinium* in Texas, but three other *Vaccinium* species occur in east Texas: *V. corymbosum* (bluish berry), *V. fuscatum* (blackish berry), and *V. stramineum* (dark reddish berry).

Uses/history/comments: Farkleberry (also known as sparkleberry) is our most common blueberry relative in Texas. While the small black fruits may not look like blueberries, they are in the same genus. The fruits are usually drier and mealier than a blueberry but taste excellent when ripe in fall. Farkleberries fruit in abundance and stay on the tree into winter if the birds don't get to them. We eat them by the handful when we find them on a hike but have also made tasty jams.

RECIPE

Farkleberry Jam

Mash ½ cup farkleberries in a small saucepan. Add 3 tbsp. lemon juice, 3 tbsp. honey, and ½ cup water and let sit for approximately 10 minutes to macerate. Then put the saucepan over low heat for 2½ minutes while stirring. The resulting jam tastes similar to Concord grape jam and is great when added to yogurt.

OCOTILLO (*Fouquieria splendens*)

Family: Fouquieriaceae

Edible part and harvest time: Flowers are available in early spring and periodically after rains nearly throughout the year; seeds typically found in summer.

Toxic lookalikes: None in Texas

Identification: Ocotillo is a **spiny desert shrub** with many long, wand-like branches, which, when viewed collectively, are arranged in an **inverted cone shape**. The erect branches are stiff, spiny, and woody, reaching up to 30 feet long and up to 2.25 inches wide. The bark has a grayish outer layer and **waxy yellow inner layers** that are exposed on older branches. The deciduous, obovate, green leaves and the **bright red, tubular flowers** (which grow in clusters at the ends of branches) are periodic, not seasonal. The **leaves and flowers flush the plant when sufficient rainfall occurs**, and the presence of leaves is a good indication of recent rainfall [25]. The 2-inch-long flowers give way to a tan, flaky, persistent capsule with skinny seeds inside that are covered in whitish hairs.

Range and habitat: Ocotillo is found in the Trans-Pecos and a few neighboring counties to the east. It is a common feature of the Chihuahuan Desert and can be found in a number of different desert habitats including rocky slopes and mesas as well as dry desert flats.

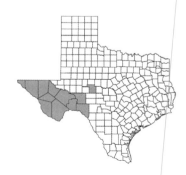

Related edible species: None in Texas

Uses/history/comments: Ocotillo is one of the most iconic plant species found in the desert Southwest. This tall, inverse-cone-shaped shrub has numerous long, spindly stalks that end in bright red flowers after rains. The flowers can be eaten raw and are sweet and sometimes tart. The flowers are sweetest when they first open, when a clear, goopy nectar is exuded. The unopened flowers are not as sweet, but still tasty. Harvesting the flowers is easy: Just bend a stalk (carefully, watch the spines) over until you can reach the flowers and snap off the whole inflorescence. We put freshly harvested flowers directly into a jar or other closed container, as the sweet nectar tends to adsorb into cloth if you use a bag, which means you lose some of the sweetness. Flowers can be added raw to salads or other dishes for a burst of color, dried and

Bright red flowers at ends of branches after rains

Leaves appear after rains and drop during persistent hot, dry weather.

used for tea, or cold-brewed fresh. Ocotillo seeds are also edible and can be harvested in the summer. You will want to parch the seeds and then grind them to make a seed flour that can be used in baking.

Additionally, ocotillo outer bark and root have a history of medicinal usage. For example, the Apache tribe reportedly bathed in and drank the root tea to relieve fatigue and sore limbs [26]. The outer bark from the base of old ocotillos also contains a natural wax and can be handy for starting fires, as it burns for quite some time [27].

RECIPE

Ocotillo Tea

Harvest enough flowers to completely fill a 1-liter jar (or whatever size you have available). Pour water over the flowers until the jar is full. Leave the jar in the fridge overnight or covered in the sun for a few hours. Then strain out the flowers for a sweet, tangy beverage. Don't forget, you can still use the flowers after this cold-steep. Usually, we will throw them into a smoothie, stew, or other dish to add some color.

GOLDEN CURRANT (*Ribes aureum*)

Family: Grossulariaceae

Edible part and harvest time: Fruits ripen in late spring or early summer (usually May and June in Texas).

Toxic lookalikes: None in Texas

Identification: Golden currant is a shrub up to 6 feet tall with smallish (less than 2 inches wide), alternate, **three-lobed leaves (each lobe has two or three teeth)**. The stems and fruits are **thornless**, unlike some other *Ribes* species. Clustered flowers are **bright yellow with an elongated tube** and five yellow sepals. The fruits are globose and start out green and **turn orange and then nearly black** when very ripe.

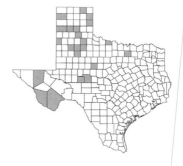

Range and habitat: Golden currant is more common in the western US but is found scattered throughout the panhandle and west Texas. In Texas, it is normally found near lakes or reservoirs or along creeks.

Related edible species: Cultivated *Ribes* species include currants and gooseberries, but there are also two other wild *Ribes* species in Texas, although neither are as common: *R. curvatum* (east Texas) and *R. mescalerium* (west Texas).

Golden current flowers are yellow and tubular.

This is the flower of the related *Ribes curvatum* from east Texas, which also has edible fruits.

Uses/history/comments: Wild currants and gooseberries are more common in other parts of the US (especially the western states), but Texas has one of the more abundant species in golden currant. Easily overlooked when not flowering or fruiting, look for

RECIPE

Currant Fruit Leather

For every 2 cups of ripe fresh currants, you'll need ¼ cup water, 1½ tsp. sugar or honey, and 1½ tsp. lemon juice (adjust the ratio of lemon juice and sugar depending on how ripe the currants are; if very ripe currants are used, you may not need to add sugar). First, add the water and currants to a saucepan and mash the berries with a potato masher. Then bring the pulpy mix to a simmer, cover, and cook on low heat for 10 minutes. Mash the mixture again, this time more thoroughly, and add the lemon juice and sugar (or honey). We like to add a pinch of cinnamon at this step. Simmer for about 5 additional minutes, until the sugar is dissolved and the mixture has thickened. Pour this cooked mash into a blender and puree until smooth. Line a dehydrator tray with plastic wrap and pour the puree into the tray and spread thin; dehydrate for 12–24 hours depending on how chewy you want it. You can also use a baking sheet and oven on the lowest setting for this.

golden currant in the panhandle of Texas near water. We have found it near lakes and reservoirs, where it grows within about 100 feet of the shoreline. The bright yellow flowers are easy to find in spring. Return trips to these plants in May and June can reap rewards in the form of plump orange currants. Even though they are usually not done ripening when orange, these still taste great with a pleasant tartness. If you wait longer, the fruits will get darker and sweeter over time, but birds and other animals tend to get to them before that point.

Currants and gooseberries are common names applied to various species of *Ribes*. Generally speaking, "currants" do not have prickles, whereas "gooseberries" do. The flavors of *Ribes* species (prickles or not) are similar, however.

BARBADOS CHERRY (*Malpighia glabra*)

Family: Malpighiaceae

Edible part and harvest time: Fruits can be found throughout much of the year in south Texas.

Toxic lookalikes: There are no especially toxic lookalikes in Texas, but the ornamental crepe myrtle (*Lagerstroemia indica*) can be mistaken for Barbados cherry. Note that crepe myrtle has alternate leaves, flowers much more profusely than Barbados cherry, and has a woody, brownish fruit, unlike the red fruit of Barbados cherry. Also, the naked, smooth bark of crepe myrtle is easy to distinguish from the rougher, gray-brown bark of Barbados cherry.

The delicate pink flowers have five petals; note the opposite leaves.

The rougher, gray-brown bark contrasts with the nonnative lookalike, crepe myrtle, which has smooth, naked bark.

Identification: Barbados cherry is an **unarmed**, semievergreen shrub up to 9 feet tall. The **opposite**, ovate leaves are up to 2.75 inches long (but typically smaller) and have smooth margins. The **delicate pink flowers** arise from the leaf axils, have **five petals**, and are about 0.25 inch wide. The round to ovoid, red fruit has one pit inside and can appear on the shrub while other parts of the plant are still flowering.

Range and habitat: Frequently cultivated for its attractive foliage, Barbados cherry grows wild in south Texas brushland, thickets, and palm groves.

Related edible species: There are no other wild *Malpighia* in Texas, but a tropical relative, *M. emarginata*, which is also called Barbados cherry or acerola, may be found planted in south Texas. Acerola is cultivated for its larger and juicier fruits, which are high in vitamin C.

Uses/history/comments: As mentioned above, Barbados cherry shares a common name with a tropical relative that has a more desirable fruit. In contrast, the native Barbados cherry is smaller and less juicy and flavorful than its tropical counterpart. However, the small red fruits are edible and enjoyable when made into preserves or used in other recipes. The main reason

Barbados Cherry Powder

Many people add supplemental doses of powdered *M. emarginata* (acerola) to smoothies or other healthy snacks. We recommend the same for our native *M. glabra*. Dry the fruits and powder them in a Vitamix or similar blender and add to whatever health drink or recipe you prefer. It won't add much flavor but can boost the nutritional value considerably. We like to add it to lemonade.

for consuming it, though, is for its vitamin content and health benefits. The tropical relative (*M. emarginata*) is well known under the name "acerola" in health circles for its high vitamin C and antioxidant content [28]. Some researchers have published nutritional data that lumps *M. glabra* in with studies on *M. emarginata*. Whether that is done erroneously or on purpose, we're not sure. But regardless, it is likely that our native *M. glabra* shares many of the same nutritional benefits as *M. emarginata*. While not especially flavorful, the native Barbados cherry is a good edible to have in your foraging knowledge tool kit. Edible plants are not just about interesting or unique flavors, but about nutritional benefits as well.

TURK'S CAP (*Malvaviscus arboreus*)

Family: Malvaceae

Edible part and harvest time: Flowers, fruits, and young leaves can be found in spring, summer, and fall depending on latitude.

Toxic lookalikes: None in Texas

Identification: Turk's cap is a mostly non-woody (except near the base) shrub with large, alternate, grapelike leaves with palmate venation. Each leaf (up to 3.5 inches wide) has **three angled lobes**, coarse teeth along the margins, and is **soft to the touch**. The **erect, bright red flowers** (1 inch tall) have five petals that are arranged in an **overlapping spiral** around the red stamen and pistil column, which reaches up beyond the petals. The round-ish fruits **ripen from green to red** and have a white, mealy flesh. Each fruit is five-celled when broken apart, with tan seeds.

Range and habitat: Turk's cap is frequently used in landscaping so can be found throughout much of Texas in urban areas, except the dry west and panhandle of Texas. It can be found growing wild in much of central, southeast, and south Texas in shaded, moist woodlands, near wooded creeks, and in palm groves.

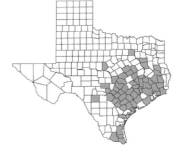

Related edible species: There is a larger introduced Central American species with hanging flowers, *M. penduliflorus*, that has escaped in south Texas and around Houston. Note that *M. drummondii*, as many

Note the red petals arranged in a spiral around the stamen and pistil column.

The ripe, red fruits look somewhat like miniature apples.

know Turk's cap by, is synonymous with *M. arboreus* and some refer to it as a variety: *M. arboreus* var. *drummondii*.

Uses/history/comments: Turk's cap is a common landscaping plant in much of the eastern half of Texas but also grows wild. There are a few different edible parts to consider, including the young leaf, flower, and (our favorite) the fruit. Each of these edible parts (to varying degrees) have a mucilaginous mouthfeel when chewed. This is because Turk's cap is in the mallow family (Malvaceae), which is also the taxonomic home of okra (*Abelmoschus esculentus*); many mallow species have a similar slimy texture. Some find this off-putting, but we love it. To be clear, though, Turk's cap is much less "slimy" than okra, and most people easily enjoy it.

To start with, the very young, somewhat fuzzy leaves can be eaten raw or added to salads and taste somewhat like cucumber. Older leaves should be avoided, as they will be too tough and fibrous. The bright red, erect flowers are also edible and are great in salads or used in tea in place of hibiscus flowers. The ripe red fruits are akin to a small, mealy, thin-skinned apple with a softer texture. The flavor is somewhere between an apple and a watermelon and is easily enjoyed. It does have a few seeds inside, but these are safe to eat and add a nice crunch. We frequently eat the fruits raw as a trail snack, but they can also be gathered in quantity for use in recipes.

As a side note, the mature leaves make serviceable toilet paper in a pinch. Not as luxurious as mullein leaf (*Verbascum thapsus*), but soft and useful nonetheless.

RECIPE

Turk's Cap Flowers + Goat Cheese

Pick a handful of bright red Turk's cap flowers and remove and discard the green sepals at the base. Then take your favorite goat cheese (or similar crumbly or spreadable cheese) and stuff the flowers. These little treasures make excellent wild-harvested hors d'oeuvres and are simple to prepare.

PURPLE PASSIONFLOWER (*Passiflora incarnata*)

Family: Passifloraceae

Edible part and harvest time: Flowers and leaves are available in spring, summer, and fall for tea; fruits ripen in fall.

Toxic lookalikes: None in Texas

Identification: Purple passionflower is a vigorous climbing or trailing perennial vine with **axillary tendrils** that wrap around surrounding vegetation. It's a hairless vine with alternate, finely serrated, and **deeply three- to five-lobed leaves** up to 6 inches long. The large, axillary, **incredibly intricate flowers** are difficult to describe but easy to identify after you've seen them once. They are a little less than 3 inches wide and have 5 sepals and 5 petals that are white and purple and look nearly identical, which makes it look like they have 10 petals. Above the sepals and petals are many **white- or purple-fringed filaments** and then five stamens and a three-parted pistil rising above the rest of the flower. The hanging fruits are **smooth, green when young, and egg shaped**. Fully ripe fruits can turn yellowish and have black seeds with a see-through pulp surrounding each individual seed.

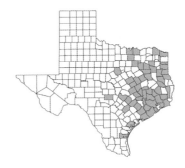

Range and habitat: Purple passionflower can be found in the eastern half of Texas, where it vines over old fields, roadsides, along creeks, and in urban settings. It is considered "weedy" in much of east Texas.

Related edible species: Texas has a number of other *Passiflora* species, but many are too small or are too rarely encountered to be worthwhile foraging. *P. foetida* is commonly found in south Texas and in Travis and Harris Counties and is worthwhile foraging for its bright red fruits.

Uses/history/comments: Passionflower, also known as maypop, has one of the most intricate and impressive flowers in the plant kingdom and can go toe-to-toe with even the most exotic rainforest species. In addition to its stunning flower, purple passionflower is a useful wild edible and medicinal that grows abundantly in the eastern half of Texas.

This is a young fruit, not quite ready for eating.

Purple passionflower tendrils and very new growth can be eaten raw in small quantities, steamed, or added to stir-fries and soups. The flavor is deep and grassy and lacks bitterness. All aboveground parts of the plant (flowers, tendrils, buds, stems, leaves, etc.) can also be used as a pleasant, calming, lightly sedative tea. We drink it before bed or to decompress after a stressful day. Passionflower tea can be made using fresh or dried plant material.

The fruits of purple passionflower are like small versions of the commercially available passionfruit (*P. edulis*) and are light green to yellowish and start to shrivel/wrinkle when ripe. When you find a ripe fruit, look closely for more in the same patch, as they can be well hidden behind leaves. Cut the fruit in half, scoop out the pulp, seeds and all, and

---

RECIPE

Passionfruit Salad Dressing

Scrape the pulp (seeds and all) from 6 ripe passionfruits. Heat the pulp in a small saucepan on low heat while stirring frequently until nearly boiling. Then remove from heat and press the pulp/seed mixture through a sieve to remove the seeds and collect the juice. Let the juice cool down and then blend with ½ cup olive oil, 1½ tsp. lime juice, ½ tbsp. apple cider vinegar, 1 tbsp. honey, and a dash of salt until smooth. Store this excellent, tangy salad dressing in a glass jar for up to a week. This is great on salads that incorporate cheese, berries, and nuts.

eat on the spot. The pleasantly crunchy seeds contrast nicely with the smooth, juicy pulp. If the fruits are still green but fully grown, you can also harvest them and put them on a windowsill for a week or so until the rind starts to wrinkle and dry out. The insides will have ripened by this time, which can be verified when cut open by the intensely tropical smell. The rind of the fruit is not good to eat.

Ripe fruits have black seeds inside that are encased in a see-through, sweet pulp.

BRASIL (*Condalia hookeri*)

Family: Rhamnaceae

Edible part and harvest time: Ripe fruits can be found from the second half of summer to fall.

Toxic lookalikes: While not known to be especially toxic, there are several similar-looking shrubs that grow in the same south Texas habitats that you should avoid when harvesting *Condalia*. These include amargosa (*Castela erecta*), which has flattish red fruits; narrowleaf elbowbush (*Forestiera angustifolia*), which has bluish fruits and no thorns; hogplum (*Colubrina texensis*), which has a woody fruit and no thorns; and guayacan (*Guaiacum angustifolia*), which has flattish red fruits and denser foliage. Brasil fruits will be shiny and black when ripe, so it's easy to avoid the above plants when harvesting.

Bushy, gangly habit of brasil

Identification: Brasil is a **thorny**, deciduous shrub up to 15 feet tall with light gray bark. The **leafy stems themselves essentially end as stout thorns**. The small (0.75 inch), alternate (sometimes fascicled), **obovate leaves** have a rounded but mucronate apex and smooth margins. The tiny **yellowish flowers are solitary or paired at the base of the leaves**. The nearly spherical fruits can be reddish when young but **ripen to shiny black** and are 0.25 inch wide with one hard seed.

Flowers at the base of the leaves; note how the leafy stems often end as thorns.

Range and habitat: Brasil is frequent in the Edwards Plateau and south Texas scrublands. Look for it in dry upland areas or along dry streambeds.

Related edible species: There are several other edible *Condalia* species in Texas including *C. spathulata* (counties along the Rio Grande east of Trans-Pecos) and *C. warnockii* (Trans-Pecos).

Uses/history/comments: Brasil and other edible *Condalia* species can fruit prolifically given the right conditions, especially in south Texas in late summer and early fall. But the dense, thorny branches and fairly delicate fruits make harvesting somewhat challenging. Though time-consuming, we prefer to carefully pick each fruit one by one so as not to accidentally squish them or get clawed to bits by the branches. Collect in a basket or bag that won't squish the fruits together. The fruits (technically drupes) are ripe when shiny black; they should not have any reddish tint remaining. Some of the other related species may still have some red to them when ripe. Ripe fruits will be juicy and sweet, with a hard seed inside that can be eaten or spit out. Due to the hard seed, adding the fruits whole to certain recipes is not ideal. We've made some excellent-tasting brasil muffins, but the hard seeds left the texture and mouthfeel lacking. So, if you use brasil in recipes, consider removing the seeds unless you want some extra crunch.

RECIPE

Brasil Trail Mix

Thoroughly dehydrate fresh brasil fruits and add to a trail mix with coconut flakes, semisweet dark chocolate chips, and Brazil nuts (an unrelated South American tree species, *Bertholletia excelsa*). The ratio should be roughly equal amounts of each component.

*FIRETHORN (*Pyracantha* spp.)

White flower clusters in spring

Family: Rosaceae
Edible part and harvest time: Fruits ripen in fall and can stay on through winter.
Toxic lookalikes: None in Texas

Identification: *Pyracantha* species are **evergreen** shrubs with **stout but sometimes hidden thorns**. The simple, **oblanceolate leathery leaves** (1–2 inches long) grow in clusters along the branches. Leaf margins are smooth to sparsely dentate. The **white flowers** have five petals and bloom in late spring, giving way to small, 0.5-inch-wide **red fruits** that grow in large clusters that weigh down the branches in fall. **Fruits look like very small apples** and are mealy when squished, with small seeds inside.

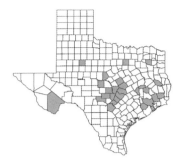

Range and habitat: The invasive firethorn is common in urban environments due to its popular use in landscaping, but also regularly escapes into the wild. In Texas, we find it primarily in dry woods near urban areas (particularly around Austin, San Antonio, and Houston) as well as along fencerows and in pastures.

Related edible species: There are three *Pyracantha* species (all nonnative) in Texas: **P. coccinea* (native to Europe), **P. fortuneana* (native to China), and **P. koidzumii* (native to Taiwan). All three look similar to each other, so we have grouped them together in this species account.

Uses/history/comments: Firethorn species are commonly used in landscaping but have unfortunately escaped and become invasive in parts of Texas. The fruits are one of the easiest to harvest in abundance,

The weight of firethorn berry clusters often bends branches over in winter.

as you can simply cut off a heavily fruiting branch (usually drooping from the weight) and then remove the fruits individually when you get home. When raw, the fruits are nothing special (bland, mealy, and seedy), but we still enjoy them that way. When dried or cooked, however, they become an excellent treat. Simply dehydrating firethorn fruits brings out a bit more sweetness, which makes them great for adding to granola or yogurt. That said, the below jam recipe is our favorite way to prepare them.

RECIPE

Firethorn Jam

Mash ½ cup firethorn fruits in a small saucepan. Add ¼ cup lemon juice, ⅓ cup sugar, and ⅛ cup water and let sit for approximately 10 minutes to macerate. Then put the saucepan over low heat for about 4 minutes while stirring the entire time. This super-easy recipe makes a very nice, cranberry-colored jam that has a pleasant texture (due to the small crunchy seeds). Great with butter on your favorite toast.

DEWBERRY (*Rubus trivialis*)

Family: Rosaceae

Edible part and harvest time: Fruits ripen late spring to early summer.

Toxic lookalikes: Dewberry superficially resembles poison ivy to the untrained eye, but dewberry has prickles, whereas poison ivy has no thorns, spines, or prickles at all. Additionally, dewberry leaves have more serrated leaves and, of course, the fruit looks like a blackberry, whereas poison ivy fruits are white, round berries. Also make sure not to mistake *Lantana* spp. fruits for dewberry. *Lantana* species are small to medium-sized shrubs with highly aromatic leaves, no spines or prickles, and fruits that superficially resemble dewberries but have more of a bluish hue.

Identification: Dewberry is a low (less than 3 feet tall), semievergreen, **trailing shrub** with slender, wiry branches covered with both **straight and curved prickles**. It tends to grow in dense patches that can overtake roadsides and fields. The alternate leaves are compound with **three to five coarsely toothed leaflets**. The **white flowers** (1 inch wide) have five petals and bloom in spring. The fruits look **nearly identical to blackberries** and are black when ripe but still edible when younger and red.

Range and habitat: Dewberry is common in much of the southeastern half of Texas. It is not found in the Trans-Pecos or panhandle and only in certain counties in south Texas but is abundant in much of the rest of the state. Habitat varies widely but includes thickets, riverbanks, roadsides, fencerows, and other disturbed areas.

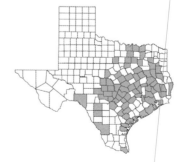

Related edible species: *R. trivialis* is the most common *Rubus* species in Texas, but there are several others that all have edible fruits. Some of the more common include *R. aboriginum* (eastern half of Texas), *R. argutus* (east Texas), and *R. riograndis* (south Texas and band between central and east Texas).

Dewberry flowers in early spring; note the often-trifoliate leaves.

Uses/history/comments: Dewberries are one of our native blackberry relatives and are ubiquitous in many parts of Texas. The delicious ripe fruits can be found most abundantly in late April and May and change from red to black when ripe. Reddish fruits can still be eaten but are more tart than sweet. Both visually and flavor-wise, ripe dewberries are very similar to store-bought blackberries. Dewberries are typically found growing in large vining patches, where many fruits can be picked at once. Sometimes, dewberry can dominate a large patch of ground near forest edges, where it can become the dominant ground cover. Note that although dewberry is related to blackberries, the plants are much smaller and vinier than some of the larger blackberry species in the eastern and western US. Be careful while harvesting, as the prickly stems and leaves can catch on fingers, clothing, and shoes; it's best to wear gloves if you are harvesting a large number of dewberries.

Large dewberry patches can take over open areas, forming impenetrable mats.

We usually pick them and eat them raw as is, but dewberries make excellent jams, wines, and desserts and can be used in place of blackberries in any recipe. Stacy is very into paleo baked goods, and the recipe described below did not disappoint.

Dewberry leaves have also been used similarly to raspberry leaves in tea as a urinary tract tonic [11].

RECIPE

Paleo Dewberry Muffins

Whisk 2 cups almond flour, ½ cup tapioca starch, and ¾ tsp. baking soda together in a large bowl. Add 1 raw egg, ⅓ cup almond milk, ½ cup raw honey, 3 tbsp. olive oil, 1 tbsp. vanilla extract, and 2 tbsp. apple cider vinegar. Whisk until the batter is smooth. Add about 1 cup fresh dewberries and mix evenly throughout the batter. Pour the batter into cupcake tins with liners about two-thirds full and bake at 350°F for about 25 minutes. You can obviously substitute more-traditional ingredients if you so choose, but these muffins are excellent.

COMA (*Sideroxylon celastrinum*)

Note the sticky, whitish sap exuding from the fruits.

Family: Sapotaceae
Edible part and harvest time: Fruits are available in late spring and early summer.

Toxic lookalikes: There are several other fairly nondescript thorny shrubs in south Texas that could be confused with coma that are toxic or otherwise not edible. These include *Castela erecta* (which has flattish red fruits) and *Koeberlinia spinosa* (which as its common name, allthorn, implies, has no leaves for much of the year). *Forestiera angustifolia* is a thornless lookalike that is best distinguished by its lack of thorns. It does have similar-looking fruits, though, so take note.

Crowded flowering coma branches

Identification: Coma is a **thorny** semievergreen shrub or small tree up to 20 feet tall, but often shorter, with **branches that end in sharp spines**. The alternate, often fascicled, **oblanceolate to ovate leaves** are less than 1 inch long, **glossy, and smooth margined**. Other than the midrib, the leaf veins are not prominent. The small white flowers are clustered on pedicels, typically at the leaf axils. The oblong 0.5-inch fruits are green when young, ripen to **dark bluish purple**, and **often exude a sticky, whitish sap when ripe**.

Bushy, thorny habit typical of coma

Range and habitat: Coma is found in the South Texas Plains and a few scattered counties farther up the Gulf Coast. It can grow in a variety of soil types and can be found abundantly in the thornbrush thickets of the Lower Rio Grande Valley.

Related edible species: There are two other edible *Sideroxylon* species in Texas: *S. lanuginosum* (which is a small tree common throughout much of Texas except for the panhandle and extreme south Texas) and *S. lycioides* (which is only found in far southeast Texas counties).

Uses/history/comments: The *Sideroxylon* genus is represented by three species in Texas. Coma is the second-most-commonly encountered; we did not choose to showcase the most commonly encountered, *S. lanuginosum*, also known as gum bumelia, because we only find it fruiting abundantly on an infrequent basis. Meanwhile, *S. celastrinum* produces larger fruit more abundantly and reliably in south Texas. Regardless, gum bumelia and coma can be used interchangeably, but we will focus on coma here.

Coma fruit turn dark bluish purple when ripe in late spring and early summer (usually April through June) in south Texas and can be picked and eaten straight off the bush. Many times, when we harvest them, there will be a white, sticky sap that exudes from the fruit. This is normal but can be an annoyance when harvesting. We recommend collecting in a glass jar or similar container to avoid a messy, sticky harvest bag. The fruits are somewhat sweet and overall enjoyable, with an almost cucumbery aftertaste. When dried, they are slightly sweet, with a slightly bitter note.

RECIPE

Coma Jam

Simmer 3 cups fresh coma fruits in a pot of water (just enough water to cover the fruits) for about 15 minutes while stirring occasionally. Remove the pot from the stove and break up the fruits with a potato masher or similar utensil until the juices have released into the water. Strain the juice through a cheesecloth to remove the seeds and skins. Add the juice back to the pot along with 3 tbsp. lemon juice and ¼ cup sugar. Bring to a boil while stirring continuously until the mixture thickens into a jam consistency (about 3 minutes or so). Let cool and then scoop the jam into a jar and refrigerate for later use. Use within a few weeks.

CENIZO (*Leucophyllum frutescens*)

Family: Scrophulariaceae

Edible part and harvest time: Leaves can be harvested for tea year-round; flowers available after rains.

Toxic lookalikes: None in Texas

Identification: Cenizo is an unarmed, evergreen, rounded shrub that grows up to 8 feet tall. The simple, sessile, **silvery-gray leaves** can be alternate, opposite, or whorled, so leaf arrangement is not especially helpful for identification. The leaves are fuzzy, obovate, and less than 1 inch long. The axillary **pink or purple bell-shaped flowers** have five lobes and are prevalent after rains. The small brownish fruit capsules have many seeds and split into two sections to release them, as with most Scrophulariaceae family plants.

Range and habitat: Cenizo grows primarily in the southwestern third of Texas and is most common on limestone hills and brushlands of the South Texas Plains, Hill Country, and Trans-Pecos. It's also frequently used in landscaping throughout much of Texas.

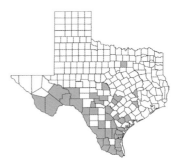

Related edible species: There are a few less common *Leucophyllum* species that can be used similarly to *L. frutescens* in Texas, although some of them have limited ranges, so it is best to stick with *L. frutescens*. That said, *L. candidium* and *L. minus* can be found in parts of the Trans-Pecos, while *L. zygophyllum* is found in

Bushy cenizo habit

the Lower Rio Grande Valley. They all look similar (with whitish-gray leaves) but differ in leaf size and flower color, among other things.

Uses/history/comments: Cenizo is also known as Texas sage and Texas ranger. It is common wild in many of the drier parts of Texas, but most Texans will be familiar with this plant as one of the more common landscaping plants, especially for water-conscious or xeriscape landscaping due to its drought tolerance. Cenizo is one of our most pleasant and enjoyable wild "tea" plants that are available year-round, along with yaupon. When steeped, cenizo leaves have a pleasant and calming quality to them. The flowers, which can

Cenizo often flowers after rains.

RECIPE

Cenizo Tea

Pick the last 2 inches or so of a leafy stem of cenizo (with or without flowers) and strip the leaves/flowers from the woody stem, discarding the stem. Steep the leaves/flowers in a cup of almost boiling water for 10 minutes while covered. After steeping, remove the plant material and add a few drops of honey. Mix well with a spoon and sip slowly.

appear sporadically throughout the year after rains, can also be used as a tea. Cenizo tea is a reliably enjoyable, simple brew that can easily replace store-bought herbal teas in your kitchen.

Cenizo is also useful for colds and fevers and is widely used for this purpose in many parts of northern Mexico [26].

GREENBRIAR (*Smilax bona-nox*)

Family: Smilacaceae

Edible part and harvest time: Tender young shoots and leaves are available in spring and summer.

Toxic lookalikes: There are three toxic vines that look somewhat similar to greenbriar: Canadian moonseed (*Menispermum canadense*) grows in a limited number of counties in central Texas along with Harris and Dallas Counties; Carolina snailseed (*Cocculus carolinus*) grows in central, north, and east Texas; and its cousin variable leaf snailseed (*Cocculus diversifolius)* grows in south Texas. However, each of these are easily distinguished from greenbriar and other edible *Smilax* species, as they lack thorns. Our native *Smilax* species have thorns, although sometimes they are missing from younger portions of the stem. If you're not sure because you can't find any thorns, it's best to stay away and assume it's not *Smilax*. Also, note that the dark bluish-purple greenbriar fruits are not edible.

Identification: Greenbriar is a vigorous vining monocot that climbs using pairs of tendrils that arise from the leaf petioles. The **older, tougher vines are angled and covered in sharp prickles**, while the newer stems are flexible and tender (new stems have prickles

The young, tender growing tips of greenbriar are choice.

The prickly stems of greenbriar and mottled splotches on the leaf are helpful for identification; note the young leaves are sometimes reddish.

too, but they are soft and flexible when young). The simple, variably shaped (from triangular to nearly heart shaped), late deciduous leaves are up to 4 inches long. The leaves are smooth and green (sometimes reddish when young) with entire or prickly margins and are **often mottled with lighter splotches**. The small green to yellowish flowers are inconspicuous in axillary umbels. The spherical berries ripen in clusters from green to black and have a large, hard seed inside.

Range and habitat: Greenbriar can be found in central, north, and east Texas as well as the Lower Rio Grande Valley. It can be found in many habitats, most frequently in thickets, fencerows, and open woods.

Related edible species: There are several other edible *Smilax* species found primarily in the eastern two-thirds of Texas. These include *S. glauca*, *S. hispida*, *S. laurifolia*, *S. pumila*, *S. rotundifolia*, *S. smallii*, and *S. walteri*.

Uses/history/comments: The thorn-covered woody vines of greenbriar do not seem a likely place to find tender wild edibles. Greenbriar and other *Smilax* species can form impenetrable tangles and thickets. If you've ever walked into a greenbriar thicket by accident or while bushwhacking, you know that it's nearly impossible to extricate yourself from its grasp without ripping some clothing or coming out looking like you got in a fight with a weed whacker.

Greenbriar "Asparagus"

Harvest the young but robust shoots in spring. Try to find the larger shoots that come off established, mature plants that are around ¼ inch in diameter. Using a pot and steamer basket, steam for about 5 minutes until tender and serve with melted butter and a pinch of salt.

Surprisingly, greenbriar produces one of the most common trailside snacks in many parts of central and east Texas. Most abundant in spring and summer, the new grow-ing tips are vibrant green, tender, and delicious. The new growth will even be covered in thorns like the mature parts of the vine below, but the thorns, stem, and leaves are flexible and tender when young. Make sure that your "greenbriar" has at least some thorns before harvesting, as the toxic lookalikes mentioned above lack thorns. Sometimes certain sec-tions of the vine will be thornless, so make sure to follow the vine down to its base, where it is typically thornier. If you're not sure because you don't see any thorns, avoid it.

To harvest, simply find where the new growth gradually transitions to the stiff, woody, mature growth and pull off the new growth. Most new-growth stems are a couple millimeters wide, but very robust leaders can be 0.25 inch wide and look similar to a stalk of asparagus. Most commonly, we eat these raw while hiking, but you can harvest large amounts of greenbriar tips to use in soups, stir-fries, or chopped in salads.

CHILE PEQUÍN (*Capsicum annuum*)

Family: Solanaceae

Edible part and harvest time: Fruits ripen late summer to winter.

Toxic lookalikes: Pigeonberry (*Rivina humilis*) superficially resembles chile pequín but does not have erect fruits; pigeonberries fruit on a raceme and are somewhat transparent, whereas chile pequíns fruit on individual pedicels and are an opaque red. Additionally, there are toxic red-fruited *Solanum* species (particularly *Solanum triquetrum*) that could potentially get confused with chile pequín, but these fruits hang from the stems rather than stand erect like chile pequíns.

Identification: Chile pequín is a short (2–5-foot) perennial (sometimes annual) shrub. The slender branches often have a zigzag growth pattern and 1–2-inch-long ovate leaves. Small, five-petaled **white flowers** bloom year-round and **often nod downward**. The ovoid fruits stand erect on fruiting stalks. Fruits start out green and ripen to a **bright red**.

Range and habitat: Chile pequín has a scattered distribution across the southern half of Texas. It can be found in upland wooded areas but is most common near human settlements (historic and current).

Related edible species: There are no other wild *Capsicum* species in Texas, but many cultivated chili peppers are cultivars of *Capsicum annuum*, including cayenne, Hatch, and jalapeño. Other cultivated *Capsicum* species include *Capsicum frutescens* (including Tabasco and Thai pepper cultivars) and *Capsicum chinense* (including habanero cultivars).

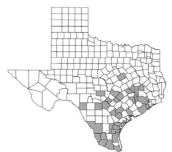

Uses/history/comments: Chile pequín (also known as bird pepper or chiltepín) is a very hot native chili

Note how the fruits stand erect on the fruit stalks, unlike some of its toxic lookalikes.

Note how the small white flowers tend to nod downward.

pepper. It is the apparent ancestor to the cultivated peppers classified under *Capsicum annum* (including cayenne). Chile pequíns were likely first domesticated by ancient Mesoamericans thousands of years ago, which allowed time for selection and breeding to create the array of cultivars we find today [13].

Wild chile pequíns rate high on the Scoville pungency scale (50,000–100,000 Scoville heat units) and regularly surprise most first-time foragers (you've been warned). We are lightweights when it comes to spicy food, but we can handle one or two pequíns at a time. Our preference, however, is to swallow the pill-sized fruits without chewing. This method removes the spiciness from the equation but still imparts the medicinal benefits (high in

RECIPE

Chile Pequín Fire Cider

Chop ¼ cup of fresh garlic, ¼ cup of fresh ginger, and 2 tbsp. of raw chile pequíns. Add to a large glass jar along with enough apple cider vinegar to cover the garlic/ginger/pequín mix by about 3 inches. It is best to select a jar with a tight-fitting plastic lid for this, as metal lids tend to corrode from interacting with the vinegar. Screw on the lid and let this mixture sit unrefrigerated for 3 weeks (shaking it once every few days), then strain out the pulp and save the remaining liquid. Feel free to add raw honey to make it easier to drink. Keep the liquid refrigerated and use during cold/flu season daily (we take 1 tbsp. every day or two as an immune booster). This simple fire cider recipe can be amended with medicinal herbs including horseradish, onion, turmeric, echinacea, and cinnamon.

vitamins A, C, and E). We often swallow pequíns as a general immune booster when we come across a fruiting bush. They can also be added to salsas and sauces or dried and ground as chili pepper flakes. We use them in an immune-boosting "fire cider," which is essentially a strong vinegar brew using garlic, ginger, and peppers.

CHRISTMAS BERRY (*Lycium carolinianum*)

Family: Solanaceae
Edible part and harvest time: Berries ripen in winter (hence the name).
Toxic lookalikes: Christmas berry is distinguished by its spines and succulent narrow leaves, but other red-fruited nightshade family plants growing wild in Texas, including *Solanum triquetrum* and **S. pseudocapsicum*, are toxic and could be mistaken if you don't look at the leaves or confirm the spines.
Identification: Christmas berry is a short, sparsely branched, **spiny shrub** about 3 feet tall. Approximately 0.5-inch-long spines are sparingly distributed along the branches. Leaves are **somewhat succulent**, linear to narrowly spathulate, glabrous, and nearly sessile. Flowers are 0.5–0.75 inch in diameter with **four lavender-colored petals**. The **ripe red berries** are ovoid, 0.25 inch long, and pendant.
Range and habitat: Christmas berry is found in all coastal counties in Texas along with a few additional

Small lavender flowers can appear at the same time as the fruit.

Note the spines and fleshy, succulent leaves; the toxic lookalikes in Texas lack these characteristics.

counties in central and south Texas. This species is normally found in or around wetlands, ditches, ponds, marshes, and salt flats in coastal counties.

Related edible species: Christmas berry is closely related to the famous goji berries (*L. chinense* and *L. barbarum*) from East Asia. Other native relatives with edible fruit in Texas include *L. berlandieri* (south, central, and west Texas) as well as *L. pallidum* and *L. torreyi* (both in the Trans-Pecos).

Uses/history/comments: Christmas berry (and other native *Lycium* species) are relatives of goji berries and have a similar consistency and flavor when dried. The fruits are also edible raw and taste somewhat like a small, sweet tomato. The flavor really shines, though, when dried. In our opinion, they have a superior flavor compared to goji berries, although

RECIPE

Christmas Trail Mix

Collect ripe Christmas berries and dehydrate them. Drying can take a while, as the berries are fairly resistant to dehydration; it takes about 24 hours in a dehydrator on low (95°F) to dehydrate them completely. Mix equal parts dried Christmas berries, pecan halves, coconut chips, and dried mulberries and take on your next adventure.

they are smaller. Christmas berries are not the easiest to find in abundance; we usually just snack on them if we come across them on the trail.

Interestingly, the leaves of Christmas berry stay on through winter, but they sometimes drop during summer droughts (referred to as "drought deciduous"—a trait found in many desert-dwelling species). But because the leaves are on the plant when the fruits are ripe, identification is made easier, as other red-fruited toxic nightshades in Texas have significantly different leaves (and no spines).

AMERICAN BEAUTYBERRY (*Callicarpa americana*)

Family: Verbenaceae

Edible part and harvest time: Fruits ripen in fall.

Toxic lookalikes: Care should be taken to distinguish beautyberry from the various *Lantana* species, which are also in the Verbenaceae family. *Lantana* fruits may be toxic, especially when green. Beautyberry fruits are easily distinguished by color (distinctly bright pink to purple as opposed to the bluish-black berries of *Lantana*) and by the arrangement of the fruits (beautyberries cluster in bunches along the stem, whereas *Lantana* berries look almost like a bluish blackberry arranged at the end of a fruiting branch).

Identification: Beautyberry is a deciduous shrub up to 9 feet tall with arching branches. The relatively large (up to 9 inches) leaves are opposite (occasionally with a third leaf), ovate, coarsely toothed, and lightly fuzzy. The small white to pink **flowers are arranged in compact cymes close to the stem**. The small, spherical fruits are showy and **densely clustered in ball-like groupings along the stem**. The fruits are most commonly **bright magenta**, but can be bluish, purple, or even white when ripe.

Range and habitat: American beautyberry is found in much of the eastern half of Texas in woods, thickets, and bottomlands, where it prefers shady, moist areas. It is also a common landscaping plant in Texas and can be found in urban settings.

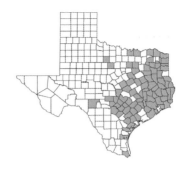

Related edible species: There are no other *Callicarpa* species in Texas, but there are other medicinal species in the Verbenaceae family, including *Glandularia* and *Verbena* species.

Uses/history/comments: With such an unnatural fruit color, many Texans assume that beautyberry is toxic. However, American beautyberry has a history of edible and medicinal uses. The most obvious are the magenta fruits, which ripen in fall. The fruits are small but can easily be gathered en masse by snipping off a few fruiting branches and then taking them home to separate the fruits from the stems. The fruits can be eaten raw, but we have read accounts of foragers getting an upset stomach from eating large quantities of raw beautyberries. We like the unique, almost minty flavor of the berries, but we never feel compelled to eat large quantities of the raw fruits anyway. If the fruits are cooked, they can be safely eaten in larger quantities as jams or jellies. Our favorite recipe for beautyberry is the pink salad dressing described below.

White or pinkish flowers grow in clusters along the stem; note the opposite leaves.

RECIPE

Beautyberry Salad Dressing

Add ¼ cup fresh beautyberries, 1 tbsp. lemon juice, 2 tbsp. olive oil, 1 tbsp. water, and a pinch of salt to a food processor or blender. Blend on medium until mostly smooth and pink, with some flecks of beautyberry skin remaining for texture. Add to any salad. We don't know why, but the flavor ends up tasting a little bit like strawberries. We assume it's the sweetness of the lemon interacting with the unique flavor of beautyberry that produces this unexpected result.

PEPPERVINE (*Ampelopsis arborea*)

Family: Vitaceae

Edible part and harvest time: Fruits ripen in fall.

Toxic lookalikes: There are several similar-looking vines that are toxic or potentially toxic and should be avoided. Virginia creeper (*Parthenocissus quinquefolia*) grows in similar habitats to peppervine and also has clusters of dark fruits. Virginia creeper is toxic, and ingestion of the fruits has caused fatalities and kidney damage [29]. Distinguishing it from peppervine is simple if you study the leaves. Virginia creeper leaves are palmately compound and have five to seven distinct leaflets that radiate from a single point, whereas peppervine leaves are bipinnate. Cow-itch vine (*Cissus incisa*) is another toxic lookalike. It has thick, succulent, trifoliate leaves that have an unpleasant odor when crushed. Heartleaf peppervine (*Ampelopsis cordata*) is closely related to *Ampelopsis arborea* and has similar pinkish immature fruits but has bluish-purple mature fruits and the leaves look more like grape leaves. While we have not found reports of toxicity in heartleaf peppervine, the fruits taste bad and should not be eaten. *Clematis* species can also have similar-looking leaves, but they lack fleshy berries so could not easily be confused with peppervine.

Identification: Peppervine is a perennial, deciduous, woody, climbing vine. It has alternate, dissected, **bipinnate leaves** that are overall triangular in outline and up to 6 inches long. The leaflets are glabrous, ovate, acute at the apices, and coarsely toothed. The small greenish flowers have five petals each and grow in clustered cymes. The **spherical fruits ripen from pinkish when immature to black and shiny**. Often there will be some ripe black fruits and some immature pink fruits in the same fruiting cluster. Ripe fruits are 0.5 inch in diameter and have one seed inside. The fruit is thinner skinned than most native grape species.

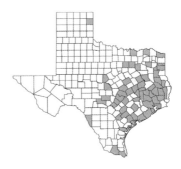

Range and habitat: Peppervine is found in the eastern half of Texas in a variety of habitats. In urban settings, it grows along fencerows and disturbed, overgrown areas, while in wilder areas, it can be found in thickets, streamsides, and moist woods. It often grows up and over shrubs and can reach high into trees.

Related edible species: There are no other edible *Ampelopsis* species in Texas, but refer to the notes on the related heartleaf peppervine (*A. cordata*) in the "Toxic lookalikes" section above and be sure to avoid it.

Uses/history/comments: Peppervine is a confounding plant for most. So many new foragers mistake it for a wild grape, and to be fair, it is in the same family. However, the bipinnate, dissected leaves are very different from our native grapes. The sweet, juicy, grapelike fruit itself is also polarizing. Some authors dismiss it as inedible, while others relish it. We take a middle stance. It is edible and delicious when processed sufficiently but can be frustrating to eat if you don't take proper precautions. This is because the fruit contains small, sharp calcium oxalate crystals (known as raphides) as a defense mechanism. It is thought that this defense (common in *Ampelopsis* species) promotes consumption by birds, and therefore wider distribution of seeds, while repelling mammal consumption. The raphides irritate a chewing mammal's mouth and esophagus, while birds typically swallow fruits whole, where stomach acids can dissolve the oxalic acid crystals without irritation [30].

Therefore, when you eat the fruit raw, you will notice a slight irritation in the back of your throat. It's not painful but is irritating enough that it is not uncommon to cough after eating a few fruits. We recommend eating only a couple raw fruits at a time. This is where many foragers stop and consider it more or less inedible. However, when processed, the raphides can be reduced considerably (although we have not been able to remove them entirely). To reduce the raphides, you will have to first mash up the fruits to make a juice. Be careful here, as the raphides can irritate your skin, so use gloves when handling the juice. After mashing or juicing, you can

Small greenish flowers grow in clusters; note the leaves are not palmately compound like one of its toxic lookalikes, Virginia creeper.

strain, settle, or heat the juice to reduce the raphides to an acceptable level. We prefer a combination and typically strain the pulpy juice through a cheesecloth; let it settle overnight in the fridge; decant the liquid so the raphides, which settle to the bottom, are left behind; and then cook the remaining juice into a jam. The resulting jam is delicious and does not irritate your mouth or throat in reasonable amounts.

RECIPE

Peppervine Jam

Harvest 2 cups of ripe peppervine berries and blend on high with 2 cups water. Put on latex gloves and strain the resulting juice through multiple layers of cheesecloth or a nut milk bag into a jar, squeezing to get all the juice out and into the jar. Put the jar in the refrigerator overnight to let the raphides settle. The next day, decant the juice into a saucepan, making sure to leave the bottom contents of the jar undisturbed, as this contains many of the irritating raphides. Add 2 tbsp. sugar and 1 tbsp. lemon juice to the pot and bring everything to a boil while stirring continuously. Reduce to medium heat and continue stirring for about 20 minutes, until the mixture thickens to desired jam consistency. Scoop the jam into a clean jar and store refrigerated for up to a few weeks. Delicious on toast with butter.

MUSTANG GRAPE (*Vitis mustangensis*)

Family: Vitaceae

Edible part and harvest time: Fruits ripen in summer (usually late June through July).

Toxic lookalikes: There are a few similar-looking vines that are toxic or potentially toxic and should be avoided. Virginia creeper (*Parthenocissus quinquefolia*) grows in similar habitats to grape species and also has clusters of purple fruits. Virginia creeper is toxic, and ingestion of the fruits has caused fatalities and kidney damage [29]. Distinguishing it from grape species is simple if you study the leaves; Virginia creeper leaves are palmately compound and have five to seven distinct leaflets that radiate from a single point, whereas grape leaves may be strongly lobed but are not compound or otherwise separated into leaflets. Cow-itch vine (*Cissus incisa*) is another toxic lookalike. It has thick, succulent, trifoliate leaves that have an unpleasant odor when crushed. The purple fruits of cow-itch can be deceptive, so make sure to check the leaf. If you see a thick, succulent-leaved "grape vine" with an unpleasant odor, please avoid. Heartleaf peppervine (*Ampelopsis cordata*) is the most deceptive grape mimic in Texas; the leaves look very similar to the untrained eye and the fruits look relatively similar, too. However, in heartleaf peppervine, typically some of the fruits in a cluster will be more pink than purple or black. While we have not found reports of toxicity, the fruits taste bad and should not be eaten. Greenbriar (*Smilax bonanox*) is discussed on page 181 but note that you should not eat the fruits. It's easy to distinguish from grape species because greenbriar stems have thorns but grapes do not.

Identification: Mustang grape is a woody vine that clambers over bushes or climbs high into trees using tendrils at the tips of new growth. The older, woody stems can be a

Note the white, feltlike underside of the leaves.

few inches wide with furrowed bark, while the younger stems can be thin, flexible, and covered in white matted hairs. The alternate leaves are **dark green above and densely white and feltlike below**. There are two types of leaves found. Most common are the broad, three-angled leaves (up to 5.5 inches) that most people might recognize as a grape leaf. The less common type of leaf can be found in vigorous new growth in full sun and is deeply lobed into three to five parts. The small white to yellowish flowers grow in dense **clusters that arise from directly opposite a leaf**. Fruits grow in recognizable **grapelike clusters** but are spherical instead of elongated as in most table grapes. The skin of mustang grape is thick, and the flesh inside is clear with small crunchy seeds in the center.

Range and habitat: Mustang grape is found in the southeastern half of Texas in a variety of dry and wet habitats including bottomlands, thickets, streamsides, and woodlands. It frequently grows over the tops of junipers and other shorter trees and bushes almost like kudzu vine to form large, amorphous masses.

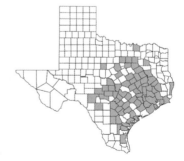

Related edible species: Texas has many other native species of *Vitis* (all of which are edible) including *V. acerifolia* (panhandle), *V. aestivalis* (eastern half of Texas), *V. arizonica* (Trans-Pecos), *V. cinerea* (Edwards Plateau and east Texas), *V. monticola* (Edwards Plateau), *V. palmata* (east Texas), *V. riparia* (east and north Texas), *V. rotundifolia* (east Texas), and *V. vulpina* (east and north Texas). Most of these (except *V. rotundifolia*, muscadine grape) have smaller fruits than *V. mustangensis*.

Uses/history/comments: Texas has more species of grapes than any other state in the country, with an impressive display of diversity in the *Vitis* genus. There are small endemic grapes like *V. monticola*, large sour grapes like *V. mustangensis*, and even sweet musky grapes like *V. rotundifolia*. Mustang grape is probably the most abundant in Texas, but the sour flavor can put some foragers off. We love the sourness and can eat handfuls with no problem, but some people can only eat one or two at a time. Regardless of how many you prefer to eat raw, all the native wild grapes can be used in jams, pies, juices, jellies, and wines. And, of course, you can dry any of them into raisins. Note that native grape species do not conform to many people's idea of a grape, which is usually centered around seed-less, plump, watery grapes from the grocery store. Native grapes have thicker skins and small seeds inside, and usually have a more robust flavor (for better or worse).

While all native grapes are edible, mustang and muscadine grapes are the easiest to gather in quantity (a friend of ours once filled up two five-gallon buckets of mustang grapes in about 20 minutes during peak season). For this reason, we rarely seek out the smaller grape species, but will eat them when we come across them on the trail.

RECIPE

Mustang Grape Juice

Harvest 2 lbs. of ripe mustang grapes per 16 oz. of juice you want to make. Rinse the grapes and remove them carefully from the stem so that the skin does not detach from the inside of the grape. Mash the grapes with a potato masher or similar utensil in a large pot until the grapes are pulverized and all liquid has been released (it

Mashing mustang grapes to make juice

looks like a purple chunky soup at this point). Place the pot of mashed grapes on the stove and bring it to a simmer on medium heat for 10 minutes while stirring occasionally. Lay a folded cheesecloth over a separate large pot and pour the mash over the top. Once cool enough to touch, squeeze the cheesecloth to get the remainder of the juice out and into the pot. Transfer the pot with the strained juice to the stovetop and put on low while stirring in 1 cup water, ½ cup lemon juice, and 3 tbsp. honey to taste (amounts are per 2 lbs. of grapes you started with) until dissolved. Put the juice in the fridge overnight and serve cold. Note: This makes a pretty thick juice, but you can always dilute with water to your desired consistency.

HERBS/WILDFLOWERS/FORBS

For the purposes of this book, herbs and forbs are generally defined as herbaceous, non-woody, non-vining plants and can be annual or perennial. "Wildflower" is not an especially descriptive name, at least botanically, but because it is a commonly used term, we include it here to refer to wild, showy, flowering herbs/forbs. Essentially, this section includes non-woody plants that are not vines or aquatic (at least not fully) and are not one of the oddballs (cacti, yuccas, agaves, sotols, or palmettos) included in the Shrubs/Vines section.

SEA PURSLANE (*Sesuvium portulacastrum*)

Family: Aizoaceae

Edible part and harvest time: Aboveground parts are available year-round.

Toxic lookalikes: None in Texas

Identification: Sea purslane is a perennial **succulent** herb with a trailing or prostrate, patch-forming growth habit. The stems are fleshy and tend to root at the nodes. The **opposite leaves** are fleshy and narrowly oblong (up to 2 inches). **Flowers are solitary and pink**, with five sepals (which look like petals). The fruits are inconspicuous green capsules containing small black seeds.

Range and habitat: Sea purslane is found on beaches, dunes, fringes of coastal wetlands, and disturbed areas near the coast.

Related edible species: There are two other edible *Sesuvium* species in Texas. *S. maritimum* (an annual species with lighter-colored flowers) is found more sporadically along the Gulf Coast, while *S. verrucosum* (which looks similar to *S. portulacastrum*) is typically found growing in wetlands in south Texas, the Trans-Pecos, and parts of the panhandle.

Uses/history/comments: Sea purslane is common in tropical and subtropical coastal areas nearly world-wide. We have eaten sea purslane from many parts of the world, and it's always comforting to find on travel adventures. The leaf's crisp, salty nature is easily enjoyed raw, but make sure to brush or rinse off any sand that may be stuck to it. The stem and flower are also edible, but the stem can be fibrous and the flower doesn't offer much; we stick to the leaves. The whole plant is specially adapted for saline, sandy habitats; its thick, succulent leaves help prevent water loss and desiccation. Note: Please do not pull up whole plants, root and all, from sand dunes, as these plants are critical to the formation and stabilization of the dunes.

The scientific and common name both allude to *Portulaca*, which its growth habit and leaves somewhat resemble (see purslane species account on page 266). However, sea purslane is a larger, more robust plant with hot pink flowers and thicker leaves, whereas *Portulaca* is smaller and has yellow flowers. The two plants are from different plant families but are both edible.

Note the thick, succulent, opposite leaves.

We normally eat sea purslane leaves raw as a beach snack, but they can also be sautéed, boiled, and steamed. Coastal cultures around the world have their own preparation methods. In the Philippines, the leaves are pickled and used similarly to sauerkraut as a side dish.

RECIPE

Simple Sea Purslane Sauté

Rinse and clean 2 cups sea purslane leaves and tender stems to thoroughly remove all sand and grit. In a skillet, melt 2 tbsp. butter on medium heat. Add the sea purslane along with a pinch of black pepper and dash of dried sage to the skillet and sauté for 1–2 minutes (it cooks quickly). Remove from skillet and plate. Squeeze lemon juice over top. No need to add salt, as the sea purslane is naturally salty. This pairs well with grilled fish.

AMARANTH (*Amaranthus* spp.)

Family: Amaranthaceae

Edible part and harvest time: Greens are available from spring to summer; seeds are available late summer to fall.

Toxic lookalikes: There are no toxic lookalikes in Texas, but some people confuse giant ragweed (*Ambrosia trifida*) with the taller amaranth species. Giant ragweed is not toxic (and actually has edible seeds), but the pollen can trigger allergies. It is easy to tell them apart since giant ragweed has trilobed leaves like a trident, while amaranth does not. Also note that many *Amaranthus* species are considered "weeds" and may be targeted for herbicide use in some areas, so use caution where you harvest. Some studies have shown that *Amaranthus* species can hyperaccumulate arsenic, so it is best not to harvest from potentially polluted areas [31]. *Amaranthus* species can also accumulate high concentrations of nitrates, which are not necessarily a major issue for healthy adults but should not be consumed by infants [9]. It's best to avoid consuming large amounts of amaranth from farm fields or other heavily fertilized areas.

Identification: Amaranth species are variable but are generally erect annual herbs (some species are prostrate). Some species can reach 4–5 feet tall, while others are much lower. Stems are usually **glabrous but grooved**. The alternate leaves are often more or less **rhombic**, have smooth margins, and often have a **silvery, shiny quality to the underside of the leaves**. Leaves coming off the main stem often have **younger shoots of leaves above the base of the relatively long petioles**. Some species have a light V-shaped pattern on the top of the leaf as well. The tiny green flowers are in **dense terminal or axillary**

spikes. The dried, brown flower spikes are prickly to the touch and release the dark, shiny, lentil-shaped seeds that are about the size of a poppy seed.

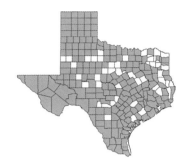

Range and habitat: There are many *Amaranthus* species in Texas, some native and some introduced. Collectively, they can be found in almost every county in Texas and are frequently found in disturbed areas, farm fields, gardens, and urban settings where they are often considered "weeds."

Related edible species: Texas has many *Amaranthus* species. Some of the more common native species include *A. albus*, *A. arenicola*, *A. blitoides*, *A. palmeri*, *A. polygonoides*, *A. spinosus*, and *A. tuberculatus*. Some of the introduced species include **A. hybridus*, **A. retroflexus*, and **A. viridus*. All furnish edible greens and seeds. Store-bought amaranth seeds (sold as "amaranth grain") come from cultivated species, which have larger seeds than those found in our wild species.

Uses/history/comments: Amaranth is a highly nutritious ancient food used by numerous indigenous peoples of North and South America, including the Aztec and Inca of Mexico. Due to its astounding food uses, it has since been spread to many parts of the world. It's now cultivated in many parts of Africa, Southeast Asia, and India and forms a significant component of many people's diet around the world. Health food stores sell amaranth seeds from cultivated varieties since they are nutritious and gluten-free. In many parts of the Caribbean, amaranth

Note the grooved stems, silvery leaf underside, and clusters of small leaves at the leaf axils. This species also shows the V-shaped pattern found on some *Amaranthus* leaves.

greens are the central ingredient in a traditional dish called "callaloo," which is a delicious green stew with many variations.

It's not hard to see why this plant has become so widespread and popular. The greens can be eaten raw but are excellent steamed, in soups, or in stir-fries. They can replace spinach in most recipes. The small seeds are excellent and can be harvested fairly easily in late summer and into fall (depending on the species). You can either strip the seeds from the fruiting spikes or break off the entire spike and put it inside an old pillowcase then beat it to release the seeds. The latter method works well when you have collected numerous seed-laden spikes. Either way, we highly recommend wearing gloves while handling the seed heads (especially dried seed heads), as the chaff can be prickly and irritating. After separating the seeds and chaff from the spikes, remove the remaining chaff by winnowing (see general winnowing method in the cedar elm species account, page 105).

Rubbing the chaff releases the small dark seeds.

The seeds can then be used as you would most grains (although amaranth is not technically a grain in the same way that wheat and barley are). They can be made into porridge, used in baking, or (our favorite) popped and sweetened, as is common in Mexico. Mexicans relish this amaranth treat they call *alegría*, which means simply "joy." Note that making *alegría* using wild amaranth seeds does not result in an exact replica of the commercial version, which uses the larger cultivated amaranth seeds that tend to pop and puff a little better.

RECIPE

Wild Alegría

Heat a pot over high heat until very hot and then add 1 tbsp. amaranth seeds. Put the lid on quickly and start shaking the pot from side to side. The seeds should start popping pretty quickly. Once the popping rate slows, pour this batch into a bowl and repeat the above process with another tablespoon of seeds until you have the amount you want. Then drizzle honey or maple syrup at a ratio of about 4:1 amaranth seed to sweetener by volume. After mixing well, you can either roll into balls or layer into tin pans for drying. No further cooking is needed. They can be eaten immediately or saved for later. You can also get creative with other additives including cinnamon, cocoa powder, and mesquite flower.

LAMB'S QUARTERS (*Chenopodium album*)

Family: Amaranthaceae

Edible part and harvest time: Young leaves are available spring to summer; seeds ripen fall to winter.

Toxic lookalikes: Poison suckleya (*Suckleya suckleyana*) is an uncommon, toxic lookalike from the panhandle that grows in wet conditions around playa lakes and other depressions. It has succulent stems and grows prostrate or ascending unlike *Chenopodium* species, which are upright and non-succulent. Poison suckleya contains cyanogenic glycosides, which have caused deaths in cows and sheep, so be cautious when harvesting *Chenopodium* in wet areas of the panhandle [32].

Identification: Lamb's quarters is a tall, annual, pale green, weedy herb with a **strong, musky scent**. It can grow up to 10 feet tall but is often shorter. Young stems are green (or sometimes reddish, especially near the axils) and **grooved**. The alternate leaves (up to 3 inches) are often rhombic, but sometimes ovate or lanceolate, and **usually have three lobes and irregular, wavy teeth**. Upper leaves are often lanceolate and smaller than lower leaves. The leaves also have a **whitish bloom on the surface**. Small, inconspicuous flowers occur in terminal or axillary clusters or spikes. The seeds, once chaff is removed, are similar to amaranth seeds: **shiny, dark, lentil shaped**, and about the size of a poppy seed.

Range and habitat: *C. album* is common in disturbed areas, fields, and gardens and has a scattered distribution in Texas that is likely expanding. At least one of the various *Chenopodium* species can be found throughout much of Texas.

Related edible species: There are numerous other *Chenopodium* species in Texas. *C. berlandieri* and *C. pratercola* are the most common and are scattered throughout the state, though rarely in east Texas, and look very similar to *C. album*. The *Chenopodium* genus also contains *C. quinoa*, from which the nutritious quinoa "grain" (actually a seed) is harvested. Quinoa is native to the Andes of South America. Another related edible is the nonnative *epazote (*Dysphania ambrosioides*), which now grows throughout much of the eastern half of Texas. This is a pungent herb frequently used in Mexican cuisine.

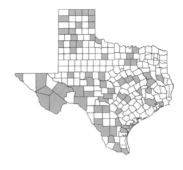

Uses/history/comments: Lamb's quarters (also known as pigweed) is one of our favorite wild greens in Texas. Young leaves and stems can be steamed like spinach or scrambled with eggs. Even older leaves are still palatable until they start to shrivel and die back in fall, but our favorite are the young, new plants that are 6–12 inches tall. Mature plants usually have some red/purple tinge to the underside of the leaves or to the stem. The leaves also have a white powdery substance that can be wiped off but does not need to be removed before eating. The whole plant has a pungent smell to it, but this smell doesn't seem to cross over into taste much when eaten. There are some species of *Chenopodium* that are downright funky, though; some even smell fishy but still taste good.

Flower clusters developing in spring

Note the grooved stems and reddish color often found near the leaf axils.

Lamb's Quarters Scramble

Collect 1 cup of fresh, young lamb's quarters greens in summer before the plant has flowered. Chop coarsely and add to a simple breakfast scramble with 4 eggs, ¼ diced onion, and a dash of salt and pepper in an oiled pan. This is one of our go-to breakfasts when in season and approximates a spinach scramble.

Lamb's quarters furnishes tiny edible seeds as well. We typically harvest these in fall, but they can stick around on the plant until winter. Harvest when the seed spikes start turning a tannish or grayish color in fall and easily fall off the plant if the branch is shaken a bit. Because the seeds grow in spikes at the tips of branches, it is easiest to grab the base of a spike and strip the seeds off in one motion to collect in a collection bag or bucket. You can quickly harvest a fair amount of seeds this way if there is a large patch. After harvesting, you'll have a bunch of tan or grayish looking seeds, but the tan/gray part is actually just the chaff. The chaff, though bitter, is edible too, so if you don't want to spend extra time processing, just use the seeds without removing the chaff. That said, the taste is better if you winnow out the chaff. The general idea and process of winnowing is described in the cedar elm species account on page 105. Successful winnowing of lamb's quarters seeds will result in a pile of tiny dark seeds. You can use the seeds in flours or cooked on their own and used in any quinoa recipe.

WILD ONION (*Allium canadense*)

Note the flowers do not have bright yellow stamens like its toxic lookalike crow poison; bulbils are also visible in the background.

The stalk on the left is what wild onion looks like in spring, but bulbils can sprout their own stalks too, as with the stalk in the center.

Family: Amaryllidaceae

Edible part and harvest time: Bulbs and greens are available in spring.

Toxic lookalikes: Wild onions have a few toxic lookalikes that grow in similar habitats and also have bulbs, so caution is advised when harvesting. You will want to avoid the ominously named crow poison (*Nothoscordum bivalve*) and Nuttall's deathcamas (*Toxicoscordion nuttallii*). Crow poison looks very much like a wild onion, but it has bright yellow anthers, whereas *Allium* species in Texas have muted non-yellow anthers. Crow poison grows in nearly identical habitats as wild onions and can even grow within and among wild onion patches, so caution must be taken to correctly identify each individual wild onion when harvesting. Nuttall's deathcamas is a more robust plant, has flowers arranged in a raceme, and has stem leaves, whereas *Allium* species flowers are arranged in an umbel and lack stem leaves. Luckily, there is another helpful trick to remember. Wild onions always have a garlic or onion odor when the leaves are crushed, while the dangerous lookalikes do not. So, if you pick what you think is an onion but it doesn't smell like an onion, you should assume it's poisonous and you should not consume it. One downfall of the smell method is that it only works once or twice per foraging expedition since your fingers will start to smell like onions. To avoid this, you can get creative and crush the onion leaves with a new stick or similar item every time you check for smell.

Identification: Wild onion is perennial but is only seen in spring when it shoots out new leaves and flowers; it then dies back, leaving the bulb to repeat the process the following year. All parts of the plant **smell distinctly like onions**. The white ovoid bulb peels into layers like its commercial cousin but is less than 1 inch in diameter. Each bulb sprouts three or more long, **basal, grasslike leaves** and one hollow flowering stalk up to 1.5 feet tall. Most varieties of *A. canadense* have white flowers in terminal umbels with six tepals. Each flower has six lavender or **pale stamens (not bright yellow)**. In a common variety, *A. canadense* var. *canadense*, all or most of the flowers are replaced with small (0.5-inch) green or reddish

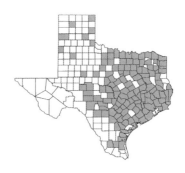

bulbils. These are basically just miniature bulbs that fall to the ground eventually to reproduce without seeds. For varieties that *do* go to seed, they are small, wrinkled, and black.

Range and habitat: *A. canadense* can be found in the eastern two-thirds of Texas, usually in shaded areas with relatively moist soils and often near streams, ponds, or other wet areas. It can also be found in meadows, woodlands, and along roadsides.

Related edible species: Other *Allium* species can be found in Texas, although many are smaller than *A. canadense*. Common species include *A. drummondii* (much of Texas), *A. kunthii* (Trans-Pecos), *A. perdulce* (west Texas and panhandle), and *A. runyonii* (South Texas Plains).

Uses/history/comments: Wild onions are an absolute treat in the spring. Their abundance can prompt the forager to try a little too hard to incorporate onions into every dish. However, as mentioned in the "Toxic lookalikes" section above, caution should be used when harvesting any wild onion.

Wild onion leaves are excellent substitutes for green onions in any recipe, and the small bulbs work well in soups, stews, scrambles, etc. Wild onion flowers are also edible and can be used as a garnish or thrown in stews and soups. Another interesting edible can be found on one of the subspecies of wild onion, *A. canadense* var. *canadense*. This subspecies produces bulbils from the top of the plant. Bulbils are like mini onion bulbs that replace most of the flowers on this subspecies and fall off to reproduce vegetatively rather than through flowers and seeds. The bulbils are even more pungent and strongly

RECIPE

Creamed Wild Onions

Harvest about 20 wild onion bulbs (keeping the greens attached) in spring, rinse off the dirt, and remove the papery bulb sheath and the roots. Sauté the wild onions whole with 1 tbsp. butter on high heat for about 7–10 minutes until soft but still aromatic. Reduce to medium heat and add ⅔ cup heavy cream and cook for another 2 minutes. Season with salt and pepper to taste and serve over rice, potatoes, or chicken. This adaptable recipe can be incorporated into many dishes.

onion-flavored than the bulbs or leaves. The underground bulbs of all wild onions are easy to harvest, as they don't grow too far below the surface. In sandy or loose soils, you can usually just pull up on the entire plant and the bulb will come with it, but in thick, clayey soils, you'll have to dig it out.

*WILD CARROT (*Daucus carota*)

Family: Apiaceae

Edible part and harvest time: The root is edible year-round but should only be harvested during flowering in spring, when identification is easier.

Toxic lookalikes: Use extreme caution when harvesting wild carrots. Two of the most dangerous plants in the country can look very similar to the untrained eye: poison hemlock (*Conium maculatum*) and water hemlock (*Cicuta maculata*). Both lookalikes can be fatal even in small, accidental doses. We strongly recommend that new foragers avoid wild carrot until they develop strong botany skills and familiarity with the two hemlock species. The leaves, flowers, and overall appearance of the hemlocks are similar to wild carrot, so following are a few key distinguishing characteristics: (1) Both hemlocks have glabrous (no hairs) stems, while wild carrot stems are usually hairy. (2) Poison hemlock has sickly looking purple dots and splotches on the stem and grows much taller than the other two species. (3) Water hemlock always grows in water or wetland areas; avoid "wild carrots" from such inundated areas. (4) In wild carrot, the central flower in the umbel is normally maroon or rose colored; all flowers of the hemlock species are white, so avoid "wild carrots" that do not have a central maroon flower in the middle of the umbel. Note that there

Note that the central flower in the compound umbel is maroon.

are other less toxic species in Texas that can look similar to wild carrot, but none share the four characteristics described above, and the fourth point regarding the central maroon flower is especially unique to wild carrot. As a beginner forager, we would highly recommend avoiding all carrot family (Apiaceae) species, as there is a relatively high percentage of toxic genera that can be difficult to distinguish.

Identification: Wild carrot is a tall biennial herb up to 4 feet tall with **hairy, green, hollow stems**. The alternate, fernlike leaves are **pinnately to bipinnately compound** up to 6 inches long and 3 inches wide. The small white flowers are arranged in large, terminal, flat or domed, compound umbels up to 5 inches wide. Each compound umbel has numerous umbellets, which in turn have numerous individual flowers. Uniquely, the **central flower of the compound umbel is maroon or rose colored**. The compound umbels have **linear, pinnately divided bracts** underneath. After flowering, brown, ridged, bristly, dry seeds develop. The roots of wild carrot are brown to white on the exterior, white on the inside, and **smell like carrots**.

Range and habitat: Wild carrot is an introduced species from Europe that now grows in much of the country, including east Texas. It's frequent along roadsides and other disturbed areas, where it can sometimes be found in large stands.

Related edible species: There is one other edible

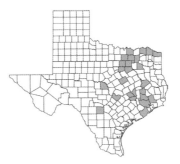

The fernlike pinnately compound leaves arise from hairy stalks.

Daucus species in Texas. American wild carrot (*Daucus pusillus*) is a smaller native carrot species found in many plains ecosystems in Texas. Its smaller size and its tendency to grow in rocky soils make the roots small, fibrous, and sometimes challenging to harvest. That, along with the fact that it lacks the central maroon flower like its larger cousin, makes it difficult for many novice foragers to identify consistently, so we generally do not recommend it.

Uses/history/comments: If you ask someone which wild edible plants they have heard of, chances are one of the first plants they mention is wild carrot, also known as Queen Anne's lace. If you ask them what it looks like, they may know it has tiny white flowers clustered into a large head and may know it has divided, fernlike leaves. But guess what? So do two of the most toxic plant species in the country (water hemlock and poison hemlock) as well as several other less toxic species in the same plant family. The fact is, most people, including beginning foragers, have little or no idea how to distinguish the deadly from the edible when it comes to wild carrot. Meanwhile, the desire to find a wild carrot is unreasonably high compared to other more easily identifiable wild edibles. For this reason, we recommend that beginning foragers skip wild carrot until they develop their botany skills and plant identification abilities. If none of the above deters you, please at least read and memorize the four key distinguishing characteristics described above in the "Toxic lookalikes" section and carefully study as many pictures of the two deadly hemlocks as you can find before venturing out. Additionally, we only recommend harvesting wild carrot when it is flowering and the central maroon flower can be easily seen. Identifying wild carrot without the flower can be challenging even for trained botanists.

Wild carrots are white or cream colored, unlike the grocery store varieties, but they smell distinctly carroty.

Emphasis on the potential dangers of misidentification aside, wild carrot is an excellent edible to know about and utilize in Texas. It's invasive, so you can harvest as much as you like, and the soils it grows in are usually fairly loose. This makes it easy to harvest the roots by simply pulling up on a stalk. Clayey soils may necessitate digging for the roots. We frequently find wild carrot on the sides of rural roads in east Texas. If you harvest from these types of areas, avoid harvesting from lower areas, as potential pollutants tend to accumulate here; seek out the hillsides above the roadway or adjacent fields and open spaces. Though *Daucus carota* is the same species name as the cultivated garden and store-bought carrots, the wild variety has white roots, not orange. In loose or soft soils, the roots can approach the size of garden carrots but are often smaller and spindlier. The taste is pretty much the same as garden carrots, but they can be more fibrous. Use them like store-bought carrots: steamed, roasted, raw, in soups, etc.

RECIPE

Roasted Wild Carrots

Harvest a handful of wild carrots and coat them in olive oil on a piece of parchment paper. Sprinkle a pinch of salt and black pepper to taste. Bake on a baking sheet at 425°F for about 15–20 minutes (depending on diameter of the carrots). Drizzle with balsamic vinegar and enjoy!

ATLANTIC CAMAS (*Camassia scilloides*)

Family: Asparagaceae

Edible part and harvest time: Bulbs can be harvested in spring when in flower.

Toxic lookalikes: There are a few toxic lookalikes, but harvesting when the plant is in flower easily distinguishes two of the most toxic, Nuttall's deathcamas (*Toxicoscordion nuttallii*) and crow poison (*Nothoscordum bivalve*), both of which have white flowers, unlike *Camassia*. Another native lookalike is funnel-flower (*Androstephium coeruleum*), but we have not found evidence that this is particularly toxic. To be safe, avoid this one; funnel-flower has a shorter (3–10-inch) flowering stalk than *Camassia*, and the flower has a unique central column of perianth segments encircling the anthers, which *Camassia* lacks. There is also the toxic nonnative *hyacinth (*Hyacinthus* spp.), which is primarily cultivated but can escape. Hyacinth has fuller, denser flowering stalks, often with more fragrant and vibrant purple or pink flowers (although they can also be similar in color to *Camassia* depending on cultivar), and the petals are often recurved, whereas *Camassia* petals usually spread out sideways or even slightly forward.

Identification: Atlantic camas is a perennial but is only seen in spring when it shoots out new leaves and flowers; it then dies back, leaving the bulb to repeat the process the following year. The **long, grasslike, arching basal leaves** are about 1 foot long, while the erect flowering stalks are 1–2.5 feet tall. The terminal raceme of **lavender to pale blue flowers** will have opened and unopened flowers on the same stalk, as they do not all open at the same time. Flowers are about 0.75 inch wide and have six "petals," **six bright yellow anthers, and a light green center**. The fruit is a three-parted capsule with small, black, shiny seeds inside.

Range and habitat: Atlantic camas grows in central and north-central Texas and ranges into parts of east Texas. In Texas, it is typically found in rocky or sandy fields, prairies, or open woods.

Related edible species: There is one other *Camassia* species in Texas that has nearly the same distribution as Atlantic camas: *C. angusta*, known as prairie camas. Prairie camas looks nearly identical to Atlantic camas and can be used the same way. In the Pacific Northwest, the bulbs of *C. quamash* were/are an important staple for local indigenous tribes.

Uses/history/comments: The native camas species of Texas do not have nearly as robust of a food history as do the camas species of the Pacific Northwest. Nonetheless, our camas species can be prepared the same way and are similarly delicious. Traditionally, in the Pacific Northwest, camas bulbs were steamed in earthen fire pits for about 24 hours, similar to the method described in the Texas sotol species account in this book. The bulbs, which look like small onion bulbs, can be steamed whole or mashed into cakes before steaming [33].

The distinctly lavender-colored flowers distinguish Atlantic camas from some of its lookalikes, which have white flowers or deeper purple flowers.

The smallish bulbs of related camas species from the Pacific Northwest were a staple for many tribes; our native species is not as abundant.

Because our native Texas species are much less common and usually don't grow in large patches, we recommend only harvesting small amounts from any camas stand. For example, if you see a patch of 20 or so plants, just harvest 2 bulbs (10 percent) and move on. We want to make sure to take on the caretaker role and ensure the survival of each patch we harvest from. Better yet, grow your own native camas beds from seed. There is an excellent company called Native American Seed (www.seedsource.com) that has *Camassia scilloides* seeds for sale (note that they call it wild hyacinth, another common name). On that note, camas species can be confused with a few very toxic species (see the "Toxic lookalikes" section above). That's why we highly recommend you only harvest camas bulbs when in flower or right after flowering, as is the custom of indigenous people of the Pacific Northwest [33].

Harvesting camas bulbs can be time-consuming but is best done with a sturdy digging stick. Dig about 1–2 inches away from the base of a flowering stalk and go straight down about 6 inches. You should be able to reach in with your hand at this point and pull the bulb out from the side of the hole, as bulbs are usually 4–5 inches deep. Bulbs can be eaten raw but are high in bland-tasting inulin (a difficult-to-digest carbohydrate), so we recommend cooking. By prolonged cooking, inulin can be broken down into sugars that are both easier to digest and tastier.

RECIPE

Steamed Camas Mashers

Harvest a handful of camas bulbs and peel off the brown, papery outer skins. Steam in a vegetable steamer for 45 minutes (or longer if you want them to be sweeter). Mash the steamed bulbs and eat with butter.

TEXAS THISTLE (*Cirsium texanum*)

Family: Asteraceae

Edible part and harvest time: Tender young leaves and stems are available in spring; taproots can be found year-round.

Toxic lookalikes: There are a few other "thistley" plants in Texas that could be mistaken for *Cirsium*. Two of the potentially toxic lookalikes include the prickly poppies (*Argemone* spp.) and star thistles (*Centaurea* spp.). *Argemone* species are easily distinguished from *Cirsium* species by the orange sap they exude when cut and the poppy-like flowers with large white or yellow petals. *Centaurea* species are usually smaller than *Cirsium* species and many have yellow flowers and no spines on the leaves or stem, whereas *Cirsium* typically has purple flowers and spiny leaves and stems. However, basket-flower (*Centaurea americana*) is taller and has a purple flower that can be mistaken for thistle. Luckily, the leaves of basket-flower, which contain hydrocyanic acid [5], do not have spines or prickles, so distinguishing them is easy.

Identification: Texas thistle is a tall, biennial (or sometimes perennial), **spiny herb** up to 4.5 feet tall. Stems are solitary at the base but usually split into numerous erect and adjacent branches. The alternate leaves vary but are often narrowly obovate with three to nine spiny lobes on each side. Leaves are up to 10 inches long and clasp the stem at the base. Each leaf is glabrous or with loose hairs on top but **densely woolly on the bottom**. Leaves near the top of the stem are smaller. The **pink flowering heads** are prickly underneath and have fuzzy-looking disk flowers on top that are grouped into a round head.

Range and habitat: Texas thistle is common throughout much of Texas except for the most northern part of the panhandle, far east Texas, and far west Texas. It's found in a number of habitats but is most commonly associated with disturbed soils, roadsides, and pastureland.

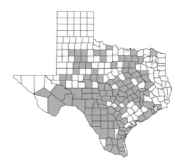

Related edible species: As far as we have found, all thistles in the *Cirsium* genus in Texas are edible, although some are better tasting than others. Some of the more common species include *C. horridulum* (east Texas), *C. ochrocentrum* (west Texas), *C. undulatum* (west Texas), and **C. vulgare* (a nonnative found in the Dallas and San Antonio areas). Other nonnative but related and similar-looking edible genera in Texas include **Carduus* (musk thistles), which can be used almost the same way as *Cirsium* species, and **Silybum* (milk thistles), which are mainly used medicinally but also have edible stalks, leaves, seeds, and roots.

Uses/history/comments: Most people would not think of thistle as a possible edible plant, but it is one of the more abundant and reliable wild greens in many parts of Texas. Though there are many *Cirsium* species in Texas, *C. texanum* is one of the most common and widespread.

Spiny stems and leaves; the central stem can be peeled and eaten like celery.

Thistles furnish multiple foraging options: young leaves, young stalks, and roots. Whatever part you eat, thick gloves are highly recommended during harvest. In order to eat the leaves, all the spines must be removed. For most species, this is more work than it's worth, since many species have very spiny leaves. However, instead of painstakingly removing the spines, you can also just peel the midrib of the leaf away from the rest of the spiny leaf and eat the midrib raw or in various cooked dishes. Roots can be harvested year-round but are typically largest in spring or fall. Cut the stalk at the base and discard, then start digging adjacent to the root. The root can go fairly deep but is easily obtained in loose soils. Clayey or rocky soils make the cost-benefit ratio less appealing.

Our favorite part of the thistle is the young stalk. Harvest the young, still-flexible stalk before it gets fibrous (typically

Typical weedy habit of Texas thistle

after flowering) and cut off all leaves. The stalk will still have some spiny parts, so these will need to be removed by peeling the entire stalk with a knife until all outer skin and spines are removed. The resulting smooth, green stalk is excellent raw or cooked and is a suitable replacement for celery since it's also hollow. In fact, when harvested in peak season, thistle stalks are sweeter and juicier than celery. Eat them as is or use them in place of celery in any recipe.

COMMON SUNFLOWER (*Helianthus annuus*)

Family: Asteraceae
Edible part and harvest time: Seeds ripen in fall.
Toxic lookalikes: There are no especially toxic lookalikes in Texas, but a few related Asteraceae genera could be mistaken for *Helianthus*. For example, the rosinweeds (*Silphium* spp.) can be tall with large yellow flowers and rough stems like *Helianthus*, but are easily distinguished by their opposite leaves (*Helianthus* leaves are alternate). Other potential lookalikes are generally much shorter than *Helianthus annuus*.
Identification: Common sunflower is a robust annual up to 8 feet tall with a **rough, stiff-haired stalk**. The **alternate leaves are ovate with nearly heart-shaped bases**, dentate and wavy margins, and up to nearly 1 foot long and nearly as wide. Leaf petioles are nearly as long as the leaf. The large flower heads are about 4 inches in diameter and have **yellow ray flowers and brown disk flowers**; there are usually numerous flower heads on one plant arising from separate flowering stalks. The **phyllaries are broad, fringed on the edges, and have an abruptly narrowed tip**. The seeds, compactly arranged in the flower

head, are like **miniature store-bought sunflower seeds** but the shells are black, without the striping seen on commercial sunflower seeds.

Range and habitat: Common sunflower is found throughout much of Texas and is even considered an unwanted weed in many areas. It's most commonly seen along roadsides and other disturbed areas but can also be found in pastures and prairies.

Related edible species: Texas has many *Helianthus* species, but only a few have edible histories. Three that do are *H. maximiliani* (central Texas and parts of east and north Texas), *H. strumosus* (northeast corner of Texas), and *H. tuberosus* (Dallas–Fort Worth area). These three species have edible tubers, but the seeds are generally too small to warrant harvesting.

Uses/history/comments: Common sunflower is the same species that produces store-bought sunflower seeds, but these are produced from cultivars with giant seed heads and giant seeds (relative to the wild ones). The wild variety found so abundantly on many Texas roadsides has similar edible seeds but on a smaller scale. You won't be cracking open wild sunflower seeds and just eating the kernel, as this would be extremely tedious. We usually just pick a ripe, partially dried seed head in the fall and pick out the seeds and eat them husk and all. The wild sunflower husks are much thinner, so eating them whole is not as unpleasant as it sounds. You can eat the seeds at any stage of development. We sometimes pick seed heads that still have the ray flowers and bite out the little, black, partially developed seeds. You can gather dried seed heads quickly from large stands with a pair of clippers and a bucket. Processing the seed heads en masse is a chore but can be

Split in half, the flower reveals the developing black seeds; note the phyllaries at the bottom of the photo, which are broad and abruptly narrowed at the tip, with fringed edges.

done fairly quickly by scraping the seeds out of each seed head with a spoon into a bowl or pan and then winnowing out the chaff in the breeze or using a fan.

Common sunflower is a frequent, tall weed along roadways in Texas.

A less often used part of the plant is the young flower bud in spring. We don't care for them much, as they are fairly rough textured. But, nonetheless, you can steam and eat them.

RECIPE

Toasted Sunflower Seeds

Harvest ripened sunflower seed heads as they start to turn brown in late summer or early fall. With your fingers or a spoon, brush out the black seeds into a bowl and winnow out any chaff that remains. Mix ¼ cup sunflower seeds (shell and all) in a bowl with ⅛ tsp. garlic powder, ⅛ tsp. onion powder, ⅛ tsp. cumin powder, and a dash of salt. Heat a cast-iron skillet with 1 tbsp. olive oil and add the seed and spice mix. Stir the mix in the oil constantly for a few minutes and pull from the stove before they start to burn. Even with the shells on, these tiny toasted sunflower seeds are great on their own or on salads.

*PRICKLY LETTUCE (*Lactuca serriola*)

Family: Asteraceae

Edible part and harvest time: Young leaves are best harvested in late winter or early spring. Flowers are available in spring and summer.

Toxic lookalikes: A young prickly lettuce could be mistaken for a prickly poppy (*Argemone* spp.), but prickly poppy has bright orange sap (*Lactuca* has white sap) and white or yellow poppy-like flowers with large petals (*Lactuca* has smaller yellow composite flowers that look more like a dandelion flower).

Identification: Prickly lettuce is an erect, annual, **weedy herb** up to 6 feet tall (often shorter) that exudes **a milky latex when cut**. The alternate, pinnately lobed leaves are somewhat spiny on the margins and have a **distinct row of bristles on the bottom of the midrib**. The leaves often clasp the stem, are up to 1 foot long, and turn from fresh green when young to bluish green when older. Flower heads are arranged in panicles from the central stem and side stems. Individual flower heads are less than 0.5 inch in diameter and have approximately 20 yellow ray flowers (each with five petal teeth) and a smaller number of disc flowers. The achenes have dandelion-like tufts of white hairs.

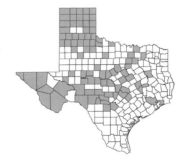

Range and habitat: *L. serriola* grows as a weed in disturbed areas in central Texas, north Texas, the Trans-Pecos, and the panhandle. South Texas lacks many *Lactuca* species.

The midrib of the leaf has a distinct line of bristles on the underside.

The small yellow flowers indicate the leaves are probably too tough and bitter at this stage. It's better to eat the leaves before flowering occurs.

Related edible species: A few other *Lactuca* species are found in Texas but are less widespread than *L. serriola*. They include *L. canadensis* (eastern half of Texas), *L. floridana* (east and central Texas), *L. graminifolia* and **L. tatarica* (Trans-Pecos), *L. hirsuta* (southeast Texas), and *L. ludoviciana* (central Texas). Many *Lactuca* species have a line of prickles on the underside of the midrib of each leaf, which makes identification fairly simple. Note that the common garden lettuce is a cultivated form of *L. sativa* from Eurasia.

Uses/history/comments: Prickly lettuce, also known as wild lettuce, is a common weed of disturbed areas. The line of prickles on the midrib on the underside of each leaf makes identification straightforward. Fair warning: The leaves can be very bitter, especially on older plants. Very young leaves are still somewhat bitter, similar to certain cultivated lettuce varieties and dandelion greens. We like to eat these raw in salads, but they are also useful as a potherb, in soups, or steamed. Again, though, don't try eating the older, tougher leaves, which get grayish green, somewhat waxy, and terribly bitter. The flowers are also bitter but add a nice splash of color to salads.

Lactuca species have been used medicinally in teas and tinctures as a mild sedative and analgesic. The white latex sap from *Lactuca* species is known as lactucarium and can be time-consumingly harvested, dried, and used for its very mild opiate-like effect [26].

RECIPE

White Bean and Prickly Lettuce Soup

In early spring, harvest enough young prickly lettuce leaves to amount to 3 loosely packed cups after coarsely chopping the leaves. Melt 1 tbsp. butter in a pot over medium-high heat and sauté 1 chopped onion until slippery and tender (5–10 minutes). Then stir 2 cups vegetable broth and a chopped tomato in with the onions. Bring the mixture to a near boil, then stir the chopped young prickly lettuce leaves in and completely submerge them. Cook for about 5 minutes and then add 1 cup canned white beans and heat for a few more minutes. Add other spices if you wish; red pepper flakes work well. Enjoy on cold early spring nights.

GOLDENROD (*Solidago* spp.)

Family: Asteraceae

Edible part and harvest time: Leaves and flowers can be harvested for tea in spring, summer, and fall depending on the species and region.

Toxic lookalikes: There are many yellow-flowered Asteraceae species that can resemble *Solidago* species to the untrained eye. Some of the ones to avoid include the *Senecio* species, which generally have a scragglier appearance with ragged, lobed leaves, larger and less numerous flowers, and black-tipped bracts below the flowers. *Senecio* flowers are not arranged in the same terminal, orderly manner as *Solidago* species. **Senecio vulgaris* is an introduced, potentially toxic weed with deeply lobed, ragged leaves and a messy cluster of flowers. *Senecio riddellii* is a native potentially toxic species from west and south Texas that has lower leaves dissected into linear segments, unlike *Solidago* species, and has larger ray flowers. *Senecio flaccidus* is another west Texas species that also has lower leaves dissected into linear segments and larger ray flowers. These three *Senecio* species have been documented in livestock poisonings and should be avoided, but other *Senecio* species may be toxic as well [5]. There is also a potentially toxic fungal rust (*Coleosporium asterum*) that can infest the leaves of some species of *Solidago*, so avoid harvesting leaves with orange spots or an otherwise diseased appearance [34].

Identification: Goldenrod species are **erect to arching** perennials (up to 7 feet tall) with slender woody stalks. The **alternate, sessile leaves** are often narrowly lanceolate, three-nerved, and **rough to the touch**. Each **stalk is solitary** up until near the tip, where it branches out; this branching crown near the tip is where flowering occurs. The **small**

yellow flowers are arranged on numerous horizontal sprays of flowering branchlets. Each tiny flower head has small yellow disk and ray flowers.

Range and habitat: *Solidago* species can be found throughout much of Texas except for the South Texas Plains and parts of west Texas. Habitats vary among species, but goldenrods are often found in moist or wet areas near water. Some species are common in drier areas along roadsides and fence lines.

Horizontal sprays of the small yellow flowers

Goldenrod leaves and flowers vary by species, but flowers are often arranged similar to this specimen.

Related edible species: There are numerous *Solidago* species in Texas, all of which can be used in tea, though some taste better than others. Some common species include *S. altissima* (east, central, and west Texas), *S. gigantea* (east, central, north, and west Texas), *S. juliae* (Hill Country and Trans-Pecos), *S. nemoralis* (central and north Texas), *S. odora* (east Texas), *S. radula* (eastern half of Texas), *S. rugosa* (east Texas), and *S. sempervirens* (coastal Texas) . These can be difficult to distinguish from one another (partially due to hybridization), but they generally have similar inflorescences, leaves, and habits.

Uses/history/comments: Goldenrod is one of our better-tasting wild tea plants. The leaves and flowers make an excellent calming brew and have a long history of use in the US. In fact, one species that grows in east Texas, *S. odora*, is also common on the East Coast and was one of the native plants used in "liberty tea" after the 1773 Boston Tea Party [35]. And, of course, it was used long before that by indigenous tribes.

Goldenrod leaves and flowers can be used in teas either fresh or dried. Just be careful to avoid plants with orange spots on the leaves or otherwise diseased plants as noted in the "Toxic lookalikes"

Goldenrod Vinegar

Harvest fall goldenrod leaves and flowers and thoroughly dry in a dehydrator. Chop the dried material coarsely. Add 1 cup of the chopped goldenrod to a clean glass jar along with 4 cups of apple cider vinegar and mix well. Then screw the cap on tightly. It's best to select a jar with a tight-fitting plastic lid, as metal lids tend to corrode from interacting with the vinegar. Let the mixture sit at room temperature for a few weeks while swirling and mixing the contents every day or two. Then strain out the plant material and pour the vinegar into a clean glass bottle or jar. Use on salads or any other way you would use pure apple cider vinegar. This is an easy way to add some of goldenrod's health-giving properties to your diet.

section above. Simply pick or strip some of the terminal flowers and adjacent leaves and brew as you would a normal cup of tea. Medicinally, goldenrod tea is known to act as a tonic to the urinary tract and can be helpful for allergy sufferers [11].

*PRICKLY SOW-THISTLE (*Sonchus asper*)

Family: Asteraceae
Edible part and harvest time: Young leaves are best in late winter or early spring. Flowers are available in spring.

When about to go to seed, the leaves are more bitter.

Note the ear-like auricles that are curled under at the base of the leaf.

Toxic lookalikes: A young sow-thistle could be mistaken for a prickly poppy (*Argemone* spp.), but prickly poppy species have bright orange sap (*Sonchus* has white sap) and white or yellow poppy-like flowers with large petals (*Sonchus* has smaller yellow composite flowers that look much like a dandelion flower).

Identification: Prickly sow-thistle is an erect, annual herb up to 2 feet tall that exudes a **milky latex when cut**. The alternate leaves are prickly, dentate, and often wavy on the margins, with a few pinnate lobes or none at all. The leaves (up to 8 inches long) **clasp the stem with curled, rounded, ear-like projections** (known as auricles) and are reduced in size near the top of the plant. The upper portions of the stem branch, with each branch terminating in a **yellow flower head** (0.75 inch in diameter). Each flower head has numerous **ray flowers but no disk flowers** to speak of. The dark achenes each have tufts of fluffy white hairs.

Range and habitat: Prickly sow-thistle is nonnative and can be found throughout much of Texas in disturbed areas including vacant lots, lawns, gardens, and roadsides.

Related edible species: *S. oleraceus* is another nonnative species that looks similar to *S. asper* and is edible in the same way. *S. asper* has curled and rounded auricles at the base of the leaf, whereas *S. oleraceus* has acute auricles that point straight backward.

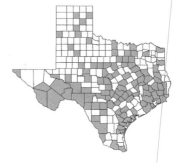

WHITEMOUTH DAYFLOWER (*Commelina erecta*)

Family: Commelinaceae

Edible part and harvest time: Flowers, leaves, and stems are available in spring and fall primarily; tubers are available year-round but hard to find without flowers.

Toxic lookalikes: There are no toxic lookalikes in Texas, but one related native species found in the Edwards Plateau region is easy to confuse with dayflower: false dayflower (*Tinantia anomala*). False dayflower is in the same family and looks similar except it's taller (up to 2 feet), erect, and has lavender-colored petals. The erect growth habit is the easiest distinguisher, as dayflowers are usually clambering, but another key differentiator is that the stamens on false dayflower are covered in tufts of yellow and purple hairs, whereas dayflowers lack these tufts. We have not found historical documentation that false day-flower is edible, but being curious, we have tried it ourselves due to its close relation to the edible dayflowers and spiderworts. It tastes about the same as those two, and we did not notice any ill effects. But because this is not a well-researched edible plant, we advise caution.

Identification: Dayflower is an unbranched or scantily branched perennial herb that dies back and overwinters with a tuberous root system. The **weak stems** are erect at first and then decumbent; the plant rarely reaches 2 feet tall and usually only if supported by other vegetation. The stem is glabrous and somewhat succulent, with sporadic, alternate leaves that can be linear to lanceolate and up to 6 inches long. The **usually solitary flowers** can be axillary but are most often terminal and consist of **two large, rounded blue petals above and one small, white, inconspicuous petal below**. There are both bright yellow and grayish or purple anthers on each flower. Each flower is borne from a green, **curved, hairy spathe** (bract). The fruit is a three-celled capsule, each with a single brown seed.

This taller lookalike, false dayflower (*Tinantia anomala*), resembles dayflower but has more lavender-colored flowers with tufts of yellow hairs on the stamens.

Range and habitat: *C. erecta* is found nearly throughout Texas in both disturbed and natural habitats. Look for it in prairies, vacant lots, sparse woodlands, or in your backyard or garden.

Related edible species: *C. erecta* is the most common dayflower encountered, but there are several other species found in Texas with similar edible properties. These include *C. caroliniana* (southeast Texas), *C. dianthifolia* (Trans-Pecos), and *C. diffusa* and *C. virginica* (both east Texas). *Commelina* is closely related to the spiderworts (*Tradescantia* spp.), which are covered in the next species account.

Uses/history/comments: Dayflower is one of those happy little flowers that just makes you smile. They're abundant, and the flowers, leaves, stems, and tubers are all edible. The blue flowers are most often eaten in salads or used as garnish or for other aesthetic food purposes. They don't taste like much so will not affect the flavoring of most dishes. The leaves and stems are also edible but are slimy and mucilaginous, so if you are a texture-sensitive eater, beware. The leaves and stems also don't taste like much but can be added

The weak stems mean this plant is erect initially but often slumps over as it gets taller.

to stir-fries, stews, or soups. Due to their mucilaginous quality, the leaves and stems are excellent first aids for scrapes and cuts when water is not readily available in the backcountry. The juicy stems and leaves can be crushed and rubbed over the wound to help clean it out. The narrow tubers can be dug up year-round, but it can be very difficult to find them when the plant is not flowering. The small whitish tubers are somewhat spicy and are best cooked, not eaten raw.

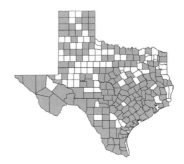

RECIPE

Dayflower Ice Cubes

Using your favorite silicone ice cube mold, add ½ inch water to the bottom of each compartment and add 1–2 dayflowers so they are floating on top. Put the mold in the freezer until frozen and then pull the mold and fill with more water to the top of each compartment and freeze again. These fancy ice cubes are great in iced teas, lemonade, and adult beverages.

SPIDERWORT (*Tradescantia* spp.)

Family: Commelinaceae

Edible part and harvest time: Flowers and leaves are available in spring and early summer.

Toxic lookalikes: See the discussion in the preceding species account on false dayflower (*Tinantia anomala*), which looks similar but has two petals instead of three, among other differences.

Identification: Spiderwort species are variable, with some very low, trailing species and several erect species up to 3 feet tall. All are herbaceous, **semi-succulent** perennials with alternate, sessile leaves and **purple flowers** with **three rounded petals and six yellow stamens**. Species can be glabrous or hairy, and most have **long, grasslike leaves** with parallel veins. The flowers are arranged in terminal clusters, often with only **one or two flowers blooming at any given time on a single plant**. In many species the inflorescence is spider-like, with many arching flower pedicels underneath the open flowers. The seed capsules are three-celled, with small seeds inside.

Range and habitat: At least one species of spiderwort can be found in nearly every part of Texas, and each species has different habitat requirements. Some of the larger, non-hairy species are found in prairies, thickets, and woodlands. Other species are found in rockier and drier areas in west Texas. Often, they are found in relatively moist micro-habitats compared to their surroundings.

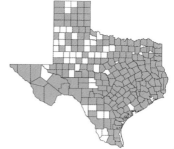

easily harvested, tasting a little like a mellowed-out carrot. They're bright white when cut open and are not fibrous or tough like some other wild edible roots. Winecup roots can be eaten raw or cooked in any dish in place of carrots or turnips. We prefer roasting them like baby carrots.

---

*CHEESEWEED (*Malva* spp.)

Malva leaves are best harvested at this early stage in winter before flowering occurs.

Family: Malvaceae

Edible part and harvest time: Young leaves are available in winter and early spring, while flowers can be found in spring.

Toxic lookalikes: It is possible to confuse *Malva* species with toxic *Ranunculus* species. *Malva* leaves are generally darker green and have accordion-like folds in the leaf (alternating up and down from vein to vein). If you're not sure, wait until they flower; *Malva* flowers are white to purple, while *Ranunculus* flowers are yellow.

Identification: *Malva* species can be either annual or perennial herbs up to 3 feet tall. The alternate, **circular or kidney-shaped leaves** are palmately veined and dentate, with distinct, **accordion-like folds** in the leaf. Individual leaves are up to 2.5 inches long and wide and often have a **reddish spot on the top of the leaf at the point where the long petiole meets the leaf**. The small, **axillary, white, pinkish, or purple flowers** have five petals that each have two teeth at the tips. The fruit is round, **disk shaped**, and splits into wedges.

Malva flowers are often light pink; note the green, disk-shaped fruit below.

Range and habitat: Cheeseweed is found sporadically in central, north-central, south, and west Texas and the panhandle. Habitat includes most disturbed areas such as vacant lots, lawns, mowed grassy areas, and roadsides.

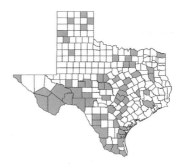

Related edible species: The two common *Malva* species in Texas are *M. neglecta and *M. parviflora, which look very similar to one another. *M. pusilla and *M. sylvestris are others that occur sporadically in Texas. All *Malva* species in Texas are nonnative but edible.

Uses/history/comments:

Cheeseweed gets its name not from the flavor but from the shape of the fruits, which look like little cheese wheels and even have partitions that look like wedges of cheese. This is a common nonnative "weed" that pops up in lawns and other mowed grassy areas. The flowers are fun added to salads but are small. The leaves are the most substantial and available edible part of cheeseweed and

Note the accordion-like folds in the leaves of *Malva* spp.; a toxic lookalike, *Ranunculus* spp., lacks this feature.

can be used raw, steamed, or sautéed. We prefer cheeseweed leaves very young (in winter and early spring) and cooked, as they get more fibrous through spring. When young in January/February, we also have harvested robust stems, which are excellent steamed like asparagus. Steamed greens with butter are a great spinach substitute, but most commonly, we scramble them with eggs.

RECIPE

Cheeseweed Scramble

Chop approximately 2 handfuls of young cheeseweed leaves harvested in winter or early spring. Scramble with 5 eggs and add salt and pepper to taste. This is a winter staple in our house.

PINK EVENING PRIMROSE (*Oenothera speciosa*)

Family: Onagraceae

Edible part and harvest time: Young leaves and flowers are available from early spring to early summer.

Toxic lookalikes: While there are other plants with light pink flowers that somewhat resemble pink evening primrose, their flowers are much smaller (for example, native *Mirabilis* flowers). *Mirabilis jalapa* has large flowers, but they are either hot pink or white and have a long flower tube, unlike *Oenothera*. There are also some vining spe-

Note the diamond-shaped fruit forming at the very base of the flower.

cies in the Convolvulaceae (morning glory) family that maybe be confusing for new foragers, but flower color and growth habit (vining versus not) make them easy to distinguish.

Identification: Pink evening primrose is a sprawling perennial herb up to 1.5 feet tall but often lower. The stems often fall over horizontally, with the ends more erect. The alternate leaves (up to 3 inches) are lanceolate to oblanceolate and **shallowly and pinnately lobed**. The showy flowers arise from upper leaf axils and are **most often pink** but can be white or more rose colored. Each flower is up to 3 inches wide and has four large, broad petals, eight yellow or white stamens, and **one long white stigma with four points at the tip that look like an X**. The flowers have a **yellowish center** and the petals appear wrinkled. The often diamond-shaped fruits are four angled and contain many small seeds inside.

Range and habitat: Pink evening primrose is common throughout much of Texas and can be found along roadsides, in vacant lots, and in other disturbed areas and is even considered a weedy species in some areas. It is also a common component of prairies and sparse woodlands.

Related edible species: There are numerous *Oenothera* species in Texas but limited or no history of edibility for many, so we don't recommend consuming them. That said, many Onagraceae family species are edible in some form, so further study and experimentation is needed. Two of the more commonly consumed *Oenothera* species are not especially common in Texas: *O. biennis* and *O. elata* are upright, tall, yellow-flowered species with edible taproots found in parts of east and west Texas.

Uses/history/comments: *Oenothera speciosa* will be familiar to many Texans, as it is one of our most common spring wildflowers. However, what Texans call this dainty flower is not at all consistent. Common names run the gamut from pinkladies, amapola (Spanish for "poppy"), to buttercup. We like to stick with pink evening primrose, which is consistent with the common name for the Onagraceae family, but to each their own.

Pink evening primrose often grows in dense colonies.

Candied Evening Primrose Flowers

Obtain a handful of fresh-picked evening primrose flowers and lay them out on a baking sheet. In a mixing bowl, whisk 1 egg white until frothy, then add 2–3 drops of vodka to the bowl and whisk again to combine. With a small, clean, unused paintbrush, gently coat each flower petal with the egg white mixture. Sprinkle sugar on each flower and let them air-dry on the baking sheet for a day or two. Once dried, the delicate, brittle flowers can be stored in an airtight container for later use. These make good garnishes for various desserts.

Regardless of what you call it, the spring flowers are abundant and make for an excellent wild edible flower to add to salads or use as a garnish. The large pink petals are pleasant, with a slightly bitter aftertaste that goes well with leafy greens, olive oil, and balsamic vinegar. The young evening primrose leaves themselves are also edible, though somewhat bitter; they can be boiled or steamed to lessen this. The tiny seeds are edible as well and contain high amounts of essential fatty acids. The seeds of some *Oenothera* species (including *O. biennis*) are even used in dietary supplements due to their fatty acid content.

DRUMMOND'S WOOD-SORREL (*Oxalis drummondii*)

Family: Oxalidaceae

Edible part and harvest time:
Leaves are available from spring to fall, while flowers can be found in fall; bulbs are available year-round but easiest to find when flowering.

The white bulb has a brown sheath that should be removed prior to eating.

Toxic lookalikes: There are no toxic lookalikes in Texas, but many people confuse bur-clover (*Medicago* spp.) and clover (*Trifolium* spp.) species with *Oxalis*. The small, pealike flowers easily distinguish these pea family plants from *Oxalis*, but if those are not present, the leaves help distinguish. In the two pea family species mentioned, the leaves are trifoliate, but the two side leaflets arise from lower on the petiole, while the terminal leaflet arises at the tip of the petiole. In most *Oxalis* species, including *O. drummondii*, each of the three leaflets arise from a common point. Additionally, *Oxalis* species have more heart-shaped leaflets, while the two pea family species are more club shaped and lack a defined cleft in the middle. If you accidentally eat a bur-clover or clover, it's fine, as these are not toxic (at least in small quantities) but are also not very palatable in our opinion.

Identification: Drummond's wood-sorrel is a perennial herb arising from a **small white bulb with a brownish sheath**. **Leaves are solitary on individual stalks** up to 5 inches tall, while flower stalks are separate and reach up to 1 foot tall. Each leaf is 2 inches wide and composed of **three strongly V-shaped to heart-shaped leaflets that arise out of a common point** where the leafstalk meets the leaf. The leaflets can be solid green or may have reddish markings below the notch. The taller flowering stalks have clusters of **pink, five-petaled flowers** with yellow centers borne on long pedicels. The seed capsules are broadly oblong, five sided, and split open forcefully to launch seeds when ripe.

Range and habitat: Drummond's wood-sorrel is most commonly found in limestone or sandy soils in the Edwards Plateau and Rio Grande Valley but is also found in the Trans-Pecos. It's frequently found in oak woodlands.

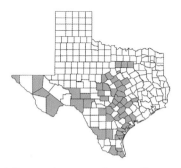

Related edible species: There are numerous other *Oxalis* species in Texas, all of which are edible. Some of the more commonly encountered ones include *O. corniculata* (much of Texas), **O. debilis* (southeast Texas), *O. dillenii* (much of Texas), *O. texana* (east Texas), and *O. violacea* (eastern half of Texas). Some of these have pink flowers, but many have yellow flowers. All of the species listed above have trifoliate leaves like *O. drummondii*, but there are other species in Texas with abnormal (for *Oxalis*) non-trifoliate leaves.

Uses/history/comments: Texas has numerous wood-sorrel species, but our favorite is Drummond's wood-sorrel. This unbranched species has thick, juicy stems, large pink flowers, and oversized leaves that pack quite a sour punch. The unexpected burst of flavor surprises and delights adults and kids alike and has led some students to refer to them as "skittles-of-the-woods." We find the flavor superior to other wood-sorrels, but all wood-sorrels in Texas have a similar flavor. On top of this, *O. drummondii* has an edible bulb at the base of each stalk. You have to dig a bit to get to it, but it looks kind of like a wild onion, with a thin brown sheath that can be removed prior to eating. It isn't as sour packed as the aboveground parts of the plant, but is tasty raw or cooked. *Oxalis* species have distinct fruits that look kind of like miniature okras. These stand erect and burst open forcefully when ripe to distribute the small seeds.

Leaves, stems, flowers, and fruit capsules are best eaten raw, as the sour flavor diminishes with cooking. They are best suited as accents to salads, as a garnish, or as a trailside snack. They can also be crushed and added to your water bottle to quench your thirst on a hike.

Other *Oxalis* species have smaller, rounder leaflet lobes than *O. drummondii* and often have yellow flowers. Note how all three leaflets arise out of one point, unlike bur-clover and clover species.

Note that all wood-sorrel species contain oxalic acid, which is responsible for some of the sourness. Some wild foragers sound the alarm for any plant containing oxalic acid or oxalates. We have found that many of these warnings are largely overblown. Yes, it is good to be aware of foods containing oxalic acid, but the reality is, people have been eating foods containing oxalic acid in various quantities forever. Spinach and rhubarb are two examples of common foods that contain oxalic acid. In reasonable quantities, foods containing oxalic acid are completely safe unless you have some kind of underlying health issue that makes you more susceptible to oxalate-rich foods. For healthy individuals, eat these foods in reasonable quantities and you have nothing to worry about.

RECIPE

Wood-Sorrel and Cucumber Tapas

Cut a cucumber into ¼-inch slices and lay out on a plate. Drizzle a drop of olive oil in the center of each cucumber slice and then place crushed, fresh wood-sorrel leaves on top of each slice. Add a dash of salt and pepper to each and enjoy this crisp, refreshing starter. This recipe was adapted from a friend and fellow forager, Aaron Bollinger. Thanks, Aaron!

AMERICAN POKEWEED (*Phytolacca americana*)

Family: Phytolaccaceae

Edible part and harvest time: Young shoots are available in early spring after properly cooking. Read the "Uses/history/comments" section below before harvesting or consuming.

Toxic lookalikes: Pokeweed itself is toxic if eaten raw or if not prepared properly (see below). The related pigeonberry (*Rivina humilis*) is a smaller plant but should be avoided. Pigeonberry has small red fruits and smaller leaves than pokeweed.

Identification: Pokeweed is a large, **hairless**, herbaceous perennial up to 9 feet tall. It dies back to the rootstock in cold weather but reemerges in spring with vigorous new shoots. Stems are robust, smooth, rounded, and **green when young and then turn reddish**. The alternate leaves are broadly lanceolate, smooth margined, and up to 10 inches long and 4 inches wide. The small white or

Harvest young pokeweed greens in early spring when they are less than 10 inches tall and lack red coloration in the stem.

pink flowers are arranged in erect or drooping racemes at the ends of branches. Each small flower has five sepals. The flower stalks and pedicels can be pink, white, or green depending on the season and stage of development. When fruiting, the pedicels and flower stalk are often hot pink. The unripe fruits are green but mature to look like a dark purple blueberry. The **hot pink flower stalks and dark purple berries** are striking and make a good indicator for pokeweed.

Range and habitat: Pokeweed grows in east and central Texas but also ranges to parts of the panhandle and Trans-Pecos. It can be weedy in rich bottomlands but also occurs on various disturbed soils and spoil piles throughout its range. We also find it on sandbars along or in the middle of creeks and rivers.

Related edible species: None in Texas

Uses/history/comments: Pokeweed should not be the first wild edible green you seek when learning to forage. This is because, first and foremost, pokeweed itself is toxic if eaten raw or improperly prepared. Secondly, you can only harvest pokeweed when it is very young and has not yet developed fruits or flowers, which aid in identification, so knowing how to identify pokeweed without those aids is critical. So, why is pokeweed in this book then? Well, it has a fairly long history of use as a *cooked* green. Proper boiling removes the toxic compounds from the young leaves and renders them safe to eat.

All parts of the mature pokeweed plant are toxic, including the fruits.

It is important to only harvest very young shoots in early spring (usually early March). We recommend noting where pokeweed is growing when it is easy to identify in summer and fall and then coming back to the same location in early spring to look for the new shoots, which are hairless and green with thick stems. Generally, we harvest shoots that are less than 10 inches tall and have not yet developed any reddish coloration in the stem or leaves. Some authors recommend even smaller shoots (6 inches tall), and it's recommended to err on the side of shorter, younger shoots. Many authors recommend different boiling times and methods, but we have found it safe to boil young pokeweed shoots in two changes of water for 15 minutes each. Boil for 15 minutes, strain and add fresh water, boil again for 15 minutes, strain and rinse.

Every part of the pokeweed contains some level of toxicity, but the roots and seeds are the most toxic. The root, while toxic, is also used as a medicine in very small doses.

There are many other wild greens that, in our opinion, taste better, are easier to prepare, and are less potentially dangerous. That's why we don't eat pokeweed nearly as much as we do lamb's quarters, cheeseweed, or amaranth leaves as potherbs. That said, every serious forager is bound to take a shot at the famous "poke salat" eventually.

RECIPE

Poke Salat

There are many poke salat (pokeweed salad) recipes, but this is the one that we use most often due to its simplicity. Harvest a handful of young (less than 10 inches tall) pokeweed shoots that have not yet developed any red in the stem or leaves. Boil a pot of water and reduce to a simmer, then add the pokeweed and simmer for 15 minutes. Pour off the water, add fresh water, and repeat the 15-minute simmer, then strain through a colander and rinse with fresh water. Add butter or ghee and any spices you prefer (chili flakes are a great addition) to the spinach-like dish and enjoy!

PLANTAIN (*Plantago* spp.)

Family: Plantaginaceae
Edible part and harvest time: Young leaves are available in spring and summer, while seeds can be found in summer and into fall.

Plantain fruiting spikes contain numerous tan seeds that can be eaten.

Toxic lookalikes: None in Texas

Identification: *Plantago* species are either annual or perennial herbs consisting of a **basal rosette** of leaves and an erect flowering stalk that can be up to 8 inches tall. Depending on species, the leaves can be long and narrow, ovate, or small and hairy. Regardless of leaf shape, *Plantago* species have **prominent parallel leaf veins**. Leaves are often smooth margined but can be wavy or dentate depending on species. Flower spikes contain many small, sessile, and inconspicuous greenish flowers. The wind-pollinated flowers develop into small, **oval-shaped seeds that are green initially and then mature to a tan color**.

Range and habitat: At least one *Plantago* species can be found in nearly every county in Texas. Western species are often found on dry caliche, while eastern and introduced species are found in a wide

Plantago species have parallel veins, unlike many dicots.

variety of habitats including disturbed, urban areas and low, wet fields and ditches.

Related edible species: There are many *Plantago* species in Texas and all have edible leaves and seeds, although some have leaves that are too small and hairy to consume enjoyably. Some of the best species to eat in Texas include *P. lanceolata* and *P. major* (both nonnative and found in disturbed areas) and *P. rhodosperma* (native and probably our most common *Plantago* found throughout much of Texas).

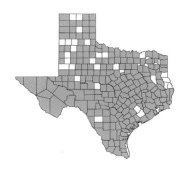

Uses/history/comments: Not to be confused with the banana-like plantain (*Musa* × *paradisiaca*), the much smaller unrelated plantain described here is common around trails, lawns, and vacant areas throughout much of Texas. The leaves are nothing special but serviceable in salads when young or steamed, but there are usually at least five other wild greens available in the same area that we prefer, so we rarely eat them. However, the seeds of plantain are a fun trailside nibble. The seeds are found on the stalks in summer and can be picked off one by one and eaten. You can pick the stalk when still green (the seeds will still be green but are edible) or when mature (the stalk and seeds will be tan). We find eating these "seeds on a stick" to be a pleasantly meditative activity when hiking.

The *Plantago* genus contains the psylliums (*P. ovata* and *P. psyllium*) that are used as a source of soluble fiber and mucilage for relieving constipation. We have not experimented with eating large quantities of plantain seeds at once, but we would imagine they would have a similar effect, as they are notably mucilaginous when wet. This property also makes them a substitute for chia seeds, as they form a similar gelatinous mass when soaked.

Fresh plantain leaves are excellent when used as a poultice on cuts, scrapes, burns, and bug bites. Crush up the leaves in your hands until they start to release juice, then hold on to the wound manually or with a wrap. This will usually stain your skin a dark green for a bit but helps tremendously with keeping wounds clean and helps promote healing.

RECIPE

Plantain Seeds on a Stick

This is not so much a recipe, but a simple way of eating plantain seeds. Grab a spike of plantain seeds (ripe or still green), then eat the seeds one by one as you hike. This meditative consumption of tiny seeds is similar to how many long-distance drivers use sunflower seeds.

*CURLY DOCK (*Rumex crispus*)

Family: Polygonaceae

Edible part and harvest time: Young leaves and shoots are available in late winter and early spring; seeds are available in summer.

Toxic lookalikes: Be sure to distinguish young new growth from pokeweed, which is toxic if not cooked properly (discussed on page 260). New growth on curly dock in early spring will consist of a basal rosette and will not be erect or have as robust of a stem as pokeweed. Pokeweed does not form a basal rosette of leaves, and its leaves are not wavy margined.

Identification: Curly dock is an herbaceous perennial that reaches up to 3 feet tall. In winter and early spring, it consists solely of a **basal rosette of oblong leaves** (up to 1 foot long) that can be smooth margined but are **more often wavy and wrinkled**. Each leaf has a prominent, wide central midrib. Later in spring, a grooved flower stalk bolts up from the center of the basal rosette. The flower stalk has stem leaves similar to the basal leaves but smaller. The flowering stalk forms large, densely clustered panicles of whorled flowers. The small **yellowish-green flowers hang in clusters around the stem**. Each flower develops into a dry, oval-shaped seed

Leaves are often wavy or wrinkled along the margin but can be smooth like this one.

that has three ovate or heart-shaped wings (called valves) that enclose the seed and form a capsule-like structure. The **capsule looks like a three-sided, pointed top with a central, lighter oval (the seed) in the center**. At first the valves are green and the seed light colored, but at maturity the valves turn brown and papery and the seed looks tan.

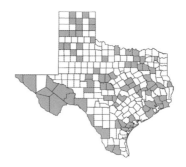

Range and habitat: Curly dock is a nonnative species that is now scattered throughout much of Texas. It can be found in disturbed areas, cultivated fields, and forested areas and is most frequently found in moist soils.

Related edible species: There are a number of other edible *Rumex* species in Texas (many of them nonnative). Some of the more common ones include *R. altissimus* (much of Texas), **R. chrysocarpus* (mostly along the coast), *R. hastatulus* (eastern half of Texas), *R. hymenosepalus* (west Texas and panhandle), and **R. pulcher* (southeastern half of Texas).

Uses/history/comments: Curly dock (also known as yellow dock) and other native or invasive *Rumex* species in Texas furnish reliable potherbs in late winter and early spring. The trick is identifying the plants at this early state, when the basal leaves are likely the only part of the plant to have developed. It is best to identify a stand of *Rumex* species the season before (which are evident by their dried stalks with clusters of the unique seed capsules). After identifying a patch in summer or fall the year prior, the basal rosettes of large simple leaves with a prominent central vein and often curly or wavy leaf margins become much easier to identify. It is best to harvest only tender, young leaves, as the older leaves can be bitter and tough. Very young leaves can be eaten in small quantities raw and have a pleasant sour flavor due to the oxalic acid content. But the leaves are much better, in our opinion, when steamed or cooked into soups or stir-fries. We prefer to steam them like spinach and eat with melted butter.

The seeds are also edible but require more work to harvest and prepare than the leaves. If you are feeling industrious, the seeds can be separated from the papery, winged capsules by crushing and then winnowing. Seeds can then be eaten as is, mixed into granolas or oatmeal, or ground into a flour for use in baking.

Dried curly dock seeds encased in the winged capsules

It's also worth noting that the juicy leaves of the canaigre (*R. hymenosepalus*), which grows in dry, sandy areas of west Texas and the panhandle, can be used effectively in place of aloe vera. These leaves can be crushed and rubbed on sunburns, rashes, and bug bites to good effect.

PURSLANE (*Portulaca oleracea*)

Family: Portulacaceae
Edible part and harvest time: The whole plant can be eaten in spring and summer.
Toxic lookalikes: None in Texas

Note how the leaves can vary in shape compared to the first photo.

Identification: Purslane is a low, mat-forming annual herb with fleshy, **succulent leaves and stems**. The prostrate, glabrous stems spread out radially from the center of the plant. The alternate or nearly opposite leaves are **sessile, oblong to oblanceolate**, and about 1 inch long. The leaves are often green but can turn reddish or purplish in very sunny areas. The terminal **yellow flowers** can be solitary to a few at the ends of each branch. Each flower is about 0.25 inch wide, with five yellow petals with two lobes each. Seed capsules are pointed and split in half along the circumference to release the small black seeds.

Range and habitat: Purslane is a common weed of disturbed areas around cities and towns. We frequently find it popping up through the joints and cracks in sidewalks and pavement. It's also common in farm fields and can be found scattered throughout Texas.

Related edible species: Other *Portulaca* species in Texas include *P. halimoides* (west Texas), *P. pilosa* (much of Texas), *P. suffrutescens* (west Texas), and *P. umbraticola* (west, central, and south Texas).

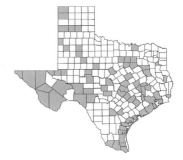

Uses/history/comments: Purslane is famously known as Gandhi's favorite food. We can see why: Even in drought conditions, the succulent, plump leaves and stems are deliciously sour and cooling. All above-ground parts of the plant have about the same texture and flavor, but the thick stems can be especially tasty when young. A true survivor of a plant, purslane can be found in the most unlikely urban settings as it struggles up through cracks in pavement. While these urban specimens may

Purslane can turn reddish in very sunny areas.

not be ideal for eating due to proximity to pollutants, the ones volunteering in your yard or local green space are excellent raw, added to salads, pickled, or used in stir-fries. We prefer purslane raw, as the flavor seems to diminish with cooking.

Purslane is a rich source of potassium, magnesium, calcium, omega-3 fatty acids, and alpha-linolenic acid (ALA) and reportedly contains the highest content of vitamin A among leafy green vegetables [37]. Interestingly, it is unclear whether purslane is native or introduced to North America. It's widespread throughout much of the Old World and may have been in North America prior to 1492 [38].

RECIPE

Purslane Salad

Gather 1 cup of purslane, chop coarsely, and add to a salad bowl. Slice 1 medium-sized cucumber into thin slices and add to the bowl along with a few leaves' worth of chopped mint and cilantro and a few sprinkles of chopped pecans. Mix well and add your favorite oil-and-vinegar-based salad dressing.

CLEAVERS (*Galium aparine*)

Family: Rubiaceae

Edible part and harvest time: The whole plant is edible from winter to early spring.

Toxic lookalikes: None in Texas. However, the closely related *Sherardia arvensis* (some actually group this in the *Galium* genus) looks similar but has light blue to purple flowers. *Sherardia arvensis* is not known to be edible but is also not known to be toxic.

Identification: Cleavers is an upright or sprawling annual herb with a weak and slender root system. **Leaves are arranged in whorls around the angled stem**; each node consists of six to eight linear-oblanceolate leaves, each 1–2.5 inches long. The most distinguishing aspect is the **tiny hook-like hairs that cover the stem and leaves**. These hairs act like Velcro and stick to nearly everything. The **tiny white flowers have four petals** (as with many Rubiaceae family plants) and give way to pairs of small, **ball-like seeds covered in stiff hairs**. Cleavers die back quickly after going to seed.

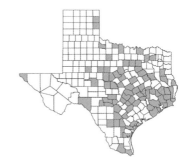

Range and habitat: Cleavers can be found in much of central, south, north, and east Texas but is absent in the Trans-Pecos and panhandle. Other *Galium* species can be found in the Trans-Pecos. Habitat for cleavers includes disturbed areas, thickets, and rich woods in semi-shaded areas.

Related edible species: The other *Galium* species in Texas are also edible, but none are as abundant as *G.*

Whorled leaves of cleavers

The small white flowers each have four petals.

aparine. They all have the same basic identifiers: whorled leaves (varying from three to eight leaves depending on species), Velcro-like hairs (some are stickier than others), and small white flowers. They include *G. circaezans* (southeast and north Texas), *G. obtusum* (east Texas), *G. pilosum* (eastern half of Texas), *G. proliferum* (west and south Texas), *G. texense* (central Texas), *G. tinctorium* (east Texas), and *G. virgatum* (much of Texas).

Uses/history/comments: Cleavers (also known as bedstraw, catchweed, or Velcro plant) are not around most of the year, but when they are, they're abundant. For a relatively short time from December to March (before it starts to go to seed and die back), cleavers run riot over vacant lots, forest edges, and other common habitats. Due to its small hooked hairs on the stems and leaves, it readily sticks to clothes, hair, and pets. Its root system is extremely weak, so entire patches can be pulled out relatively easily. As environmental educators, we've experienced a number of successful "cleaver fights," which are essentially snowball fights but with balled-up wads of cleavers in place of snow.

While cleavers are undoubtedly fun, they are also edible. All parts of cleavers

RECIPE

Raw Cleavers Juice

Take a large handful of cleavers before it has gone to seed and add with 2 cups of water to a strong blender. Blend on high until smooth (you may need to use a blender tamper to get all of it to blend well) and then pour through a fine-meshed strainer or cheesecloth to separate out the fibrous pulp. Drink as is for a free, healthy green juice or combine with other ingredients in a juice blend or smoothie. The flavor is reminiscent of wheatgrass juice.

can be eaten raw or cooked. Word of caution, though: The hook-like hairs can get caught in your throat, so make sure to chew raw cleavers *very* thoroughly before swallowing. We've made the mistake a few times, and it is not comfortable (resolved by drinking big gulps of water to wash it down). It is much better juiced so that the hairs are not an issue. Cleavers juice is an excellent spring tonic/cleansing juice that can be prepared quickly and easily.

GROUNDCHERRY (*Physalis* spp.)

Family: Solanaceae

Edible part and harvest time: Fruits ripen in fall.

Toxic lookalikes: There are several other related plants that also have inflated fruit capsules: *Quincula lobata*, *Chamaesaracha* spp., and *Margaranthus solanaceous* (which is now grouped in *Physalis* but is kept separate here for distinction). *Quincula lobata* has purple flowers, unlike the yellow *Physalis* flowers, but its fruits are apparently edible [39]. There is less information on the edibility of the other two plants (*Chamaesaracha* and *Margaranthus*), so it is best to assume these are at least somewhat toxic. *Physalis* plants are larger than the lowly *Chamaesaracha* species, although the yellow flowers are somewhat similar. *Chamaesaracha* fruits are not fully enclosed by the inflated capsules, unlike *Physalis*. *Margaranthus* has smaller purplish, bell-shaped flowers, while *Physalis* has yellow flowers. There are other toxic Solanaceae fruits that are similar in size and color, but they lack the inflated capsule, so make sure your groundcherry is enclosed in a capsule. Balloon vine (*Cardiospermum* spp.) is another plant that has an inflated capsule around the fruit, but it's a vining species with compound leaves so is not easily confused. It is not especially toxic and,

Ripe groundcherries are orange or yellow and are enveloped in an inflated, papery, lantern-like husk.

in fact, the young leaves and shoots are edible when cooked. Note that the unripe green fruits, leaves, stem, and roots of *Physalis* species themselves are toxic and have been linked to human poisonings [15]. Only consume the ripe fruit raw.

Identification: Groundcherries are annual or perennial herbs up to 2 feet tall. They can be erect or sprawling, and some species have glandular, sticky hairs along the stem, leaves, and flowers. The **alternate leave**s range from ovate to lanceolate and are dentate or entire along the margins depending on the species. The **solitary, circular, yellow flowers** arise from the leaf axils, and each has five stamens, five calyx lobes, and **dark splotches near the center of the flower**. The **flowers often nod downward**. The fruit consists of an **inflated, lantern-like capsule** (actually the remnant calyx) that envelops the round berry hanging inside. The fruit **ripens from green to orange or yellowish** and contains many small seeds.

Range and habitat: Groundcherry species range nearly throughout Texas and can be found in a wide variety of habitats including prairies, deserts, and woodlands. Almost every part of Texas will have at least one groundcherry species.

Related edible species: There are several *Physalis* species in Texas, but *P. cinerascens* is perhaps the most common and widespread. As mentioned above, the apparently edible *Quincula lobata* is related and used to be included in *Physalis*. It is found in the western

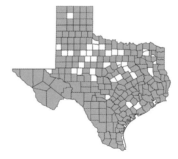

half of Texas and looks similar to other *Physalis* species but has purple flowers. A well-known cultivated relative of groundcherry is the tomatillo (*P. philadelphica* and *P. ixocarpa*). Green tomatillos are eaten raw or cooked in salsas and other Mexican dishes, but due to apparent toxicity, the wild *Physalis* species in Texas should not be eaten raw when green and unripe. Another less well-known cultivated relative is the goldenberry (*P. peruviana*), which is currently enjoying a bit of a moment in health food circles. Goldenberry fruits are about the same size as our native *Physalis* fruits.

Uses/history/comments: Groundcherries are not a well-known wild food in Texas and for good reason. The ripe fruits are literally hidden by the inflated capsules, so most people never even see the orange ripe fruits before a bird or squirrel gets to them. If you are diligent and patient, however, you will find the orange ripe fruits of groundcherry and seek them out wherever you can in fall.

Physalis cinerascens showing the nodding yellow flowers

The inflated husks surrounding the fruit begin green and stay green until the fruit is nearly ripened, when it turns brown and papery. This is the best time to harvest, but make sure the fruits are fully ripened, as the green unripe fruits are somewhat toxic, as are the other parts of the plant (leaves, stem, and roots). Nearly ripe fruits can be cooked to render safe to eat, but completely unripe green fruits should be avoided.

Our native groundcherries are not quite as sweet or sour as the cultivated goldenberries but are similar enough to warrant drying them in the same fashion for a snack. They can also be made into jams, salsas, and jellies.

RECIPE

Groundcherry Salsa

Gather 1 cup of ripe orange groundcherries and remove the outer papery husk. In a food processor, combine the groundcherries with ¼ cup chopped onion, ½ cup canned roasted tomatoes, 2 tbsp. lime juice, 1 minced garlic clove, 1 chopped jalapeño (after removing the seeds), a few cilantro leaves, ¼ tsp. salt, and a pinch of cumin powder. Pulse a few times until the mixture is well combined but still somewhat chunky. Refrigerate before eating with your favorite chips and guacamole.

EASTERN BLACK NIGHTSHADE
(*Solanum ptychanthum*)

Note how not all the fruits in a cluster ripen at the same time.

Family: Solanaceae

Edible part and harvest time: Fruits ripen midsummer to fall, while young leaves and tender shoots (which must be cooked) are available in early summer.

Toxic lookalikes: There are other *Solanum* species in Texas that are toxic and should be avoided. These include *S. triquetrum*, *S. elaeagnifolium*, *S. carolinense*, and *S. dimidiatum*, among others. Luckily for us, many of the dangerous *Solanum* species have yellow or red fruits when ripe, whereas *S. ptychanthum* (and its edible relatives) have black fruits when ripe. Additionally, none of the edible *Solanum* species related to *S. ptychanthum* have thorns, whereas many of the ones that are dangerous have thorns on the stem or on the underside of the leaves. Another toxic looka-like is belladonna (*Atropa belladonna*), which is found mainly in Europe but has escaped in parts of the East and West Coasts (but not in Texas). Belladonna has similar-looking black fruits, but they are larger (about the size of a cherry compared to the pea-size fruits of *S. ptychanthum*) and born singly (*S. ptychanthum* fruits are in clusters).

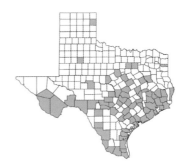

Identification: Eastern black nightshade is an annual, erect herb up to 3 feet tall with divergent branches. The

The small white flowers often nod downward.

alternate, glabrous leaves are ovate with smooth margins and are up to 4 inches long. The small, **nodding, white flowers are arranged in umbels**, and each has five petals and yellow anthers at the center. Each umbel has 3–10 flowers, which develop into small, round, smooth fruits. Each fruit starts out **green and ripens to shiny black** and has many small yellowish seeds inside. Fruits, even in the same cluster, ripen at different times, so **green and black fruits will often be found in the same cluster**.

Range and habitat: *S. ptychanthum* can be found in dry, open woods, lakeshores, and thickets but is most commonly found in disturbed areas or as a weed in gardens and crop fields. It is found in much of the southern half of Texas, while some of its close edible relatives are also found in the panhandle, south Texas, and west Texas.

Greens should be harvested in early summer before the plant flowers and should be cooked before eating.

Related edible species: Related edible "black nightshade" species found in Texas include *S. americanum* (Lower Rio Grande Valley), *S. douglasii* (south and west Texas), and *S. interius* (panhandle). The differences between these closely related species are minute, so much so that they used to be included in one species called *S. nigrum* (which has since been split). And, of course, there are related cultivated species of *Solanum* that you are more familiar with, including potatoes (*S. tuberosum*), eggplants (*S. melongena*), and tomatoes (*S. lycopersicum*).

Uses/history/comments: Many unaccustomed foragers associate the word "nightshade" with nightmarishly toxic plants. This is unfortunate, as the nightshade family (Solanaceae) is home to some of the most commonly eaten foods on the planet, including tomatoes, potatoes, peppers, and eggplants. One of the most common wild edible nightshades (both in the US and around the world) is the "black nightshade" (also known as the *Solanum nigrum* complex), which is composed of a number of closely related *Solanum* species as described in the section above. The most common in Texas is *S. ptychanthum*, which is frequently found in disturbed areas and cultivated gardens or fields.

Far from being deadly, *S. ptychanthum* and its close relatives furnish some of the most drought-resistant berries and palatable cooked greens. In fact, renowned forager Samuel Thayer suggests that the cooked greens are "perhaps the most commonly eaten wild greens in the world" [40]. Greens should be harvested in early summer before the plant flowers and should be boiled for about 10 minutes or so before eating. If the leaves are still bitter after boiling, they are best avoided, as this could indicate higher than normal levels of solanine (a bitter alkaloid that is dangerous in large amounts). Older, tougher leaves can also be bitter and should be avoided.

Greens aside, our favorite edible part of eastern black nightshade is the *ripe* berry. We emphasize the ripe black berry because the unripe green berry is potentially toxic and should be avoided. The ripe berries are delicately sweet, with a texture similar to a tiny thin-skinned tomato. These can be eaten raw or cooked into pies, jams, sauces, etc. Note that not all the fruits ripen at the same exact time. Even in one cluster of fruits, there will likely be at least one or two berries that are still green while all the others are ripe. And after you harvest the black ripe berries, be sure to come back in a few days, as the rest should ripen up soon after.

RECIPE

Black Nightshade Vinaigrette

Harvest ⅓ cup of ripe black nightshade berries and add to a blender with ½ cup olive oil and 2½ tbsp. apple cider vinegar. Blend on low to medium until the berries are pulverized and the thin skins are integrated into the mixture. The resulting quick, easy, purple vinaigrette goes great on salads or steamed veggies.

PELLITORY (*Parietaria pensylvanica*)

Family: Urticaceae

Edible part and harvest time: The whole plant is available winter through spring.

Toxic lookalikes: None in Texas

Identification: Pellitory is a **weak-stemmed** annual herb up to 1 foot tall that can be unbranched or branched just at the base. It prefers shaded or partly shaded locations and is **soft and pubescent** throughout, with semitranslucent stems when very young. The alternate leaves are lanceolate to **narrowly rhombic** and up to 2.5 inches long. The small, **inconspicuous, green flowers are arranged in sessile clusters along the stem** at the leaf axils. Achenes are small and ovoid. The **root system is very thin and weak**, which makes it easy to pull from the ground.

Range and habitat: Pellitory is found throughout most of the Texas except for much of the panhandle and far east Texas. It is most commonly found in rich, moist soils in the shade of trees or boulders. In most of Texas, it can be found under juniper or mesquite trees.

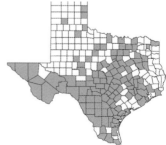

Related edible species: There are two other *Parietaria* species in Texas, although *P. pensylvanica* is by far the most common. **P. judaica* (native to Eurasia) can be found in a handful of urban areas, including Austin and Dallas. It's known as pellitory-of-the-wall for its habit of growing through cracks in ancient walls, ruins,

Note the lanceolate leaves and green flowers along the stem.

Very young pellitory plants have nearly translucent stems.

sidewalks, and other man-made structures. *P. floridana* is a native species found in parts of south Texas. *Parietaria* species in Texas can be used interchangeably with regard to food uses.

Uses/history/comments: This diminutive, overlooked herb is always a pleasant surprise for the new forager. Whenever we introduce this plant, we ask people to taste it first and share what *they* think it tastes like. We often get perplexed or surprised faces staring back at us trying to figure out the familiar flavor. Inevitably someone in the group finally latches on to it and shouts "Cucumber!" While it looks fairly nondescript and lacks flashy flowers or fruits, the flavor is excellently cucumbery. In fact, many people know this plant simply as "cucumber plant" even though it has no relation to true cucumbers. And, because it is in the nettle family, it is likely nutritionally robust, but we have not found studies that prove this definitively. Pellitory starts in winter as a very small (but still edible) plant and eventually grows up to about 1 foot tall before it starts dying back in late spring when the heat sets in. It's best harvested between those two stages when about 6 inches tall in February and March.

We have found that we can eat large amounts of young, tender pellitory when steamed and enjoy it prepared simply with butter. It loses some of its cucumber flavor when cooked, so if you want to impart a stronger flavor to any particular dish, add it raw.

RECIPE

Pellitory Pesto

Add 1 packed cup of fresh chopped young pellitory, ¼ cup pine nuts, 1 tsp. lemon juice, and 1 garlic clove to a food processor. Process until finely chopped. While the motor is still running, slowly add ⅓–½ cup olive oil (depending on consistency desired) and a pinch of salt to taste. Continue blending until smooth. This is an excellent foraged substitute for basil-based pesto. It obviously lacks the minty basil flavor but adds an excellent cucumber flavor to your favorite pesto dishes.

HEART-LEAF NETTLE (*Urtica chamaedryoides*)

Family: Urticaceae

Edible part and harvest time: Greens are available in spring.

Toxic lookalikes: Small nettle plants could potentially be mistaken for a noseburn (*Tragia* spp.), which is not especially toxic but has stinging hairs. Noseburns are smaller plants with a more vining habit rather than erect like *Urtica*. Fortunately, noseburns have alternate leaves, while nettles have opposite leaves, which makes discerning the two easy. It's also important to distinguish nettle from another stinging plant: Texas bull nettle (*Cnidoscolus texanus*). Texas bull nettle has some edible uses (see page 242), but the leaves are not edible like nettles. Texas bull nettle has large lobed leaves (typically five lobes) arranged alternately, while *Urtica* species have smaller, simple, opposite leaves.

Identification: Heart-leaf nettle is an erect annual herb covered with stinging hairs that reaches up to 2.5 feet tall. It is often unbranched except for at the base of the plant and has opposite, simple leaves. Most leaves are **broadly ovate or heart shaped**, but the uppermost leaves are lanceolate. All leaves

Note the opposite, serrated leaves and greenish flower clusters at the leaf axils.

have coarsely serrated margins and are **often purple underneath and green above**. The **clear, stinging hairs on the stems and leaves** are easily visible. The **green or purplish flower clusters arise from the leaf axils** near the top of the plant.

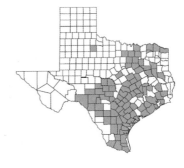

Range and habitat: Heart-leaf nettle is commonly found in bottomlands and rocky, wooded slopes throughout much of the southeastern half of Texas, though most common in central and south Texas.

Related edible species: *U. gracilenta* is another native species from far west Texas, while **U. urens* is a nonnative species found in southeast Texas and along parts of the Gulf Coast. The common nettle (*U. dioica*) is not found in Texas but has spread from Europe to many parts of the world, including most of the US (aside from Texas and the southeastern states).

Uses/history/comments: Nettle species are much maligned by non-foragers but are highly sought-after wild foods for those in the know. Nettle greens (including young leaves and flowering spikes) are highly nutritious and are one of the best-tasting wild greens. Obviously, the stinging hairs covering nettle plants make harvesting a cautious venture. We recommend wearing leather gloves, a thick long-sleeved shirt, long pants, and close-toed shoes while harvesting. If you get stung, it's usually fairly intense at the beginning but reduces in pain level quickly; however, the sting and tingly sensation can linger for quite a while (sometimes days). We recommend harvesting nettles when they are about 1 foot tall, as the stems get fibrous and tough as they get taller.

Note that there is a fun albeit limited way to enjoy nettles raw, which doubles as a party trick. It involves eating the leaves one by one after carefully plucking them off the plant in a certain way to avoid the stinging hairs. If you're up for it, see the "recipe" below.

RECIPE

Raw Nettle Leaf

Use your pointer finger and thumb to fold the top of a leaf in half taco-style while still attached to the plant so that the stinging hairs on the underside of the leaf do not touch your fingertips. Then gently pull the leaf (while folded) until you pluck it from the plant (be careful not to let the rest of the plant bend over and touch your hand as you do this; we usually hold the plant back with a stick in the other hand). After the leaf is plucked and folded taco-style, roll it between your fingers firmly so that the hairs on the underside of the leaf get crushed. You can then eat the crushed rolled-up leaf raw. If you don't crush the leaf well enough, it can sting your mouth as you chew, but for some reason, the sting is much less intense and lasts a fraction of the time when stung inside your mouth compared to on your skin.

Lower leaves are often heart shaped; note the clear stinging hairs along the petiole.

Young nettles are also excellent steamed for five minutes with a pad of butter and dash of salt on top. Additionally, if you dehydrate nettle greens and then grind them into powder, the stinging hairs are rendered harmless. The powder can then be added to smoothies, stews, baked goods, etc. We have also used nettle powder as a kind of green porridge (mixed with hot water), which sounds weird but tastes great.

AQUATICS

This section includes plants that have adapted to living in water or obligate wetland plants that only grow in water or adjacent wetlands. Be mindful of the overall health and pollutant load of the water body you plan to harvest from. Many wetland species can bioaccumulate heavy metals and other pollutants. Seek out relatively clean waters to harvest from, and avoid detention ponds, roadside ditches, and other questionable locations.

*WATERCRESS (*Nasturtium officinale*)

Family: Brassicaceae

Edible part and harvest time: Greens and flowers, typically available spring through summer.

Toxic lookalikes: There are no aquatic lookalikes in Texas.

Identification: Watercress is an aquatic or semi-aquatic perennial with stems that often **float or creep along the bank** but can be erect in emergent plants. It rarely reaches more than 1 foot above the water level. The glabrous leaves are simple on submerged stems, but **pinnately compound on emergent stems**. Each emergent leaf has one to six pairs of sessile, rounded lateral leaflets with a larger terminal leaflet. The **small white flowers have four petals** and are arranged in racemes at the ends of the stems. The **seedpods are slender and often curved upward**; they can reach up to 1 inch long.

Note the four white petals and the seed pods on the right side of the photo.

Range and habitat: Watercress is found at the water's edge of rivers and creeks throughout much of central and west Texas. It floats on top of the water or grows in saturated mud along the bank.

Related edible species: None in Texas.

Uses/history/comments: Watercress is an excellent aquatic wild green with a spiciness reminiscent of arugula. It's commonly found at the water's edge of rivers and creeks through central and much of west Texas. Watercress is originally from Europe and Asia but

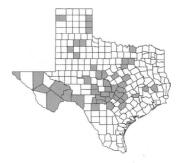

was brought over to the Americas due to its high vitamin C content, which was known to prevent scurvy [41]. Note that studies have shown that watercress can bioaccumulate zinc and copper, so take care to avoid eating watercress from polluted waterways [42]. Caution is also advised if you plan to eat watercress raw, since it can be contaminated by *Giardia* and other waterborne pathogens. For that reason, we always eat watercress cooked and seek it out near springs and other cleaner sources of water.

The tender leaves, white flowers, and green fruiting capsules of watercress can all be harvested and eaten. Watercress is best used blanched, steamed, and in soups, stews, or stir-fries. It can also be used as an accent or spice when dried. Watercress is also known to stimulate digestion and promote bile flow, as with other pungent or spicy herbs [43].

RECIPE

Blanched Watercress Salad

Gather 6 cups of the cleanest watercress leaves and young stems you can find. Coarsely chop the watercress and add to boiling water and blanch for 3 minutes. Drain the water off and rinse the watercress under cold, clean water to stop from cooking further. In a separate bowl, mix 3 tbsp. peanut butter, ½ tsp. honey, 1 tsp. apple cider vinegar, and 1 tsp. soy sauce until well incorporated. Pour this sauce over the blanched watercress, mix, and sprinkle black sesame seeds on top before serving.

AMERICAN LOTUS (*Nelumbo lutea*)

Family: Nelumbonaceae
Edible part and harvest time: Lotus nuts ripen in late summer and early fall; tubers are also available in this time frame.

Toxic lookalikes: There are no especially toxic lookalikes for American lotus, but take care not to mistake two unrelated lookalikes, *Nymphaea* spp. and *Nuphar advena*, for lotus. It's easy to distinguish these, as lotus has larger, round, peltate leaves that are usually elevated out of the water on a stalk, as are the flowers and seed heads. The flower and seed head stalks are often 2 to 3 feet above the water. In contrast, *Nymphaea* spp. and *Nuphar advena* leaves float directly on the water and can be more oval shaped, with a cleft running to the center of the leaf. *Nuphar advena* flowers are yellow, while *Nymphaea* spp. flowers can be white like the lotus flowers but are not raised as high out of the water. Both of these lookalikes have edible uses.

Large white flowers stand atop tall emergent stalks.

Identification: American lotus is an emergent aquatic perennial that spreads by seed and by rhizome. The **large, circular leaves** (up to 2.5 feet in diameter) are **peltate** (the petiole meets the leaf in the center of the circle) and either float on top of the water or, **more commonly, rise out of the water on erect, stout stalks**. The leaf is smooth margined and round with no dividing cuts or gaps, although there is **one prominent mid-vein that runs from the center to one edge of the leaf in a straight line**. Leaves can be almost 3 feet above the water level, while separate flower stalks are often taller and can reach 6 feet out of the water. **Large white to pale yellow flowers** (up to 8 inches in diameter) are borne singly at the top of the stout flowering stalks and have numerous tepals and stamens and a round, **honeycomb-like structure at the center**. The fruiting receptacle is an **inverse cone shape** with numerous round openings in the top. Each opening develops one hard, spherical nut 0.3 inch in diameter; the openings widen during ripening such that the nut can rattle around inside. The fruiting **receptacle and nuts start out green and then ripen to brown (receptacle) and purplish brown (nut).** The enlarged yellowish tubers develop at the ends of the rhizomes and are about the size and shape of bananas. When cut in cross section, each tuber has numerous round air pockets.

Range and habitat: American lotus is found in shallow ponds, lakes, reservoirs, sloughs, and

The green unripe pod on the left contrasts with the brown ripe pod on the right. Note that not all the seeds develop fully; the aborted ones are smaller and often rotten.

The ripe brown nuts are very hard and must be cracked in order to get to the tasty nut meat inside.

slow-moving streams and is scattered in the eastern half of Texas. It often grows in large colonies, which serve as prolific food providers.

Related edible species: None in Texas.

Uses/history/comments: While lotus nuts are commonly eaten in other parts of the world, many Texans are not aware we have a native lotus that provides excellent nuts and tubers. American lotus is better known as a wild food farther north, where it is more common and abundant, but Texans would do well to learn about the many uses of this aquatic wild food. And to avoid common confusion, American lotus is not the same plant as what many refer to as "water lily." Yes, they have similar roundish pads, but lotus leaves are often elevated out of the water on stalks, unlike the more common "water lily" species from the *Nymphaea* and *Nuphar* genera.

The most obvious and, in our opinion, tasty parts of the lotus are the nuts. These round nuts grow in seed heads, each with about 10–20 nuts. The nuts ripen in late summer in two distinct phases. First, they will be fully grown in size but green on the outside, and the seed head will be green as well. These nuts are excellent approximations of chestnuts when eaten raw or roasted. Just make sure to remove the green embryo in the center of the nut meat before eating, as it is quite bitter. After the green stage, the nuts will turn brown along with the seed head and start to shrink in size and get *very* hard. Harvest these before the seed head bends over and releases the nuts to the mud or water below. Simply cut the stalks of the brown seed heads and collect them in a bag to process later.

The brown lotus nutshells are *very* hard. Do not try to crack them with your teeth; more than likely, you will need a hammer or mortar and pestle to crack them. Once cracked, the nut meat tends to stick to the inner part of the hard shell. However, the flavor is excellent, even better than the younger nuts in our opinion. Note that there are often several stunted nuts in each seed head; avoid these, as they are often rotten or hollow inside. The mature brown nuts can be ground into a meal or flour and cooked as a porridge or used in various soups and baked goods. They're one of our favorite wild nuts in Texas.

Lotus tubers are also available in late summer and early fall and grow at the ends of lateral rhizomes. You will have to get muddy to harvest these banana-sized (and -shaped) tubers, as they are usually about half a foot below the mud. When cut in half crosswise, these will be easily recognizable by the symmetrical Swiss cheese–like holes throughout. Preparation of lotus tubers involves cleaning the mud off, peeling off the thick skin, and then slicing. You can eat them raw, but we don't advise this due to the questionable quality of most of the Texas waters we have found them in. We use them primarily in soups and stews, where they turn a pinkish to bluish color after cooking.

RECIPE

Quick Roasted Lotus Nuts

Gather green seed heads in late summer or early fall when the nuts have fully developed but are still green. Roast the whole seed heads by throwing directly on the coals of a campfire. Remove the seed heads from the fire, then remove the lotus nuts from the seed heads, peel off the nutshell, and eat like chestnuts. Note: The bitter, green embryo in the middle of the nut should be removed before eating.

CATTAIL (*Typha* spp.)

Family: Typhaceae

Edible part and harvest time: Spikes are available in spring, pollen is generally available in early summer, and leaf hearts are best in late spring through summer, and rhizome shoots and buds are generally available late summer through fall.

Toxic lookalikes: There are no toxic lookalikes in Texas that grow in similar wetland habitats. However, take care to harvest cattail from clean water bodies, as they can bioaccumulate and concentrate heavy metals and potentially other pollutants. That said, there is some evidence that heavy metals concentrate in the roots of cattail and may be less concentrated in aerial parts of the plant [44].

Identification: Cattails are large, emergent aquatic or wetland perennials that reach up to 9 feet tall and spread by rhizome. Each plant has 6–10 leaves that emerge from a central base.

Depending on species, leaf width ranges from 0.1–1 inch. At the base of the plant, the **leaf sheaths surround the central flowering stalk on either side**. The erect flowering stalk can be shorter or taller than the leaves depending on species. Each flowering stalk terminates in **two distinct groups of flowers** (separated by 0.5 inch of bare stalk): male flowers in a thinner terminal portion and female flowers forming the wider portion below the male flowers. The female section is what most people know as the cattail. Both male and female flower spikes turn from green to brown as they mature. The male section releases yellow pollen and then withers, while the female section remains and consists of **fluffy cattail down when pulled apart**.

Cattail leaf bases surround the central flowering stalk on either side.

Range and habitat: Cattail is present in brackish and freshwater marshes, lake edges, ponds, and riversides throughout much of Texas. Despite it not showing up in many counties on the adjacent range map, it can grow in man-made stock ponds, reservoirs, ditches, and other water features nearly throughout the state.

Related edible species: All *Typha* species in the US are edible, and Texas has three species that all look similar: **T. angustifolia* (panhandle and central Texas), *T. domingensis* (throughout Texas), and *T. latifolia* (throughout Texas).

Uses/history/comments: It is commonly known, even among non-foragers, that cattails are edible. However, most people have no idea what parts are edible or how to harvest them. Luckily, there are many edible parts and almost always at least one part of cattail that you can eat regardless of season. But prepare to get dirty: Harvesting cattails can be messy, and you're almost guaranteed to get wet.

The young flowering spikes appear toward the latter part of spring. This spike will eventually turn into the classic brown cattail head. But before it does, the immature spike will have a sheath protecting its male and female parts. After you peel off the sheath, the immature top (male) part of the spike can be snapped off, boiled, and eaten kind of like a small, green corn-on-the-cob. If you wait for the spikes to mature fully, the flowering male part will produce abundant yellow pollen, which can be gathered and added to flours to boost nutrition in baked goods. We typically put a plastic bag over the

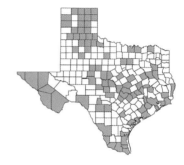

pollen-producing spike and then bend it over and shake to collect the pollen.

The leaf hearts (our favorite cattail food) are available late spring through summer. These are basically the core of the leaf bases. To harvest, grab a single plant (which consists of a bundle of 6–10 leaves) by the inner leaves, excluding the outer two leaves. Then pull forcefully, but slowly, upward until the leaf base dislocates from the rhizome. You should now have a bundle of long leaves that transition to white at the base. At the center of this white part will be the leaf heart, or core. You'll know when you get to it, as it is the perfectly white, non-fibrous central part of the leaf. As you go farther up the leaf heart/core, the outer layers will become more and more fibrous. A greater portion will be fibrous the further into the season you get, so it's best to harvest earlier in the summer. This non-fibrous heart/core is an excellent cooked vegetable that is reminiscent of heart of palm both in texture and flavor. We use it in soups, stews, and stir-fries. We don't recommend eating it raw, due to the questionable cleanliness of many Texas water bodies.

Cattail leaf heart after removing the outer leaf sheaths

The central portion, after removing all fibrous layers, is the edible heart.

The rhizome shoots and buds are also excellent eating and can be found late summer through fall. They lie under the water in the muck and can be found by locating a rhizome and following it horizontally until you reach an end point. The choice parts will be nearly white and smooth, with no rootlets. These are best eaten steamed or boiled, or used in stews and soups. The rhizomes themselves are also partially edible but require processing to coax out the starch from their core. We don't usually bother with the rhizome, as the above-mentioned parts of the cattail are more rewarding.

RECIPE

Simple Cattail Stir-Fry

Gather 1 or 2 cattail hearts, clean well, and cut into ½-inch slices. Add 2 tbsp. avocado oil to a cast-iron pan and heat on medium. Once hot, add the cattail slices, 2 minced garlic cloves, ¼ cup diced green onions, 1 cup shredded carrots, 1 cup snow peas, 1 tbsp. sesame oil, ⅛ tsp. red pepper flakes, ½ tsp. fish sauce, and 1 tbsp. soy sauce. Cook while stirring constantly for 5–10 minutes. Serve on its own or over rice. Alternatively, you can add nearly any other vegetable in place of the carrots and snow peas.

APPENDIX A: ABBREVIATED LIST OF OTHER WILD EDIBLE PLANTS IN TEXAS

While this book details many of the more common and abundant wild edible plants in Texas, we couldn't cover everything. Below is an abbreviated list of other edible wild plant species in Texas that didn't quite make the cut. This list is by no means exhaustive.

An asterisk (*) before a plant listed below denotes that it is an invasive or nonnative species.

Trees
Maple (*Acer* spp.)
American chinquapin (*Castanea pumila*)
Hawthorn (*Crataegus* spp.)
American beech (*Fagus grandifolia*)
Crabapple (*Malus* spp.)
Red bay (*Persea borbonia*)
Black locust (*Robinia pseudoacacia*)
Sassafras (*Sassafras albidum*)
American basswood (*Tilia americana*)

Shrubs/Vines
American hog-peanut (*Amphicarpaea bracteata*)
Groundnut (*Apios americana*)
New Jersey tea (*Ceanothus americanus*)
Seagrape (*Coccoloba uvifera*)
Mormon tea (*Ephedra* spp.)
Spicebush (*Lindera benzoin*)
Mangle dulce (*Maytenus phyllanthoides*)
*Kudzu (*Pureraria lobata*)
Rose (*Rosa* spp.)
Desert yaupon (*Schaefferia cuneifolium*)

Herbs/Wildflowers/Forbs
Giant ragweed (*Ambrosia trifida*)
Wright's yellowshow (*Amoreuxia wrightii*)
Searocket (*Cakile* spp.)
Bittercress (*Cardamine* spp.)
*Chicory (*Cichorium intybus*)

Spring beauty (*Claytonia virginica*)
*Coriander (*Coriandrum sativum*)
Prairie tea (*Croton monanthogynous*)
Chufa (*Cyperus esculentus*)
*Stork's-bill (*Erodium cicutarium*)
Strawberry (*Fragaria* spp.)
Sumpweed (*Iva annua*)
*Horehound (*Marrubium vulgare*)
*Mint (*Mentha* spp.)
Partridge berry (*Mitchella repens*)
Indian breadroot (*Pediomelum hypogaeum*)
*Beefsteak plant (*Perilla frutescens*)
Grasses (Poaceae)
*Indian strawberry (*Potentilla indica*)
Devil's claw (*Proboscidea* spp.)
*Tumbleweed (*Salsola* spp.)
Wild sage (*Salvia* spp.)
Brookweed (*Samolus* spp.)
Stonecrop (*Sedum* spp.)
Jewels of Opar (*Talinum paniculatum*)
Cota (*Thelesperma megapotamicum*)
*Salsify (*Tragopogon* spp.)
Clover (*Trifolium* spp.)
Corn salad (*Valerianella* spp.)
Violet (*Viola* spp.)

Aquatics
Spatterdock (*Nuphar advena*)
Water lily (*Nymphaea* spp.)
Pickerelweed (*Pontederia cordata*)
Wapato (*Sagittaria latifolia*)

APPENDIX B: HELPFUL RESOURCES AND ADDITIONAL READING

Foraging is a lifelong pursuit. We encourage everyone to learn from as many different teachers/sources as possible. Check out classes run by other local foragers, research online, and acquire as many foraging and plant identification books as possible. Below is a list of resources (available at the time of publication) that we recommend for furthering your foraging knowledge.

Texas-based companies/organizations offering local edible plant walks:
*Earth Native Wilderness School (Bastrop, TX; www.earthnativeschool.com)
Foraging Texas (Houston, TX; www.foragingtexas.com)
The Human Path (Bulverde, TX; www.thehumanpath.net)
*Lady Bird Johnson Wildflower Center (Austin, TX; www.wildflower.org)
*Local Leaf (Austin, TX; www.local-leaf.com)
Natureversity (Austin, TX; www.natureversity.org)
Primitive Texas and Louisiana (College Station, TX; www.primitivetexas.com)
Note: One of the authors runs edible plant walks/classes (at time of publication) through these organizations.

Books:
Atlas of the Vascular Plants of Texas, vols. 1–2, by Billie L. Turner, Holly Nichols, Geoffrey Denny, and Oded Doron
Botany in a Day by Tom Elpel
Cacti of Texas and Neighboring States by Del Weniger
Caribbean Wild Plants & Their Uses by Penelope N. Honychurch
Common Flora of the Playa Lakes by David Haukos and Loren Smith
Edible and Useful Plants of Texas and the Southwest by Delena Tull
Edible Wild Plants: A North American Field Guide by Thomas Elias and Peter Dykeman
Edible Wild Plants: Eastern/Central North America by Lee Allen Peterson
A Field Guide to Common South Texas Shrubs by Richard Taylor, Jimmy Rutledge, and Joe Herrera
The Forager's Harvest by Samuel Thayer
It Will Live Forever: Traditional Yosemite Indian Acorn Preparation by Beverly Ortiz and Julia Parker
Manual of the Vascular Plants of Texas by Donovan Correll and Marshall Johnston
Nature's Garden by Samuel Thayer

Plants of Deep South Texas by Alfred Richardson and Ken King

Poisonous Plants of the United States by Walter C. Muenscher

Remarkable Plants of Texas by Matt W. Turner

Shinner's Manual of the North Central Texas Flora by William F. Mahler

Southwest Foraging by John Slatterly

Trees and Shrubs of the Trans-Pecos and Adjacent Areas by Michael Powell

Trees, Shrubs, and Vines of the Texas Hill Country by Jan Wrede

Trees, Shrubs, and Woody Vines of the Southwest by Robert A. Vines

The Useful Wild Plants of Texas, the Southeastern and Southwestern United States, the Southern Plains, and Northern Mexico, vols. 1–4, by Scooter Cheatham, Marshall Johnston, and Lynn Marshall

Weeds of the West by Larry Burrill, Steven Dewey, David Cudney, Burrell Nelson, and Tom Whitson

Wild Edible Plants of Texas by Charles W. Kane

Wildflowers and Other Plants of Texas Beaches and Islands by Alfred Richardson

Wildflowers of Houston & Southeast Texas by John and Gloria Tveten

Wildflowers of Texas by Geyata Ajilvsgi

Wildflowers of the Big Bend Country, Texas by Barton Warnock

Wildflowers of the Big Thicket by Geyata Ajilvsgi

Wildflowers of the Texas Hill Country by Marshall Enquist

Wildflowers of the Western Plains by Zoe M. Kirkpatrick

Online resources:

BONAP's North American Plant Atlas (www.bonap.net/Napa/Genus/ Traditional/County)

County-level distribution maps for each species in the US. Maps indicate which plants are native, invasive, or rare/threatened/endangered in each county.

Eat the Weeds (www.eattheweeds.com)

Based in Florida, Green Deane has over sixty years of foraging experience. His website is an excellent source for understanding the history, etymology, and uses for edible plants in Florida, many of which can be found in Texas, especially in coastal and south Texas.

Flora of North America (www.efloras.org)

The Flora of North America (FNA) has helpful keys to most plant families in the US, including the technical differences between species in the same genus.

Foraging Texas (www.foragingtexas.com)

Mark "Merriwether" Vorderbruggen maintains an excellent website highlighting many of the edible plants in Texas, with a focus on plants found in southeastern

Texas. Mark also runs plant walkabouts around Texas at various nature centers, arboretums, and other locations; look for upcoming plant walkabouts on his website.

iNaturalist (www.inaturalist.org)

iNaturalist is a citizen science project and online social network for naturalists, citizen scientists, and biologists built on the concept of mapping and sharing observations of biodiversity across the globe. Helpful for recording and identifying plants. Never eat a plant solely based on the iNaturalist identification algorithm.

Lady Bird Johnson Wildflower Center, Native Plant Database (www.wild flower.org/plants)

The Native Plant Database allows you to search for plants based on habit (tree, shrub, herb, fern, etc.), state (not just Texas), bloom time, bloom color, leaf arrangement, light requirements, etc. We find the bloom time search function especially helpful for figuring out when certain plants will be in bloom.

APPENDIX C: ILLUSTRATED GLOSSARY AND BOTANICAL TERMINOLOGY

Common Leaf Arrangements (Figure 1)

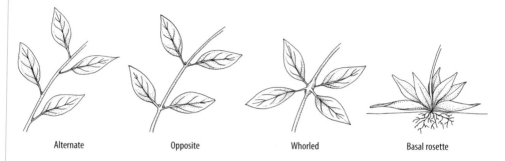

Alternate · Opposite · Whorled · Basal rosette

Common Leaf Shapes (Figure 2)

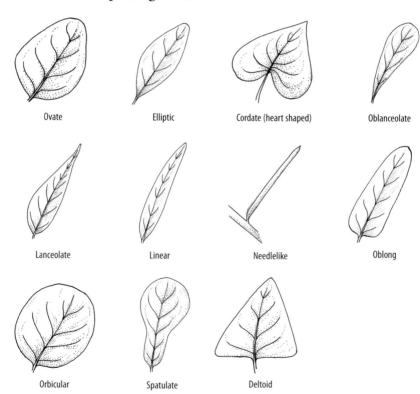

Ovate · Elliptic · Cordate (heart shaped) · Oblanceolate

Lanceolate · Linear · Needlelike · Oblong

Orbicular · Spatulate · Deltoid

Common Leaf Types (Figure 3)

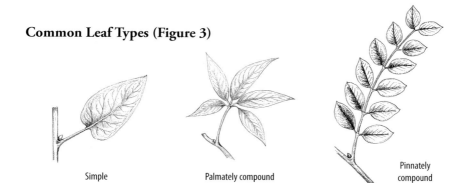

Simple   Palmately compound   Pinnately compound

Common Leaf Margins (Figure 4)

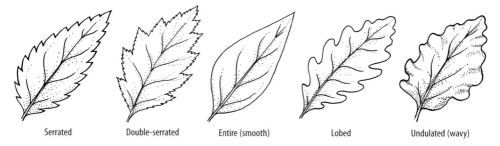

Serrated   Double-serrated   Entire (smooth)   Lobed   Undulated (wavy)

Common Inflorescence Types (Figure 5)

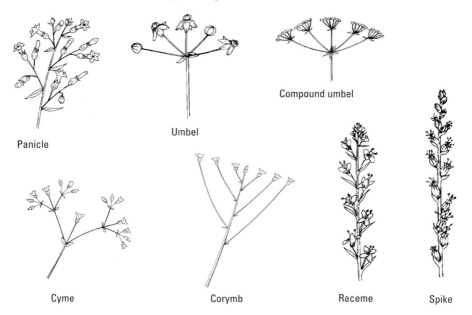

Compound umbel

Panicle

Umbel

Cyme   Corymb   Raceme   Spike

Cross Section of a Generalized Flower (Figure 6)

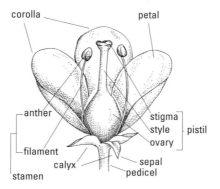

Flowers of the Sunflower Family (Asteraceae) (Figure 7)

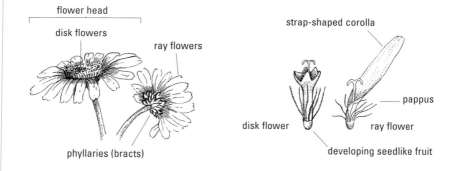

COMMON BOTANICAL TERMINOLOGY

Achene: a small, dry, one-seeded indehiscent fruit.

Alternate: any leaf arrangement along the axis other than opposite, whorled, or basal.

Annual: a plant completing its life cycle within a single year or season.

Apex: the tip of a plant part.

Areole: in Cactaceae family, a raised or depressed spot on the surface through which spines or leaves grow.

Aromatic: fragrant, spicy-pungent; usually in reference to a scent given off by crushed leaves.

Ascending: rising or curving upward.

Auricle: a small, ear-like projection from the base of a leaf or petal.

Axil: the angle formed between a leaf and the stem it attaches to.

Axillary: born or carried in the axil.

Berry: a fleshy or pulpy, non-opening fruit containing one to many seeds.

Biennial: a plant completing its life cycle in two years.

Bract: a reduced or modified leaf subtending a flower or flower cluster.

Bulb: an underground bud enclosed in numerous overlapping, thickened, leafy scales (like an onion).

Calyx: collectively, the outer whorl of flower parts, which are usually green.

Campanulate: bell shaped.

Capsule: a dry dehiscent fruit consisting of two or more carpels.

Carpel: the ovule-bearing portion of a flower; a simple pistil or one part of a compound pistil.

Catkin: a scaly deciduous spike.

Ciliate: fringed with hairs on the margin.

Clasping: basal portion of a leaf or other organ partly or wholly surrounding the stem or other structure, but not united.

Compound: leaf formation where the leaf is divided into separate leaflets; leaflets often look like individual leaves.

Connate: united at the base; usually refers to the joining of the basal part of the blades of opposite leaves.

Corolla: the inner, colored whorl of flower parts; the petals collectively.

Corymb: a flat-topped or convex flower cluster with the outer pedicels longest, the outer flowers opening first.

Crenate: a margin with rounded teeth.

Cuneate: wedge shaped, often in reference to the base of a leaf.

Decumbent: lying down with the tip ascending.

Decurrent: extending beyond normal placement, as the margin of a leaf sometimes extends past the leaf node and down the stem.

Deltoid: triangular.

Dentate: a margin with teeth that point outward but not forward.

Dichotomous: repeatedly branching in pairs.

Dicot: a member of the flowering plants, or angiosperms, that has a pair of leaves, or cotyledons, in the embryo of the seed.

Dioecious: having staminate (male) and pistillate (female) flowers on different plants of the same species.

Disk flower: a small tubular flower found on the central disk of a composite-type flower head.

Drupe: a fleshy, one-seeded, indehiscent fruit; stone fruits such as plums and cherries.

Elliptic: narrowly oval, usually twice as long as broad.

Emergent: a plant whose root system grows underwater, but whose shoots, leaves, and flowers grow above the water.

Endemic: restricted in range to a given area that may be defined politically or geographically.

Entire: a margin that is linear and unbroken.

Fascicle: a compact bundle or cluster.

Filament: the slender, threadlike stalk supporting the anther; any threadlike structure.

Glabrous: lacking hairs.

Gland: a structure on or beneath a surface that secretes a sticky or aromatic fluid.

Glaucous: covered or tinted with a whitish or colored blush, like cabbage.

Globose: spherical, rounded.

Glochids: hairlike spines or short prickles, generally barbed, found on the areoles of some cacti.

Hastate: usually refers to a leaf with basal lobes that turn outward.

Head: a dense cluster of flowers that rise from a common point on a peduncle.

Herbaceous: herblike, usually leafy and green, non-woody.

Incised: cut, often deeply.

Inflorescence: the flower cluster or flower head of a plant.

Internode: the section of stem between two nodes.

Involucre: the whorl of bracts (or phyllaries) subtending a flower or flower cluster.

Lateral: on the side of.

Leaflet: the leaflike part of a compound leaf that is borne from a leaf petiole or branch of a leaf, not from a main plant stem or branch.

Linear: long and narrow.

Lobe: any projection of a margin, often rounded, normally larger than a tooth.

Lyrate: lyre shaped; pinnately, sinuately lobed, the terminal lobe often largest.

Margin: edge; refers to the outer edge of a leaf.

Monocot: a member of the flowering plants, or angiosperms, that has one leaf, or cotyledon, in the embryo of the seed.

Monoecious: having staminate (male) and pistillate (female) flowers on the same plant.

Morphology: the form and structure of an object.

Mucronate: having a small, short projection at the tip.

Nectar: a sweet liquid produced by plants and used as food by insects.

Nerve: the vein or rib of a leaf blade.

Nodding: hanging or drooping downward.

Node: the point on a stem from which leaves arise.

Oblong: much longer than broad, with nearly parallel sides.

Orbicular: more or less round.

Ovary: the ovule-bearing part of the pistil.

Panicle: a compound, raceme-like inflorescence.

Pappus: a crown of scales or bristles on an achene.

Pedicel: the stem of a single flower or of one flower in a group of flowers.

Peduncle: the stalk of a single flower or a group of flowers.

Peltate: a type of leaf having its petiole attached to the center of the lower surface of the blade.

Pendulous: hanging.

Perennial: a plant of indefinite life span that renews itself each year.

Perfoliate: a condition with the stem apparently piercing a leaf or surrounded by basally joined opposite leaves.

Perianth: collectively, the inner and outer whorls of flower parts; used when the distinction between the two whorls is vague or difficult to determine.

Petiole: the leafstalk.

Phyllary: in the Asteraceae family, one bract of the involucre.

Pinna: one leaflet or primary division of a pinnately divided leaf.

Pinnate: a compound leaf with the leaflets symmetrically arranged on both sides of a common petiole.

Pistil: collectively, the stigma, style, and ovary; the ovule-bearing portion of a flower.

Pod: a dry, dehiscent fruit; the fruit of a legume.

Pollen: the male spores borne by the anther.

Prickle: a sharp outgrowth of the bark or epidermis of a plant.

Procumbent: trailing on the ground without rooting.

Prostrate: lying flat.

Pubescent: covered with hairs.

Raceme: a simple, elongate inflorescence, with the pedicles of the flower all nearly the same length.

Rachis: the axis of a spike, raceme, or compound leaf.

Ray flowers: the outer, petal-like flowers surrounding the disk of a member of the Asteraceae family.

Recurved: curving or bending backward or downward.

Reniform: kidney shaped.

Resin: a sticky, usually aromatic liquid produced by the glands of some plants.

Reticulate: having a netlike pattern.

Retuse: notched at the apex.

Rhizome: an underground stem capable of producing new stems or plats at its nodes.

Rhombic: diamond shaped with four sides.

Root: a usually underground part of a plant that normally anchors the plant to the substrate and functions chiefly in obtaining water and minerals.

Rosette: a circular cluster of leaves radiating from the center at or near the ground.

Rugose: wrinkled or bumpy.

Sagittate: shaped like an arrowhead.

Samara: an indehiscent winged fruit.

Scape: a flower stalk rising from the ground and carrying one or more flowers; it may bear scales or bracts, but no leaves.

Sepal: a leaflike segment of the calyx.

Serrate: a toothed margin, with the teeth pointing forward.

Sessile: a condition in which the blade of a leaf attaches directly to the stem, without a petiole.

Silique: a type of capsule found in the Brassicaceae family, either half of which peels away from a central, transparent, dividing membrane.

Simple: undivided, not branched, not compound.

Sinuate: strongly or deeply wavy, usually in reference to a leaf margin.

Spathe: a broad, sheathing bract enclosing the flower cluster of certain plants.

Spatulate: shaped like a spatula; wide and rounded at the apex but narrow at the base.

Spike: an elongate inflorescence of sessile flowers.

Spine: a sharp-pointed rigid structure, usually a highly modified leaf or stipule.

spp.: abbreviation for species (plural).

ssp.: abbreviation for subspecies.

Stalk: a general term for the usually elongated structure connecting or supporting an organ or group of organs.

Stamen: the male (pollen-bearing) organ of a flower; anther and filament collectively.

Stellate: having radiating arms, or shaped like a star.

Stem: the main stalk of a plant arising from the roots.

Stigma: the pollen-receptive part of the pistil.

Stipules: pairs of much-reduced leaflike appendages found at the base of the petiole.

Striate: having fine ridges, grooves, or lines along the axis.

Strigose: covered with rough, stiff, sharp hairs that run more or less parallel to a given surface.

Subtend: to be closely below or adjacent to.

Subulate: awl shaped.

Succulent: fleshy; soft and juicy.

Tendril: a coiling or twining organ with which a plant climbs.

Tepals: a collective term for petals and sepals, used when they cannot readily be differentiated.

Ternate: in sets of three, as a leaf composed of three leaflets.

Thorn: a sharp-pointed modified branch.

Throat: in a corolla composed of fused petals, the central opening of the flower.

Trailing: lying on the ground and elongating but not rooting.

Tribe: a subdivision of a family that is higher than genus rank.

Trifoliate: having three leaflets.

Truncate: abruptly ending in reference to a leaf, one whose blade contracts sharply, in a very short distance, at the base.

Tuber: a short, thickened underground stem that bears numerous buds.

Tubercle: a knoblike protrusion from a surface; in the Cactaceae family, a protrusion that bears an areole on or near its tip.

Umbel: a flat-topped or convex flower cluster in which the pedicels arise from a common point.

Undulate: wavy, usually in reference to a surface or margin.

var.: abbreviation for variety.

Vein: an externally visible fibrous strand; a rib.

Weed: a plant of rank, prolific, or obnoxious growth, usually growing to the detriment of a crop or more desirable species; an unwanted plant.

Whorl: a ringlike arrangement of like parts (often leaves).

Wing: a ribbonlike membrane bordering plant parts, as along stems, around seeds, etc.

Woody: having hard, persisting tissue.

Woolly: having long, soft, more or less matted hairs.

Xeric: pertaining to arid or desert conditions, implying minimal water supply.

ENDNOTES

[1] S. Cheatham, M. C. Johnston, and L. Marshall, *The Useful Wild Plants of Texas, the Southeastern and Southwestern United States, the Southern Plains, and Northern Mexico* (Austin, TX: Useful Wild Plants, 1995).

[2] D. S. Correll and M. C. Johnston, *Manual of the Vascular Plants of Texas* (Renner, TX: Texas Research Foundation, 1970).

[3] E. Frankel, *Poison Ivy, Poison Oak, Poison Sumac, and Their Relatives* (Pacific Grove, CA: Boxwood Press, 1991).

[4] J. Wrede, *Trees, Shrubs, and Vines of the Texas Hill Country* (College Station: Texas A&M University Press, 2010).

[5] W. C. Muenscher, *Poisonous Plants of the United States* (New York: Macmillan Publishing Co., 1975).

[6] S. Foster and R. Caras, *Venomous Animals & Poisonous Plants* (New York: Houghton Mifflin Company, 1994).

[7] E. Dauncey and S. Larsson, *Plants That Kill: A Natural History of the World's Most Poisonous Plants* (Princeton, NJ: Princeton University Press, 2018).

[8] M. Moore, *Medicinal Plants of the Mountain West* (Santa Fe: Museum of New Mexico Press, 2003).

[9] T. J. Elpel, *Botany in a Day: The Patterns Method of Plant Identification* (Pony, MT: HOPS Press, 2010).

[10] J. M. Poole, W. R. Carr, D. M. Price, and J. R. Singhurst, *Rare Plants of Texas* (College Station: Texas A&M University Press, 2007).

[11] N. Telkes, *Medicinal Plants of Texas* (Cedar Creek, TX: Wildflower School of Botanical Medicine Publishing, 2014).

[12] R. B. Taylor, J. Rutledge, and J. G. Herrera, *A Field Guide to Common South Texas Shrubs* (Austin: Texas Parks and Wildlife Press, 1997).

[13] M. W. Turner, *Remarkable Plants of Texas* (Austin: University of Texas Press, 2009).

[14] Lady Bird Johnson Wildflower Center, "Plant Database: Juniperus virginiana," last modified November 11, 2015, https://www.wildflower.org/plants/result.php?id_plant=juvi.

[15] K. Kindscher, *Medicinal Plants of the Prairie* (Lawrence: University Press of Kansas, 1992).

[16] R. S. Felger and M. B. Moser, *People of the Desert and Sea: Ethnobotany of the Seri Indians* (Tucson: University of Arizona Press, 1985).

[17] A. Ž. Kostić, D. D. Milinčić, M. B. Barać, M. A. Shariati, Ž. L. Tešić, and M. B. Pešić, "The Application of Pollen as a Functional Food and Feed Ingredient—The Present and Perspectives," *Biomolecules* 10, no. 1 (2020): 84.

[18] S. Coffman, *The Herbal Medic*, vol. 1 (San Antonio, TX: Human Path, 2014).

[19] L. T. Rodríguez-Ortega, H. González-Hernández, J. M. Valdez-Carrasco, A. Pro-Martínez, F. González-Cerón, and A. Rodríguez-Ortega, "Nutritional Quality of the White Worm (*Agathymus remingtoni* Stallings & Turner Lepidoptera: Hesperiidae) of Maguey Lechuguilla (*Agave lechuguilla* Torrey)," *Agroproductividad* 13, no. 8 (2020): 69–72.

[20] R. Kossah, C. Nsabimana, Z. Jianxin, C. Haiqin, T. Fengwei, and C. Wei, "Comparative Study on the Chemical Composition of Syrian Sumac (*Rhus coriaria* L.) and Chinese Sumac (*Rhus typhina* L.) Fruits," *Pakistan Journal of Nutrition* 8, no. 10 (2009): 1570–74.

[21] Food Safety Net Services, "Local Leaf—Analytical Results," Local Leaf, San Antonio, TX, 2018.

[22] D. Weniger, *Cacti of Texas and Neighboring States* (Austin: University of Texas Press, 1991).

[23] F. W. Martin, C. W. Campbell, and R. M. Ruberté, *Perennial Edible Fruit of the Tropics: An Inventory*, Agriculture Handbook No. 642, United States Department of Agriculture, 1987.

[24] W. P. Bemis, L. D. Curtis, C. W. Weber, and J. Berry, "The Feral Buffalo Gourd, *Cucurbita foetidissima*," *Economic Botany* 32, no. 1 (1978): 87–95.

[25] A. M. Powell, *Trees and Shrubs of the Trans-Pecos and Adjacent Areas* (Austin: University of Texas Press), 1998.

[26] M. Moore, *Medicinal Plants of the Desert and Canyon West* (Santa Fe: Museum of New Mexico Press, 1989).

[27] D. Alloway, *Desert Survival Skills* (Austin: University of Texas Press, 2000).

[28] T. Mezadri, D. Villaño, M. S. Fernández-Pachón, M. C. García-Parrilla, and A. M. Troncoso, "Antioxidant Compounds and Antioxidant Activity in Acerola (*Malpighia emarginata* DC.) Fruits and Derivatives," *Journal of Food Composition and Analysis* 21, no. 4 (2008): 282–90.

[29] D. Tull, *Edible and Useful Plants of Texas and the Southwest* (Austin: University of Texas Press, 1987).

[30] M. Witty, A. Yard, J. Kinard, and R. O. Adekunle, "*Ampelopsis brevipedunculata* Berries Are Simultaneously Attractive to Birds and Repulsive to Mammals," *International Journal of Botany* 6, no. 1 (2010): 35–40.

[31] J. Mellem, H. Maijnath, and B. Odhav, "Bioaccumulation of Cr, Hg, As, Pb, Cu and Ni with the Ability for Hyperaccumulation by *Amaranthus dubius*," *African Journal of Agricultural Research* 7, no. 4 (2012): 591–96.

[32] J. L. Voss, "Suckleya," Guide to Poisonous Plants, Colorado State University, 2019, https://csuvth.colostate.edu/poisonous_plants/Plants/Details/31.

[33] J. Pojar and A. MacKinnon, *Plants of the Pacific Northwest Coast* (Redmond, WA: Lone Pine Publishing, 1994).

[34] A. O. Tucker, M. J. Maciarello, and K. Clancy, "Sweet Goldenrod (*Solidago odora*, Asteraceae): A Medicine, Tea, and State Herb," *Economic Botany* 53, no. 3 (1999): 281–84.

[35] L. Perry, "Liberty Tea," Department of Plant and Soil Science, University of Vermont Extension, accessed August 23, 2020, https://pss.uvm.edu/ppp/articles/liberty.html.

[36] M. Moore, *Los Remedios: Traditional Herbal Remedies of the Southwest* (Santa Fe: Red Crane Books, 1990).

[37] M. K. Uddin, A. S. Juraimi, M. S. Hossain, M. A. Nahar, M. E. Ali, and M. M. Rahman, "Purslane Weed (*Portulaca oleracea*): A Prospective Plant Source of Nutrition, Omega-3 Fatty Acid, and Antioxidant Attributes," *Scientific World Journal*, February 10, 2014.

[38] R. Byrne and J. McAndrews, "Pre-Columbian Purslane (*Portulaca oleracea* L.) in the New World," *Nature* 253, no. 5494 (1975): 726–27.

[39] G. Ajilvsgi, *Wildflowers of Texas* (Fredericksburg, TX: Shearer Publishing, 2003).

[40] S. Thayer, *Nature's Garden* (Birchwood, WI: Forager's Harvest, 2010).

[41] J. Ritchason, *The Little Herb Encyclopedia* (Pleasant Grove, UT: Woodland Health Books, 1995).

[42] Y. Kara, "Bioaccumulation of Cu, Zn and Ni from the Wastewater by Treated *Nasturtium officinale*," *International Journal of Environmental Science and Technology* 2 (2005): 2.

[43] P. Holmes, *The Energetics of Western Herbs*, vol. 1 (Boulder, CO: Snow Lotus Press, 1997).

[44] A. Klink, A. Macioł, M. Wisłocka, and J. Krawczyk, "Metal accumulation and Distribution in the Organs of *Typha latifolia* L. (Cattail) and Their Potential Use in Bioindication," *Limnologica* 43, no. 3 (2013): 164–68.

INDEX

eggplant, 276
Ehretia anacua, 59
elderberry, 108
epazote, 202, 248
Ericaceae, 69, 156, 157
Eriobotrya japonica, 99
Erythrina herbacea, 12
escarpment live oak, 83
Euphorbiaceae, 19, 242
evergreen sumac, 119

Fabaceae, 21, 31, 70, 73, 75, 78, 80
Fagaceae, 83
Fagus grandifolia, 84
false aloes, 112
false dayflower, 238, 240
farkleberry, 156
Ferocactus spp., 140
firethorn, 172
Forestiera angustifolia, 169, 177
Fouquieriaceae, 158
Fouquieria splendens, 158
funnel-flower, 210

Galium aparine, 269
Galium circaezans, 270
Galium obtusum, 270
Galium pilosum, 270
Galium proliferum, 270
Galium texense, 270
Galium tinctorium, 270
Galium virgatum, 270
garden nasturtium, 284
Geranium, 249
giant ragweed, 198
Glandularia spp., 189
glasswort, 130
Glechoma hederacea, 245
Gleditsia aquatica, 77
Gleditsia triacanthos, 75
goji berries, 187
goldenberry, 272
golden currant, 160
goldenrod, 221

goldenseal, 133
greenbriar, 181, 193
Grossulariaceae, 160
groundcherry, 271
ground ivy, 245
Guaiacum angustifolia, 169
guayacan, 169
guayusa, 124
Gulf Coast, 44, 59, 117, 124, 129, 130, 178, 196, 197, 222, 265, 280
Gulf Prairies, 44
gum bumelia, 178

habanero pepper, 184
Hatch pepper, 184
heart-leaf nettle, 279
heartleaf peppervine, 190, 191, 193
Hechtia texensis, 111
Helianthus annuus, 216
Helianthus maximiliani, 217
Helianthus strumosus, 217
Helianthus tuberosus, 217
henbit, 245
High Plains, 45
Hill Country, 112, 121, 179, 222
hogplum, 169
honeylocust, 75
honey mesquite, 80
horsecrippler cactus, 139
horse mint, 248
Houston, TX, 99, 105, 165, 235
hyacinth, 210
Hyacinthus spp., 210
Hydrastis canadensis, 133
Hypochaeris spp., 226

Ibervillea spp., 154
Ilex coriacea, 123
Ilex cornuta, 131
Ilex decidua, 123
Ilex guayusa, 124
Ilex longipes, 123
Ilex opaca, 123, 131
Ilex paraguariensis, 124